GREAT RED DRAGON

GREAT RED DRAGON

OR LONDON MONEY POWER

L B WOOLFOLK

Published by

FacsiMile Publisher
12 Pragati Market
Ashok Vihar, Ph-2
Delhi - 110052, India
Phone: 011-47034999
Email: www.facsimilepublishers.com
info@facsimilepublishers.com

Distribution Network
gyanbooks.com
India, USA, Canada, UK, Australia

ISBN: 978-93-3289-798-4 (HB)

First Published, 1890

2nd Impression 2025

Printed at: Gyan Press, Delhi.

GREAT RED DRAGON

Author: L B WOOLFOLK

Great Red Dragon,

OR

LONDON MONEY POWER.

BY

L. B. WOOLFOLK.

CINCINNATI:
GEORGE E. STEVENS,
39 W. Fourth St.
1890.

Dedication.

TO THE AMERICAN PEOPLE:

Trusting that its publication will promote the glory of God and the highest well-being of Man:
In exposing, and leading to the overthrow of the mightiest Evil that has ever risen on the Earth; and
In revealing JEHOVAH on the side of humanity now, as of old, leading our Race in the prophetic PILLAR OF LIGHT out of the bondage of the present Era into the glorious Millennial Canaan promised to Man,

—This Work,—

As an Offering on the Altar of Consecration—and a Tribute of Philanthropy from a heart yearning with unspeakable longing and hope for the Well-being of Mankind, is respectfully inscribed by

THE AUTHOR.

PREFACE.

THIS work is divided into three parts:—

PART I gives a History of the Rise of the London Money Power.

PART II proves that this Imperialism of Capital,—the London Money Power,—is foretold in prophecy, under the symbol of the Great Red Dragon.

PART III gives the Remedy for the industrial evils that afflict our country.

There are many persons, perhaps, who will be deeply interested in Part I, and Part III, who will feel but little interest in the prophetic portion of the work. The work is so arranged that all such persons can skip Part II, and pass from Part I to Part III, without any break in the connection of thought: though they will miss the most striking delineations of the character and the activities of the Money Power.

On the other hand, those who are interested in the prophetic aspect of the work, will find its structure in proper logical arrangement as a prophetic exposition; since it is necessary to present the history of the Money Power, before the symbols of prophecy can be applied to it.

This work is the outgrowth of a life of thought, largely directed to the study of Prophecy, History, and Political Economy. Indeed, the work is the product of original thought. Its historical portion is the history of an Imperialism whose existence has been hitherto unrecognized.—Its remedy is based upon principles of Political Economy that have never before been presented to the world.—Its Prophetic Exposition is part of a System of Prophetic Interpretation that is entirely new. The Author may therefore claim the indulgence due to a pioneer, whose movement is over a pathway unsmoothed by the progress of earlier thought.

As no history of the London Money Power has ever been written, the Author has been under the necessity of gathering his facts from newspaper items, and from the statements of individuals whose reliability is above question. His store of facts has been constantly increasing down to the present time. Some important facts he has learned since the publication of this work began; other facts he learned too late for them to appear in the present edition.—No doubt, in every community facts are known which illustrate the course of the Money Power in this country. These facts will doubtless soon be published; and it is hoped that ere long a full and connected history of the Rise of the Money Power may be given to the world.

PART I.

HISTORY OF THE RISE

OF

THE LONDON MONEY POWER.

CHAPTER I.

RISE OF THE MONEY POWER—FIRST ERA.

I. INTRODUCTION.

AN Imperialism of Capital has grown up within the last two centuries from small beginnings, until it is now the mightiest power that has ever existed on the earth. It is an Imperialism mightier than the empire of the Cæsars, grander than the empire of Napoleon in the hour of his highest glory. In comparison with it all other empires sink into comparative insignificance. This titanic power is the Imperialism of Capital, which I call, by way of distinction, the Money Power.

1ST. THE MONEY POWER DEFINED.

I do not mean by the Money Power to include any persons possessed of property, who are engaged in independent business enterprise. I do not mean any American business men, or business Companies engaged in independent business enterprise, whether they be farmers, merchants, manufacturers, bankers, miners, builders, or persons engaged in any department of business enterprise. The Imperialism of Capital to which I allude is a knot of capitalists—Jews almost to a man—who have their headquarters in the Money Quarter of London, in Threadneedle street, Lombard, and other streets in that vicinity, where bankers have their habitat. These Jew capitalists have succeeded in centralizing in their own hands the industry and commerce of the earth.—They own almost all the debts of the world,—the debts of nations, states, counties, municipalities, corporations and individuals,—amounting in the aggregate, it is estimated, to seventy-five billion dollars, on which they are annually receiving about four billion dollars of interest.—They own the manufactories, the shipping, and the commerce of Great Britain, and most of the manufactures, shipping and commerce of the whole world.—They have attained control of the industry and trade of the whole earth; and are rapidly centralizing all business in their own hands. They hold possession of all the great lines of trade and business of all kinds, and they regulate all prices by their own arbitrary methods.—These Jew Money Kings have established a grand Imperialism of industry, commerce and wealth, which is thoroughly organized, and rules in the sphere of industry and trade with autocratic sway.

In our age, CAPITAL IS KING. This Money Power of the Money Quarter of London is the only grand preëminent Imperialism existing on the earth. Monarchs severally rule their own dominions, and no one of them has preëminent power. The Imperialism of Capital, in our time, stretches the arms of its power over the whole earth: it alone sways the nations with preëminent rule. It buys all the products of the earth: it fixes all prices of all commodities without regard to the law of supply and demand, by its own arbitrary will. It is Imperial over industry and trade, and none can resist it. It is rapidly progressing toward its ultimate aim, of possessing itself of all the world's wealth and all the world's property. If things remain as they are, these Jew Money Kings will, at no distant day, have achieved their aim, and will own the earth in fee simple.

2nd. Discovery of Existence of Money Power.

The world will be surprised at the statement that such a grand Imperialism of Capital exists. For it has grown up so silently, and has veiled its operations in such secrecy, that its very existence is unsuspected. The Author was as ignorant of the Money Power as all the rest of the world outside of the ring, until, when visiting England many years ago, he, through a combination of circumstances unnecessary to mention here, became acquainted with the existence of this grand centralization of Capital in England, and was given a pamphlet that was intended for private circulation. This pamphlet, and the boastful statements of the Englishman who gave it, imparted to the Author information which is carefully kept from the general public. Quotations will be made from this pamphlet later on in this work. No confidence is thereby violated, and its statements ought to be known to the world.

Thus informed of the existence of the Money Power, the Author has watched its progress for over twenty years. As events occurred, his mind, strongly magnetized, as it were, by this subject, seized upon and gathered to itself all facts bearing upon the question. A newspaper item, meaningless to others, was to him an important historical fact in the rise and growth of the Money Power. He has thus, point by point, gathered the materials for the sketch which here follows.

Before quoting from the pamphlet just mentioned, it will be better, in order to give consecutiveness to the subject, to first trace the rise of the Money Power; and then to make quotations, to show that it was already a grand Imperialism in the decade extending from 1860 to 1870.

II. FIRST ERA IN THE RISE OF THE MONEY POWER.

The Money Power of the World had origin in small beginnings, in the 18th century; but it has reached its grand development in our own age. It had its origin in the British East India Company, and has grown up so quietly that its grand centralization has not attracted the attention of mankind. Indeed, it has only become powerful enough in our own age, to produce startling effects upon the industry of the world.

In the ages before the invention of the steam engine, the chief commerce of the world consisted in the interchange between the Temperate zone and the Tropics. There was but little interchange between the different countries of the Temperate zone; for all having the same climate and agricultural productions, each country produced sufficient for its own consumption; and, all manufactures being wrought by hand, each country had enough manufactures for the supply of its own needs, except a few articles of luxurious consumption. The chief commerce of the world consisted in the exchange of some of the products of the Temperate zone, especially specie, for articles of luxurious consumption, sugar, tea, coffee, indigo, opium, and the spices, contributed by the Tropics to the commerce of the world.

This commerce has always enriched the nation which carried it on, and made its merchants the great commercial magnates of the earth.

In Ancient Times, the Phœnicians possessed it for two thousand years, and it made them the great merchants of the earth. The share of Egypt in the traffic gave to that country its great wealth in the early eras of the monarchy. In the age of Solomon, the Jews possessed the Eastern end of the traffic for a generation, and it so enriched them that silver was in Jerusalem as stones. The development of this commerce was the sphere in which was displayed the proverbial wisdom of Solomon, and it constituted the chief glory of his reign.

The power of the Assyrian Empire was largely based upon the possession of the Eastern end of this commerce; the conquests of the Empire along the Mediterranean, having broken up the old line of the trade by way of the Red sea.

To obtain possession of this commerce was the aim of the conquests of Nebuchadnezzar, the founder of the Babylonian Empire. He carried the traffic through Babylon, and up the Euphrates, across Syria and Asia Minor, and gave the Western end of the traffic to the Lydians and the Ionian Greeks. This was the origin of the proverbial wealth of Crœsus, which the Greeks, in their ignorance of the commercial relations of the East, attributed to the gold washed from the placer mines of the river Pactolus. The possession of the Western end of the trade, at this time, awakened the Greeks from the lethargy of barbarism, and started the race upon its grand career of civilization.

The hostility of the Greeks to Persia, which caused the burning of Sardis, and led to the Persian wars, no doubt originated in the fact that Persia gave the traffic back to the Phœnicians, who restored it to its old route by way of the Red sea.

After the Christian Era, the Venetians took possession of the traffic and it made them the great merchant princes of the Middle Ages.

The discovery of the passage around Cape Good Hope gave the traffic into the hands of the Portuguese, who kept it for a century. Then the Dutch, the French and the English organized trading companies which competed with each other for the possession of this great East India trade, now, since the passage around Cape Good Hope, swelled into much larger proportions than in former times.

Britain was slow to engage in it, and during the Seventeenth Century made only feeble efforts, productive of little result. In the early part of the Eighteenth Century, the British East India Company was reorganized and put in successful operation. In return for a loan of fifteen million dollars to the British government, a large sum for those days, it received a charter, giving to it the exclusive right to trade with all countries of the Indian and Pacific Oceans, between Cape Horn and Cape Good Hope.

From this time the East India Company made rapid growth in prosperity and power.

In the various wars of the Eighteenth Century between Great Britain and her commercial rivals on the Continent, the bull-dog pluck of the British sailors, and their superior nautical skill gave to British vessels so great an advantage in naval combats as secured to Britain a maritime supremacy. The British East India Company prospered, not only by the usual gains of traffic, but also by taking possession of the trading stations of its commercial rivals from which they were dispossessed by conquest.

In the great Seven Years' War, continuing from 1757 to 1764, Great Britain dispossessed France of all her colonial possessions. In India, at the same time, through the genius and energy of Clive, the British East India Company laid the foundation of its imperial greatness. Historical authorities date the rise of the East India Company to imperial power at the victory of Plassy, 1757 A. D. In 1764, it was an empire exercising imperial sway in Bengal over a territory containing a population of forty millions, and yielding larger revenues than those of the Austrian empire, at that time the greatest European power.

In 1764, the British East India Company was the grandest and richest corporation in the world. It was the only corporation which ruled a territorial empire. It was enriched by traffic, by the extension of its trade through the conquest of the trading stations of its Continental rivals, and by the wholesale plunder of India.

It had been from the first the best investment of capital to be found in the British Islands. Its stock was eagerly taken by all who had the means. The mercantile class took as much stock as they could afford; but, as we know, merchants usually have little more capital than they need for their regular business. The British Landed Aristocracy had large incomes from their estates; and being under a necessity of seeking the best investments, in order to portion their younger children, they made large investments in the East India Company. But the great Capitalists of that age were the Jews. They were the money holders. They subscribed largely to the stock; and as, in each generation, the stock of the Aristocracy was sold to portion younger children, the Jews, always economical, always full of money, and always in search of the best investments, bought the stock thrown upon the market. Thus it came to pass that the greater part of the stock of the East India Company, and of the other companies afterwards organized out of the dividends of that great company, fell into the hands of the Jews. The Jews became the great Money Kings of the world.

Under the impulse of Jew exactions, the career of the East India Company in India was a continued series of trickery, wrong, exaction, theft, robbery and murder. In the Eighteenth Century, the Mogul empire was in the last stages of decay; and the East India Company, in its dealings with the native states and Princes of India, constantly shifted its ground as expediency required, sometimes treating them as independent states, and sometimes, as dependencies of the Mogul empire. It hired its soldiers to one native prince, to enable him to conquer another: it sold its favors on every side; and when the opportunity came, it devoured the treasures and the territory of friends and foes alike. History presents no career of conquest, in which fraud, deceit and rapine were so blended as in the conquest of India by the East India Company. It was the first example in the history of the world of a trading corporation becoming an imperial power; and its imperial rule was marked by the rapacity, chicane and fraud that characterizes a great corporation in the soulless and conscienceless pursuit of gain.

From 1764, the East India Company had control of the grand trade between the Temperate zone and the Tropics. It continued its conquests in India until, in 1857, the date of the Sepoy mutiny, it ruled almost the whole peninsula. The Money Kings who controlled it, possessed an empire compared with which the possessions of the Phœnicians and Carthaginians, and all their predecessors were as nothing, and they attained a domination over industry and trade without a parallel in the annals of the world.

Chapter II.

RISE OF THE MONEY POWER, Continued: SECOND ERA.

The Money Power of the World entered upon a new and grander era of development when steam was applied to manufactures. In 1774, Watt perfected the steam engine; and this new servant of man, mightier than the Genii of oriental fable, was at once set at work propelling manufactures. The power loom, the spinning Jenny and the cotton gin were soon afterward invented, and gave a great impulse to steam manufacturing industry.

The conditions of the time threw steam manufactures entirely into the hands of the London Money Power. Great

Britain was the only country in Europe which had coal and iron for steam purposes. The capitalists of the East India Company were the only people in the world with capital to engage in the new industry; for the great trading companies of other countries had been broken down by British conquests. Enriched by the trade of the Orient and the Tropics, these London capitalists at once seized the opportunity events offered them, and embarked energetically in steam manufactures.

The East India Company, as such, did not engage in these manufactures. All the stockholders would not wish to invest in them: so large a corporation would be unwieldy; and the immensity of the monopoly might excite alarm and provoke opposition. It would be much better to operate through smaller corporations. A few capitalists might hold the stock of a great number of them without exciting jealousy; and their management would be quiet and easy. The different corporations were like the regiments of an army: it was easy to form them into brigades, and divisions, and army corps, so as to give them the compact solidity of a grand military organization. It had the flexibility of individual enterprise, and the solidity of a despotism. The Money Kings adopted the policy of single corporate companies for each special enterprise.

They built manufactories of all kinds: they started iron mills, woolen mills, cotton mills. Manufactures of all kinds sprung up on every side. The Money Kings organized new joint stock corporations which built mills and manufactories: new companies which operated mines of coal and iron: and, as commerce wonderfully expanded through manufactures wrought by steam power, they organized new companies, which built vessels to plow the waters of every ocean, and built new warehouses, and established new trading stations all over the earth.

Commerce had languished in previous ages, because the

Temperate zone had not sufficient cheap products suited to tropical demand, to offer in exchange for tropical productions. Steam manufactures opened up a new commercial era. They greatly stimulated tropical production, by offering manufactures in those markets. They also greatly stimulated industry in the Temperate zone. In all the countries of the Temperate zone, the demand for the manufactures of Britain was far beyond the ability to pay for them with exports.

The first effect of this state of things was a wave of excitement that swept over Great Britain. An industrial boom was started. Everybody who had money invested in the stock of manufacturing companies, shipping companies, trading companies. In companies for steam manufactures, the Money Kings took care to have the majority of stock: outside companies they knew they could devour at their leisure. The grand Money Kings had such advantages in their immense capital and in their perfect organization, that in commercial crises, often originated, and always manipulated by them, they managed systematically to break down rival companies, and buy them out, and to rob and plunder the minority stockholders; until, in the end, these organized capitalists got into their own hands and very cheap, all, or the greater part of the stock of the various companies, manufacturing, mercantile and shipping, that originated in steam manufactures. They thus reduced to a system and a science the art of crushing rival companies, and freezing out minority stockholders. Their whole career was a systematic course of treachery, fraud and plunder, without a parallel in history. They advanced step by step, always causing a boom in every new enterprise that enlisted much outside capital, and always managing to operate seasons of business disaster, in which they lost a few hundred thousands by falling prices, a loss which they were abundantly able to stand, while making many millions by getting cheap the stock of broken corporations and the stock sold by minority stockholders.

Dealing in futures in Boards of Trade, was then started on a grand scale, a system originated for the purpose of enabling large capitalists to force stocks up or down as they choose, by dint of capital, without any regard to the actual value—the most satanic engine of trickery, fraud and oppression ever devised to enable the strong to plunder the weak. It is the drag net with which the Money Kings destroy multitudes of men of small means, as the fisherman takes fish in his seine. They are fishermen: the rest of mankind are their prey. They are always seeking after spoil. They are always dragging their net for the destruction of the unwary.

But aside from this plunder of the weak and the trusting, the regular profits of the new age of industry were very large. In every country of the Temperate zone, the demand for British manufactures was much greater than could be paid for by exports. And the difference in the balance of trade was always systematically arranged by lending money on mortgage for that amount, or by spending the amount of the deficit in starting some business enterprise in that country. In this way, the adverse balance of trade was not felt by the country falling behind. It bought all it wanted, and the adverse balance of trade actually made times better; for it caused the profits of the Money Kings to be invested in the country, stimulating business into activity. It only had the disadvantage that the business investment did not belong to the nation, but to the Money Kings: and the prosperity it caused was not national prosperity, but was the bloated gains of the Money Kings.

This has been the regular method of the Money Kings for the last hundred years. Starting new manufactures, new shipping companies, new trading companies: getting in all the outside capital possible, and then freezing out minority stockholders, and throttling outside corporations: getting all the nations in debt to them, and making parasite investments to the amount of the deficit of the balance of trade: putting in the profits derived from the East India Company, first: and then, not only putting in its profits, but continually reinvesting all the profits of all their enterprises in the country; until their investments, accumulating like a rolling ball of snow, at last become an avalanche to bury beneath its weight the prosperity of the world.

THE ROTHSCHILD SYNDICATE.

Even in the beginning of this second era of the growth of the Money Power, it realized immense profits—profits so great as enabled the Money Kings to loan the money necessary on both sides to sustain the immense armaments of the wars of the French revolution. They let the British government and the powers warring against France have all the money they required; and they supplied to Napoleon and his allies the loans necessary for his campaigns.

At that time, for the convenience of the Money Kings, the great house of Rothschild was established. The rise of the house of Rothschild has always been shrouded in the mystery that veils all the operations of the Money Power. The house took immense contracts on both sides; and made to both sides immense loans. Where the money came from has always been a mystery. The common explanation given of it is wholly inadequate to account for the sudden rise of the house of Rothschild into such enormous wealth. The only way to account for it is to suppose that the Rothschild family was chosen by the Jew Money Kings as the head and fiscal agency of a grand

Jewish syndicate formed at that time, to concentrate under one management the money of the Jew capitalists.

It was a great convenience, and a great source of power. The Rothschilds were chosen, perhaps, in part, on account of their superior business qualifications; and perhaps, in part, because there were three brothers, who could be heads of separate banking houses in London, and Paris and Vienna. By such a syndicate the Jews could lend money and take army contracts on both sides. And if, in the end, one side should achieve a decided triumph, the Rothschild on the winning side could save the Rothschild on the losing side, and thus the money of the Jews would be safe in any event. It was a grand stroke of Jewish skill and policy, the organization of this grand syndicate; but it was the first instance of the organization of a syndicate in the world; and it was never known as such; but, with the usual readiness of mankind to believe in the sudden growth of vast fortunes from nothing, the world accepted the rise of the house of Rothschild as an individual fortune, and not a syndicate. In our time, when combination of capital into syndicates is common, the house would be recognized at once as the head of a syndicate. The rise of the house of Rothschild is memorable as the first grand combination of the Jews in a syndicate, for the transaction of a vast business in which all their capital might be combined. The Rothschilds became the head of the Jew Money Kings, and have ever since been the head of the Jews, acting as a syndicate. That house is probably at the head of the Jew Money Power of the world.

When Napoleon fell, there remained but one grand imperialism in the world,—the Imperialism of Capital,—the Jew Money Power, centered in the Money Quarter of London. Since the fall of Napoleon, the nations of Europe have been maintaining war military establishments in time of peace, at an expense far beyond their revenues. The London Money Kings have loaned them the money to make up the annual deficit. They have invested in national debts alone about twenty-six billion dollars. Besides these national debts, are the loans they have made to states, and counties, and municipalities, and corporations and individuals, amounting in the aggregate, as it is estimated, to over fifty billion dollars more.

And then, there are the immense amounts of their own investments in all the countries of the globe. The wealth of the Money Power is simply beyond calculation. It can not amount to less than $160,000,000,000. It is probably nearer two hundred billions.

CHAPTER III.

RISE OF THE MONEY POWER, CONTINUED: THIRD ERA.

The Money Power entered upon the third era of its growth with the application of steam to transportation in railroads and steamships.

The Railroad Era began about 1830; but for twenty years after steam was applied to railroads, industry languished throughout all countries of the Temperate zone, for want of sufficient money to transact the business of the world. But little progress was made in applying steam to transportation, until the mines of California first, and then the mines of Australia, and the Rocky Mountains, and old and new mines opened in Mexico and South America gave hundreds of millions of dollars to the circulating medium of the world. In 1850, the age of railroad and steamship building began on a large scale. Then the Money Power was fully embarked in this third era of its development.

The Supremacy of the Money Power over Industry, beginning with the application of steam to manufactures, was continued on a still higher plane of power, from 1850 and onward.

The new companies organized out of the dividends of the East India Company soon threw the old parent company into the shade by their gigantic enterprises. The experience of these new corporations seems to have convinced the Money Kings that the territorial sovereignty of the East India Company was a mistake. They found by experience that it was better for them to monopolize industry, commerce and wealth under the protection of a government controlled by them, than to exercise territorial sovereignty themselves. These new corporations began to trade with India, as with the rest of the world. The East India Company, having no manufactures, was eclipsed as a trading corporation by these new rivals; and it soon came to restrict itself more and more to its territorial sovereignty. The Money Kings soon found that the new corporations were much better instruments for traffic, and they eventually made the East India Company merely their shield in India, behind whose protection they carried on their traffic. That company governed India entirely in their interest; for the same stockholders operated the East India Company and the new corporations born of the new age of steam industry.

They finally found the East India Company a burden, and an embarrassment. They derived the same advantage from the protection of the British government as from the Company, and without the cost and trouble. And moreover, bonuses and other advantages given them by the British government were safe and sure, while advantages and franchises given them by the East India

Company might be subsequently annulled as unauthorized and fraudulent. To get rid of the expense and danger of maintaining the sovereignty of India, they, at the time of the Sepoy mutiny, influenced the British government to assume the government of India:—and the East India Company, having served its end in giving birth to those new corporations born of its profits, passed away. The spider's brood, true to their nature, devoured their dam.

The Money Kings Greatly Enlarged Their Operations in the new age of steam transportation. They constantly invested their gains in more manufactures, more ships, and more ware-houses, all over the earth. And when they made more profits than were needed for such investments—for their profits grew faster than the wants of commerce—they invested their surplus profits in various countries, in lands, in city houses, in building new railroads; and in buying vast bodies of lands in the Tropics, on which they opened up immense plantations, for the growth of coffee, tea, indigo, rice, opium, spices, and all tropical productions.

They started new enterprises owned by themselves in all the countries of the globe:—tea plantations in China; coffee plantations in Java and Ceylon; sheep ranches in Australia and South Africa and South America; sugar plantations in the West Indies and the Sandwich Islands; gold and silver mines in California, the Rocky Mountains, Australia, Mexico, and South America; diamond mines in India, and South Africa and Brazil; ruby mines in Burmah; lumber mills in Canada, the United States, Norway, Sweden and Poland; city buildings in all countries; and railroads all over the world. These, and many other enterprises employed the boundless capital of the London Money Kings.

City Buildings have been a favorite investment with them in countries of the Temperate zone. They derive two advantages from these investments: the buildings yield a high profit on the investment; and the Money Kings could thus put up rents in other countries, and increase the cost of living. This last point is an essential part of their industrial system.

In order to maintain the manufacturing supremacy of Great Britain, it is necessary that the cost of living should be as cheap there as in other countries. The price of food is necessarily higher in England than in other countries; and this has to be counterbalanced by cheaper rents. Rents are very low in England. By owning many buildings in foreign countries, the Money Kings are able to start a prevailing high standard of rents; which increases their profit on their investment, and raises the cost of living, till it is as high or higher, in other countries, than in England. Furthermore, these high rents increase the value of property, and start foreign capital into real estate speculation, leaving to the Money Kings the safe field of productive industry. — They are wonderfully shrewd, and understand perfectly all the points that benefit their interest, and injure the interest of the rest of the world.

Railroads are Their Favorite Investment in countries of the Temperate zone. The ownership of them not only yields a large return upon the investment, but it gives to the Money Kings entire control of the internal traffic of the countries whose railroads they own. It also enables them to build up cities at points on the railroads known beforehand to themselves; so that, by getting possession of the land around the site, they make hundreds of millions of dollars in speculations in town lots.

With incomes derived from all these various sources, and constantly reinvested—with the whole world tributary to them—it is not wonderful that they have grown so rich. Having taken possession of all the lines of business in which money is to be madė, it is no wonder that, for forty years, they have been the only people in the world who had a monied capital. No wonder that, continually impoverished by them, the nations of the earth have never had money to build railroads, or water works, or gas works, or any public buildings, but had always to issue bonds and sell them in London, to get money for all public improvements.

In the age of railroads, these Jew capitalists grew exceeding rich. At the beginning of the Era of Railroad Building, in 1850, no country had any capital, these London Money Kings excepted. The Money Kings alone of all the world had money; and they have taken special care, during the whole era, to make the world continually poorer by constantly increasing its debt to them.

Chapter IV.

FOURTH ERA.—DEVOURINGS OF MONEY POWER, SINCE 1864:

I. AGGRANDIZEMENT OF MONEY POWER: GENERAL VIEW.

The Money Power has been continually widening its operations in each successive era of its rise. The first era was the era of the East India Company; and of commerce based upon tropical products, and the exchange of those products for the productions and the specie of the countries of the Temperate zone. In the second era, the Money Power added steam manufactures to the trade with the Tropics, which it previously held. In the third era of its rise, the Money Power added to its previous sources of wealth the vast power derived from the possession of steam transportation, in railroads and steamships.

The Fourth Era of the rise of this terrible Imperialism began in 1864. In this era, armed with the immense capital derived from all its sources of wealth, the Money Power of the World entered upon its vast investments in mortgages in real estate; and began its career of monopolizing, at a stroke, whole branches of industry and vast lines of trade. This era will end, if things go on as they are, in the Money Power taking possession of all business, and owning all the property of the earth.

Since 1864, the London Jew Money Kings have been continuing their operations on the basis of boundless capital. They have, in this era, vastly extended their operations, and widened the range of their monopolies. Their command of capital is so vast, that they dominate the whole sphere of industry and trade with absolute sway. As against individual enterprises, their power is irresistible.

Like a Great Serpent, the London Money Power is, in our time, enveloping the industry of the earth in the coils of its capital, and crushing all competitors in its folds and devouring them. And it has grown so great, and its monopoly of business is so enormous, that its annual income,—from interest on loans—from rents of houses and farms—from profits of business,—is so vast, that it is able to take possession of a whole line of business at once, destroying all competitors. Woe to the men who are operating in a line of business which these Money Kings desire to monopolize: they at once envelop the feeble rivals in the folds of their capital, and crush and devour them. They now have sufficient capital to seize upon and monopolize all the business of the earth. And they are rapidly doing it.

PARASITE INVESTMENTS.

Indeed, their capital is now so vast that business operations will not afford it adequate employment. They can no longer find adequate investment for their constantly increasing income,—in extending their grand industrial enterprises—in loans to nations, states, and municipalities,—in building ships and warehouses and railroads. They can only find investment,—in building cities—in buying up city property—in purchasing and improving immense bodies of wild lands—in laying and foreclosing mortgages upon improved farms—and in buying up breweries, and flour mills, and lumber mills, and various business interests, all over the earth. They own almost all those business interests now: they will soon own the rest.

These parasite investments of the Money Kings are like the fly eggs laid in the nose of the sheep: it is an addition to the amount of bioplasm in the sheep, but, instead of being sheep bioplasm, it is foreign. The eggs will hatch; and instead of the new life adding to the health and vigor of the sheep, it consumes its life. The worms that breed from the eggs burrow into the head, and if they can not be gotten rid of, the sure result is the death of the sheep.—In the same way, the ox fly lays eggs in the back of the ox, that breed worms; which, in their development, make the ox as lively as the investments of the Money Power make the nation where its investments are made. But instead of helping the ox, they feed upon his life: they fever him: and if there are so many of these "wolves," as farmers call them, that the ox cannot bear the frenzy caused by their development, the ox will die.

But all these parasites, when full grown, do not continue to prey upon the animal whose life tissues have nursed them into growth. When full grown, they, fortunately for the animal, strive to leave the body on which they have preyed. But it is not so with the investments of the Money Kings. They keep planting more and more of their eggs in the body of all the nations; and, when the eggs hatch into parasite enterprises, the parasite enterprises continue to prey upon the country, until at last they will sap its strength, and devour its life.

These parasite enterprises of the London Money Kings are like the fly eggs deposited in the body of a caterpillar. If no egg is deposited, the caterpillar spins its cocoon, and at the proper time emerges as a butterfly. But when the fatal egg is deposited, the caterpillar lives on and spins its cocoon, as if in perfect health; but the parasite develops, and continues its work of destruction, and the caterpillar, instead of emerging from its chrysalis state, dies in its cocoon with its vitals utterly devoured.—This is what the Money Kings are now doing for all the nations. They are laying parasite eggs of capital in the body of every nation. Either the parasite must be gotten rid of, or the nations will perish.

II. DEVOURINGS OF THE MONEY POWER IN INDIA.

The Money Power of the World was nursed into imperial grandeur by the trade and wealth of India. India was its primal seat of dominion. In India, its power has always been uncontrolled and absolute. There, it has been allowed to work its will more thoroughly than anywhere else; and in India we can best perceive the ultimate outcome of its policy.

1st. Plunder of Hindoo Potentates.

Until the middle of the Eighteenth Century, the East India Company was only a mercantile corporation, having a few trading stations in India, and deriving its revenues from traffic. Rising into political power through the courage and genius of Clive, it began its career as devourer, in India, by extorting the hoarded wealth of one Hindoo potentate after another, as the price of its aid or its tolerance; and as the native rulers were successively reduced to bankruptcy and impotence in the crushing coil of the East India Company, that corporation gradually substituted its own administration for that of the native governments. In every advance, it showed the subtlety, the crawling insidious guile of the serpent. It enveloped state after state in its coil, and crushed the native governments so relentlessly, and yet so quietly, that when it finally devoured the territory of a fallen potentate, the act attracted but little attention. The East India Company continued its course of quiet gradual appropriation of territory for a century, until the Sepoy revolt in 1857.

2nd. Monopoly of Industry.

In the earlier period of its power, the East India Company took possession of all the trade and industry of the territories under its sway. But after the Age of Steam began, and the great British capitalists formed new joint stock corporations through which to carry on the grand industries arising out of steam manufactures, the East India Company lost its importance as a trading corporation. As we have seen, it finally restricted itself to its territorial sovereignty, and gave up to the new corporations the trade of India, giving them every advantage under its administration.

Under this policy, the new corporations of the London Money Kings, advancing step by step, took possession of the business industries of India.

They first took possession of the internal traffic and the foreign commerce of the country. They bought the native products at prices which yielded the wretched Hindoo producers a mere subsistence; and they sold in the India markets native products and foreign merchandise at the highest prices it was possible to extort. They made all the profits; and the entire population of India, except the officers and the agents of the Money Kings, was reduced to utter penury.

They continued their encroachments, and gradually got the industry of the country completely under their control. They superseded the old hand manufactures of the country by manufactures wrought by steam, of which these capitalists have entire possession and reap all the profits. And they broke down the old system of transportation, and substituted it by railroads owned by themselves.

For a long time, the Money Kings raised opium, and indigo, and cotton, and rice and other India products, for their commerce, upon lands owned by Hindoos. They made their profit by putting down prices to the lowest point that would yield subsistence to the Hindoo laborer. They thus kept the Hindoo population on the verge of starvation; so that, during the last forty years, frequent famines have carried off millions of the population.

We know from the Irish famines, that a modern famine is not a dearth of food, so much as the lack of means to buy bread. During one of the famines in Ireland, an American vessel entering the harbor of Cork with provisions sent by American charity to the starving Irish, met two vessels sailing out of the harbor laden with food sent from Ireland to a foreign market. The millions of Hindoos who have perished of hunger, during the last forty years, were the victims of the Money Power putting down prices of labor, and putting up the price of commodities.

3rd. Jungle Plantations.

But in the latter era of the growth of the Money Power, since the application of steam to transportation, the Money Kings have realized such vast profits from their world-wide manufactures and commerce, that they have made immense land investments in India. Vast areas of alluvial lands along the plains of the Ganges and the Bramapootra rivers have for ages been covered with the primitive jungle. Much of it is delta lands along the streams; much of it, broad alluvial plains and uplands, stretching from the sea to the foot of the Himalaya Mountains.

The Money Kings induced the government to offer these jungle lands at a very low price, and those imperial capitalists bought them. They next wished to populate these jungle lands with a race of Hindoo serfs who would till the soil for wages barely sufficient for subsistence. They offered the Hindoos the alternative of emigration to the jungles in their employment, or of starvation in their village homes.

Some Five Million Hindoos Died of Famine before they submitted. But the Money Kings triumphed; transplanted the Hindoos; and opened up grand plantations in the jungle. They built railroads; founded cities; and now they own cities, railroads and plantations. They own in fee simple a vast empire in India,—an empire of alluvial lands, more extensive than the ancient empires of Nineveh and Babylon in the valleys of the Euphrates and the Tigris—far more extensive than the Egyptian empire in the valley of the Nile—larger than Greece and Macedon combined—wider in extent than Italy—a broader domain than the whole of Great Britain. They find it cheaper to own the land and hire peasants to cultivate it, than to buy the products of free Hindoo labor. And in that wide empire of alluvial lands owned by them in fee simple, extending from the sea to the Himalayas, and from the heart of India into Burmah, those capitalists are now producing opium, and rice, and indigo, and cotton and india rubber, and quinine, and spices, and tea, and cotton and wheat.

4TH. ALL MARKETS CRUSHED BY INDIA PRODUCTS.

And they throw all these products of a teeming soil and pauper labor upon the markets of the world, making immense profits, and forcing down the price of productions all over the earth to the pauper standard of Hindoo labor. They are now publishing in our papers that they can grow wheat so cheaply upon their jungle lands, that, in competition with them, our Western farmers can only be allowed, in future, fifty cents a bushel for their wheat! Will not Omnipotent Justice blast such wrong doing?!

By the Competition of their Hindoo Plantations, tilled with Hindoo *Ryot* labor at five cents a day, they force down the price of Carolina rice and Southern cotton to the same level. Raising products upon their own lands with Hindoo pauper labor—shipping their products upon their own railroads into their own seaport cities—and transporting them in their own ships to their own warehouses in every country—these Money Kings are able to crush down the prices of productions in every country, and force the people of all countries to sell their products at any price they choose to offer!!

An Important Fact is learned from the course of the Money Power in India. The Money Kings find it more profitable to own lands and till them with pauper labor, than to buy the products reared by the free natives of the soil. They regard the purchase of cheap lands a good investment. They will doubtless continue the purchase of India lands, until they own all the lands of India, and all property of every kind, and the Hindoos become serfs, cultivating their lands, and filling positions in various departments of their service.

How can it be otherwise? Every department of industry in that country, except agriculture in part, is in their hands. They have in possession every source of profit. They and their agents realize all the profits that are made: nobody else makes more than a subsistence. The Money Power has India enveloped in its coils. It is only a question of time when the Serpent will complete the devouring of all its lands and all its property.

And we shall perceive as we proceed, that the Boa Constrictor has our country in almost the same condition as India. If things go on, in a few years more the Money Kings will own a wider empire of farming lands in the United States than in India; and the American farmer will be reduced to the condition of the Hindoo peasant laborer working for a few cents a day, or he may look on and see the lands he has lost cultivated by Chinese and Hindoos. We shall be reduced to the condition of slaves. There is a bottomless pit before us. The Money Power is preparing to plunge us into it.

CHAPTER V.

FOURTH ERA, CONTINUED:—DEVOURINGS OF THE MONEY POWER IN THE U. S.

Space will not admit of a full narration of the manner in which the Money Power is devouring industry and trade and wealth, throughout the world. While the head and the den of the Serpent are in England, its coils extend all over the earth. It is everywhere ruining business men, and taking possession of their business and property. In Europe, in Asia, in Africa, in South America, in Mexico, in Canada, in Australia, and in the Islands of the sea, it is constantly pursuing its deadly business of monopolizing the industry, trade and wealth of the world, by ruining people engaged in independent enterprise. But space will only admit of a statement, in part, of its devouring the industries of the United States.

This Knot of London Jew Capitalists is having its way in the United States more completely than anywhere else in the world, except India. In England, the Landed Aristocracy holds its own against the Money Power, in part, by the law of primogeniture, which enables it to maintain possession of the land, and much city property; and by the marriages of the sons of the landed aristocracy with the daughters of rich Englishmen associated with the Jew Money Kings and sharing their profits.

But, in America, the Money Power has had free course to ravage and devour.

I. THE MONEY POWER HAS KEPT OUR CURRENCY CONSTRICTED.

The Money Kings have always had to have American products, as the basis of their trade with the population of Britain, and with the whole earth. They needed our cotton for their English manufactures: our wheat and pork, and beef, to feed their British operatives: our hops, and barley, for the manufacture of malt liquors, for British and foreign consumption: our fats, for the manufacture of soaps; and our tobacco, for the British and foreign markets. Great Britain afforded them only coal, and iron and labor. American productions have constituted the grand basis of their world-wide manufactures and commerce.

It was, therefore, their interest to buy our products cheap; and, to that end, it was their interest to have in this country as low a scale of prices as possible. An effectual means of securing a low rate of prices for cotton, tobacco, wheat, cotton, cheese, and all our products, was to keep money scarce in this country, and its purchasing value very high.

And during almost our entire existence as a nation, the scarcity of money which the Money Kings have caused has enabled them to keep down prices to the lowest point, and cause our people to suffer from chronic hard times.

1st. The Crash of 1837.

Our people once carried the idea that industry should be left to take care of itself, to the extreme of holding that the general Government should not supply currency to the country, but should leave it to be supplied by the states, and by individuals. Our currency was on a specie basis; and it was held that the proper proportion between specie and currency was, specie to the amount of one-third of the paper circulating medium, to be kept in the vaults of banks.

This Abominable Currency System placed our currency, and the price of our products, completely under the control of the London Money Kings. For the Money Kings always had the balance of trade against us;

and they always purposely kept us drained of specie, so that, on a specie basis of one-third of the circulation, we could maintain only a sparse currency.

But, in 1836, our system of paper money was expanded to a point in some measure adequate to meet the business wants of the country. For the first time, our produce went up to a fair price, sufficient to give us prosperity. We then had a paper circulation of $136,000,000; certainly not an inflated currency for the amount of our population and trade, being less than half the amount of currency *per capita* we had in 1870.

But, we did not have Specie enough to maintain the one-third specie basis. The Money Kings had no idea of paying a fair price for the American produce they were obliged to have. It was increasing the value of our exports; and would soon enable us to pay with our products for the imports we bought of them; and we should soon have been able to secure specie enough for a safe basis for our circulating medium. They wished to keep money scarce, and prices low; so as to compel us to sell them our products so cheap as to keep the balance of trade against us. By thus keeping us in debt to them, they could keep us drained of specie, and keep money scarce and prices low, perpetually.

To this end, money must be made scarce, and times hard. The state banks were banking on a specie basis, and had not nearly specie enough to redeem their issues. It was only necessary for one prominent bank to fail, in order to cause a run on all the banks, and a suspension of specie payments; with a consequent contraction of the currency, scarcity of money and low prices, again.

The Money Kings made a heavy draft for specie on New York. A prominent bank in New York failed, and the state banks all over the country went down like a house of cards. Contraction of the currency followed at once. In 1842, five years after the panic, we had in the whole country only $64,000,000 of currency, being only a little over three dollars *per capita* of the population! It was horrible. A tide of bankruptcy without a precedent overswept the country. For thirteen years, from 1837 to 1850, scarcity of money continued, keeping our prosperity depressed, and making our prices low enough to satisfy the avarice of the London Money Kings, who got our wheat, and cotton, and pork and beef at any price they chose to offer.

The astonishing folly of our people in allowing the Money Kings to put down prices in this country by means of a scarcity of currency will excite the wonder of a later and wiser age. These Money Kings never buy anything of us they can do without. They have always had to have a certain amount of our cotton, pork and beef and wheat and barley and hops. They can not do without them. If we sustain the price at a fair rate they will have to pay it. And yet, from 1837 to 1850, we allowed them, by draining us of specie, to contract our currency to three dollars *per capita*, and put our prices down to starvation rates! What lamentable ignorance of the principles of political economy! By allowing the Money Kings to keep our currency contracted, we allowed them to cheat us out of about $100,000,000 a year in the value of our exports—to get us deeper into debt to them every year, and to keep our people oppressed with direful poverty. Our fathers showed great unwisdom. Are their children wiser?

Our produce had an actual value, which the Money Kings would have had to pay. But by basing our currency on specie, of which they could drain us, we kept our produce at *an artificially low price*. We thus lost every year a hundred million dollars by putting our products at an artificial price below their real value.

The Money Kings are wise: they no doubt laughed in their sleeve at our simplicity in thus allowing a price to be fixed upon our products below their real value.

The London Money Kings organized the crash of 1837. They drew on New York heavily for specie; just before the panic. The balance of trade is always against us and in their favor, and they could draw for specie as long and as heavily as they pleased. And they continued to draw specie, till the end they aimed at was accomplished, and the panic began. There can be no doubt that they did it with full intent to bring about the panic that followed.

2ND. THE CRASH OF 1857.

There was no expansion of the currency after 1837, till after the discovery of the gold mines of California. In 1850, the state banks again began to expand, and once more we had fair prices for produce, and prosperous times. The expansion continued till 1857. There was no undue inflation. The currency was not in excess of the legitimate needs of business, and prices were not too high.

But the currency was in excess of our capability of redeeming it in specie. All the gold taken out of the mines in California was sent direct to London, to pay, in part, the balance of trade against us. The London Money Kings took care that we should not have specie enough to constitute a one-third basis for a currency adequate to the business wants of the country. They, having the power to regulate the amount of specie we were allowed to keep, did not choose to leave in the United States specie enough to furnish a basis for an amount of currency adequate to give us fair prices.

The fall of a Trust Company Bank in Ohio, started a panic, and brought on a general crash of the state banks, with the natural result of hard times, and a cheap market, in which the Money Kings could buy our produce at their own price.

The Panic of 1857 Was, Beyond Question, Engineered by the London Money Kings. They took especial pains to get possession of the circulation of the Ohio Trust Company Bank, whose fall caused the panic, and they made extraordinary drafts upon it for specie, amounting to $5,000,000, so as to insure its fall.

Of two things one is certain: Either the Money Kings owned the Trust Company Bank, so that they could get possession of its circulation at any time, and start the panic; or else they took especial pains to gather up its circulation, so that they might drain it of specie. From the name of the institution,—"Trust Company,"—in the light of our own times, when these Money Kings are starting "Trusts" all over the world, it seems most probable that the Trust Company Bank was established by the London Money Power for the express purpose of using it as an instrument to start the panic.

In either case, they are pilloried before the eyes of our people, as making secret war upon our prosperity. It is like the secret underhanded methods of the Money Kings to start a bank in this country, in order to have it ready, at any moment they chose, to start a panic by its fall; on purpose to break down our prosperity, and give them a cheap market in which to purchase our products, necessary to their commercial system.

The Boa Constrictor thus Kept Itself Coiled about our currency system, and it has constricted our currency every time it expanded sufficiently to give us fair prices. They have thus been able to buy our products at little more than half their value, cheating us in this manner out of hundreds of millions of dollars every year, and keeping us in poverty. By the low prices thus maintained, the Money Power has kept the balance of trade hundreds of millions against us every year; and this adverse balance of trade has been kept even, by lending us money to build railroads, and to use in every form of public improvement; thus by its loans coiling around our industry and our property, and constantly devouring it.

The Money Kings are public enemies, all the more dangerous because they work by such sly, secret undermining methods.

For forty years, from 1820 to 1860, prices were kept down and times hard. Twice we were about to become prosperous, in 1836, and in 1856; when both times, the Money Kings promptly crushed our rising prosperity. In the forty years, from 1820 to 1860, they cheated us, by these low prices, out of at least four billions of dollars—enough to have made us the richest and most prosperous people on the globe.

One great Benefit of the Late War was, that it caused the Federal Government to furnish a currency that was not subject to collapse by the Money Kings withdrawing specie from the country. The Money Kings brought on the crash of 1873. But they could not do it by withdrawing specie. They were under the necessity of resorting to other means. Before presenting the means by which the crash of 1873 was brought about, it will be better to bring up the account of their working in the country to that date, so that their operations upon the currency in 1873 may be better understood.

II. THE MONEY POWER DEVOURED OUR COMMERCIAL MARINE.

The War afforded the Money Power the opportunity to strike us a deadly blow, in taking possession of our merchant shipping. The means by which they accomplished this was in perfect accord with their watchful craft and cunning. One of their ship building establishments built the steam cruisers which swept the seas, capturing many American vessels. Their depredations so raised the cost of marine insurance, that American vessels could no longer compete with those of Great Britain. Under such circumstances, American ship owners became willing to sell their ships. The Money Kings had gained so much money by their world-wide operations that, as soon as the vessels were offered for sale, they were ready to purchase them. In a few months the American ships were all purchased by the Money Kings, and transferred from the American to the British flag. At one grand gulp the Boa Constrictor swallowed down the American navy.

While we had our commercial marine, we received for our produce the ruling price in the foreign port; and the profits were divided between the American producer, the American merchant who exported the produce, and the American ship owner who carried it. But thenceforth, we only received the New York price: the Money Kings realized all the profits beyond our own shores.

But this was too much for them to be willing for us to receive. They wished to get closer to the producer, and leave to our people as small a part of the price of our products as possible. Having driven us off the ocean, they now invaded our frontiers, resolved upon conquering and taking possession of every branch of industry in the country. The history of the encroachments of the Money Power upon our industries is one long tragedy.

III. THE MONEY POWER DESTROYED OUR NEW YORK MERCHANTS.

The first step in the encroachments of the Money Power upon our national industries, was their overthrow of the great New York wholesale merchants. It began its movement against them immediately after the War. But it proceeded to the accomplishment of its aim with such subtlety and craft, that our people have not known of the destruction of the grandest merchants in the country.

I Only Found It Out in 1880, when I spent some time in New York city. The man at whose house I boarded told me one day in conversation that he had been rich, but had failed in business: he then obtained a support by taking boarders.

"Misery loves company," said he; "and the only consolation I have is that all the tall trees of the forest fell, when I went down. "Why sir," he continued, "not more than three or four business men in New York, who were prominent in business before the War, are in business now. They all failed. Nobody knew what hurt them; but, from some cause, nobody knows what, business took new channels; their business left them; and they broke. How business changed in New York since the War," he continued meditatively, "is incomprehensible to everybody."

Here was a grand effect; and I began to search out the cause. I was then familiar with the methods of the Money Kings. I had been watching their course for years in this country, and it was not difficult to find and follow their trail, on the war path against the New York merchants.

A Still Hunt was started against the New York wholesale merchants. The London Money Kings owned the English manufactures and the mercantile shipping houses. They started branch houses in New York—filled them with splendid stocks of goods—and then they started the English Drummer System in this country. The Drummer System was originated in England, over half a century ago, to accomplish the same purpose there against the old merchants of Great Britain, that was now wrought out by it in the United States. The Money Kings, by means of it, drew all the trade of the country to their own New York branch houses.

The Western and Southern merchants had been in the habit of visiting New York City, once or twice a year, to buy new stocks of goods. But now, the drummers of the Money King branch houses offered the Southern and Western merchants goods, by sample, of better quality, and at lower prices, than they could get them in New York. The old New York merchants waited for their customers to come. When, supplied by drummers, they quit coming, the old merchants, suppressed by English branch houses, failed, and retired from business.

It would be an interesting investigation to discover to what extent the Money Kings subsidized the old mercantile houses of New York City in their campaign. It is usually their custom to get some of the business interests already established on their side—reorganize them with a vast capital—take a controlling interest of the stock of the new companies to themselves—but leave them under the old name, and the old management. It seems that they adopted this policy toward only a few of the mercantile houses of New York City. The few old houses that remained standing doubtless became the allies of the Money Power. But they seem to have made almost a clean sweep, substituting new houses for the old.

In their conquest of the New York merchants, the Money Kings employed the tactics which they always use. As they availed themselves of their immense capital to put down prices on the New York merchants, so their method always is to put down prices on every business interest they assail. *The unfailing sign of their assault on a business, is a putting down of prices in the business.*

The Money Kings Always Operate Through Joint Stock Corporations in order to conceal their operations. A company is started in mercantile or other business by three or four persons associated in a joint stock corporation. It can not be known but that those persons constitute the entire company. There is nothing to indicate that the stockholders are the London Money Kings, and that the company is operated on British capital. It seems to the public that it is an American firm. But if the Company books of one of these conquering Companies that break down old business interests could be inspected, it would be found that the stockholders who furnish its unlimited capital are in London.

IV. THE MONEY POWER DEVOURED OUR RAILROADS.

The secretive methods of the Money Power are nowhere more fully displayed than in the manner in which it got possession of our railroads.

The advantages of owning our railroads were so vast and so obvious, that the Money Power, having boundless wealth, could not fail to purchase them.

1st. The Foundation of Their Ownership of Our Railroads

was laid with consummate skill and craft. They took their first steps at the time of their construction.

1. Many Lines, Like the Illinois Central,

were avowedly built and run by London capitalists.—Many lines of railroad were built by them in the West in consideration of land grants.—And many lines have been pushed by large railroad companies through new districts of country, for the sake of the trade to be obtained.

2. The Money Kings Got the Other Roads

by means of mortgages. The great Trunk Lines, and indeed, almost all the railroads east of the Mississippi, were built by the issue of bonds, and were ironed by the Money Kings for first mortgage bonds. The Money Kings always *got possession of the roads under an arrangement of the mortgage.*

Some of us recollect, along in the 50's, what hard work we had to build our railroads. We had no wealth: we had to build them with our poverty. We had no capital: we had to build them with debt. When two cities wished to link themselves with an iron girdle, they issued bonds to the extent of their credit: they induced all the counties along the line to issue bonds; and these bonds were always sold in London—the only place in the world where there was any cash capital—in order to get money to build the road-bed. Sometimes it required several issues of bonds, with intervals of despondency, and even despair, before the road-bed was completed. When the road-bed, or a considerable part of it, was completed, it was well known that the London Money Kings would furnish the iron and rolling stock, at the rate of $10,000 a mile, secured on first mortgage bonds.

I recollect that in 1855 to 1857, one of our cities was making tremendous efforts to build a railroad reaching toward a great business center. After two or three efforts made with intervals of deep despondency, over one hundred miles of the road-bed was at last completed; and one of the most distinguished citizens of the state was sent to London, to negotiate for the iron for the road. He succeeded in his object; but, being a man of enlarged views, he came back astounded. He said he found men from all over the world in London on the same business as himself: all wishing to get iron for railroads, at $10,000 a mile, secured on first mortgage bonds: and they all got the iron. He said, "These London capitalists are sure to get the railroads for the first mortgage bonds; and no man can foresee the consequences. It will certainly work a mighty change in the condition of the earth, when these capitalists get possession of all the land transportation of the world. No man can tell what the result will be."

We are now seeing some of the evils which this statesman of a generation ago dimly foreshadowed.

In this railroad financiering we have a fair specimen of the management of these Jew capitalists. When the railroads were first started, they made but little money. The system of operating them was as yet crude and imperfect; and the business that has since grown up along them, and made them profitable, was as yet in its infancy. As a rule, the Money Kings got possession of the railroads under some arrangement of the first mortgage bonds.

The Money Kings are the owners of our railroads. It is known that the Erie railroad is owned by the great house of John Bidall Martin, in Lombard street, London. A mortgage was placed upon the Milwaukee and St. Paul, last July, for $150,000,000, which was taken in Lombard street, London. John Bidall Martin was the head of a syndicate which foreclosed the mortgage on the Wabash railroad system, two years ago.

A favorite method with these capitalists of holding railroads, is to have them bonded to them on mortgage security. They never pay for these bonds more than about forty-five per cent. of their face value. Whatever else goes unpaid, the interest on these bonds must be met, or the mortgage is foreclosed. The Roads are thus mortgaged for their full value, and the owners of the bonds are really the owners of the railroads. The mortgage, together with some preferred stock on which interest is sometimes paid, absorbs the earnings of the road. The rest of the stock receives no dividends, and is of no actual value. The bond holders are practically the owners of the roads. It is only a question of time when the bond holders will take possession of their prey. They would do it at any time if the management of those who may hold the stock does not suit them. But the probability is that they keep in their hands a controlling interest of the stock, so as to secure the present control of the roads.

In the second place, it is certain that

2ND. IF THE MONEY KINGS WERE EVER IN POSSESSION OF THE RAILROADS, THEY OWN THEM STILL.

1. THE LAWS OF POLITICAL ECONOMY PROVE

that, if the London Money Kings ever got possession of the Railroads, they have them still. We could never have bought them back by any possibility, unless the Balance of Trade were in our favor. For, without such a favorable Balance of Trade, our people could never possibly have the means to buy the railroads back. But the Balance of Trade has been steadily against us all the while. Hence, it is perfectly manifest that the railroads are still in the hands of the Money Power. This is as certain as any fact in the world of nature. For the laws of political economy are as fixed as the laws of nature.

2. THE HISTORY OF THE MONEY POWER PROVES

that no Americans have ever bought back Railroads once in possession of the Money Kings. It is a fixed rule with the Money Kings never to take an interest in any business, without having a controlling interest in the stock; and having got a controlling interest in any enterprise, *they work it, and never sell it.* They are always buying property: They never sell;—except indeed, batches of stock, to gulls, in Wall street operations! If the Money Power ever got a controlling interest in American railroads, they never sold it out again, and no Americans ever had in their own ownership the controlling interest in such American railroads.

3. An Objection

may be presented here, that many American railroads, and those the most valuable, are notoriously owned by Americans: that the Vanderbilts own the New York Central system—that Jay Gould owns a large system in his own right—that Tom Scott owned the Pennsylvania Central—that Garrett owns the Baltimore and Ohio—and that Huntingdon owns the Chesapeake and Ohio and its connections.

This is a matter of such importance to the American people that it ought to be thoroughly sifted. These men have claimed to be the owners of these grand railroad systems;—but are they? Or are they merely the agents of the London Money Kings, holding the railroads in trust for them?

3rd. Circumstantial Evidence that Amounts to Scientific Demonstration

proves that these men are the agents of the London Money Kings.

It is remarkable that very many peculiar facts have come to light about these railroad magnates, which prove that our American "railroad kings," so-called, are only the agents of the London Money Kings. The proof is stronger than could be expected, when the Money Kings do everything in their power to conceal their ownership. They have always systematically concealed their track, so that no direct evidence of their ownership can be found. Their actions are always in the dark.—But a midnight murderer or a burglar can be convicted on circumstantial evidence. So, if the ownership of the railroads by the

London Money Kings were a felony, there is sufficient proof to send them to state prison.

1. Jay Gould an Agent for British Capitalists.

A large number of facts prove this:—

1) In 1873, Jay Gould and Jim Fisk were full partners in the ownership of the New York and Erie R. R. Holding $23,000,000 of railroad stocks, they were thought to be worth over $11,000,000 each. They were full partners, and were supposed to be worth about the same amount. It is perfectly evident that Fisk and Gould were not the real owners of the Erie railroad. As the trail of a serpent can only be seen when the snake crosses a dusty road, so the track of the Money Kings can usually be seen only when it runs across the grave of an agent. The settlements made at death frequently show that the reputed millionaire was only an agent of the Money Kings.

When Fisk was killed, in 1873, he, as has been stated, was thought to be worth $11,000,000, as he was holding that amount of railroad stock. But when his estate was wound up, his family received only a few thousand dollars. Thus the settlement of his estate after his death, showed conclusively that Fisk was only an agent, holding, in connection with Gould, the Erie railroad for the real stockholders in Great Britain. There can be no doubt that Jay Gould, his partner, was their agent also.

Once finding Mr. Gould acting as the agent of the Money Kings, creates a strong presumption, that, in his subsequent operations, he is also the agent of European capitalists. But the case does not rest on mere presumption. It is perfectly certain that, in all his subsequent operations, Jay Gould has been only an agent of the London Money Kings, holding the railroads ostensively owned by him in trust for them.

2) **Jay Gould's Railroad System** belongs to the Money Kings. In 1873, Jay Gould could hardly have been worth more than his partner, Jim Fisk. In the hard times that followed 1873, nobody in America could make much money. Yet, in 1878, Jay Gould came out West with forty million dollars, as it was given out through the newspapers, and bought ten thousand miles of railroad; and the American people were made to believe that it was his money, and that he himself owned, in his own right, the railroads of the Gould system. His wealth was regarded as enormous. He was reputed the richest man in America. His wealth has been estimated as high as two hundred million dollars.

But of late years, facts have transpired, which show conclusively that Jay Gould is only the agent of the Money Power, to hold and operate their railroads:—

The Wabash System is one-half of the ten thousand miles of railroad in the Gould System. Some years ago, the Wabash System became embarrassed, and was placed in the hands of a receiver. Mr. Gould no doubt supposed that it might affect his credit for the American people to suppose that he could not sustain the credit of his roads; so he had an interview with a New York reporter, which fell under my eye, in which he said that much the greater number of the stockholders of the Wabash System were in Great Britain, and only a few in the United States:—and Jay Gould is one of the few!—It is evident that Jay Gould is not the owner of the Wabash System!

The rest of the ten thousand miles of the Gould System consists of the Missouri Pacific, the Missouri Kansas and Texas, the Texas Pacific, and the Iron Mountain Railroads.—The Texas Pacific did not belong to Jay Gould, for its stockholders have had it taken out of the Gould System by process of law.—The Missouri Kansas and Texas did not belong to him; for its stockholders also, have brought suit and withdrawn the Road out of the Gould System.

Indeed, a short time since, Mr. Gould had an interview with a reporter, which I saw, in which he stated that he held more stock in the Missouri Pacific than all his other investments put together. The Missouri Pacific is a Road three hundred miles long, running from St. Louis to Kansas City. And Mr. Gould's stock in that road amounts to more than all his other investments put together! And he does not even own all of that three hundred miles of railroad.—And yet Mr. Gould was the ostensible owner of ten thousand miles of railroad and worth two hundred million dollars!!

When we find one of the ostensible great owners of a grand railroad system to be merely an agent of the Money Power, it gives rise to a strong presumption that the other reputed owners of great railroad systems are also agents of the Money Power.

2. Vanderbilt an Agent of the Money Power.

There is a large amount of cumulative evidence to prove that Commodore Vanderbilt was an agent of the Money Kings:—

1) Commodore Vanderbilt was originally a poor man. He first rose into prominence as the manager of a line of steamers, running in the Isthmus route from New York to San Francisco. But when he quit the ship line and went into Wall street speculation in railroad stocks, he was worth only one million dollars. Manifestly, therefore, he was not the owner of the steamship line, but was holding and operating it as the agent for the stockholders, who were largely English.

If Commodore Vanderbilt was the agent of the Money Kings in operating the steamship line, and was afterwards transferred by them to Wall street, to operate for them there, it will explain many things otherwise unaccountable.

2) Vanderbilt always operated in Wall street as a bull. In other words, he was always buying railroad stocks. I recollect reading a work written when his operations were the wonder of the whole country, in which the author said that Vanderbilt had an unlimited purse back of him. Nobody knew where he got his money, but the money at his command was practically without limit. Frequently he had the whole street against him, but he was always able to put down any combination that was formed against him. He had more money at his command than could be brought against him in all America.

It is idle to suppose that Vanderbilt was able to carry his vast operations through, with the one million dollars he was worth when he went into Wall street. Many of the operators there who combined against him were each far richer than he. We can only account for his immense operations, which required the command of unlimited capital to carry them to the successful issue he always attained, on the hypothesis that he was the agent of the London Money Kings to buy up railroad stocks for them.

I recollect that when Vanderbilt bought out Harlem, a little railroad some twenty odd miles long, the whole world was astonished that one man was able to buy and own an entire railroad. He soon afterwards bought the Hudson River railroad, and the New York Central; and he continued to purchase railroads, until he owned a grand system extending far into the Northwest. It was impossible for Commodore Vanderbilt to have conducted his immense operations with his own limited capital. If he was the agent of the Money Kings, all is explained.

3) At his death, Commodore Vanderbilt was reputed to be worth one hundred million dollars. When, in his will,

he divided out only three and one half millions among his children, that fact confirmed me in my belief that he was an agent of the Money Power, and that the three and one half million dollars was all he was really worth; and that, in giving the rest of the property, including the railroads, to his son Wm. H. Vanderbilt, he simply transferred the agency to him. This view was confirmed by the fact that Wm. H. Vanderbilt, immediately after his father's death, went to London, as I believed, to see his principals, and have his agency confirmed.

4) A fact which occurred in 1880, was, to my mind, conclusive evidence that Wm. H. Vanderbilt was only an agent. He then transferred a controlling interest in the New York Central System to a syndicate of New York capitalists, avowedly representing English capitalists, for $50,000,000; which he at once invested in four per cent United States bonds. Now, I do not think that Mr. Vanderbilt would have done that, if the property had been his. The transaction is contrary to all the laws of human motive.

1] The stock made him a Railroad King—one of the most influential men in America. And it was paying him far more than four per cent.

2] A man owning a grand railroad system under his own absolute control would not jeopardize his interests, by selling a controlling interest to foreign capitalists. Nor would an astute financier like Vanderbilt have sold a controlling interest in a grand railroad system which must have been paying much more than four per cent., to invest the money in four per cent. bonds. It is not in human nature to make so bad a bargain.

3] Nor does it accord with the pride of a railroad magnate thus to abdicate power, and step down and out. If Mr. Vanderbilt was a free agent, his action is inexplicable by all the laws of human motive.

4] But if he was an agent of the London Money Kings, and an order came from headquarters to make the transfer, he would have to "obey orders."

5] And this was probably the fact. Mr. Vanderbilt was a haughty irritable man, and exceedingly indiscreet in his utterances. If an agent, he was not the best man to keep in such a responsible position. His utterances, "d—— the people," and "I do not run my roads for the benefit of the people", exposed him to popular odium, and would not commend him to his principals.

6] At the next election after his transfer of stock, Mr. Vanderbilt was elected a director in all the roads of the system; but he was made president of only a subordinate road. He was evidently very much humiliated, and made a meek speech in which he said he had no doubt the new arrangement would be more agreeable to the stockholders.

7] He did with the United States bonds bought by him just what he would have done if he were an agent acting under orders from his superiors in London. What did he do with them? Did he keep them in New York, as he would naturally have done if they had been his own? No: he at once deposited them in London, in the banking house of John Bidall Martin, in Lombard street.

5) The provisions of the will of Wm. H. Vanderbilt bear out the idea that he was an agent of the London Money Kings. He divided his property among his children more equally than his father had done; but he gave to one son $56,000,000, a controlling interest in the railroad system; and he provided that all the property should remain together. This arrangement would secure the control of the railroad system to the Money Kings, as effectually as the arrangement made by his father.

I do not doubt, however, that Gould and the Vanderbilts are rich in their own right. The Money Kings pay their agents well. Their rule is to give them a large, though minority interest, in the property they manage. And then, the position of Commodore Vanderbilt, and later, of Jay Gould, and Wm. H. Vanderbilt, would give them vast opportunities of making a great deal of money for themselves in operations in Wall street. But all the cumulative facts prove that Commodore Vanderbilt was an agent of the Money Kings—facts which are wholly inconsistent with the idea that the Vanderbilt family really owns the railroads it holds in possession.

If the grand so called "Railroad King" in America, is only an agent of the London Money Kings, what a commentary upon the grandeur of those imperial capitalists!

3. **Tom Scott** was the reputed owner of the Pennsylvania Central;—but, since his death, we hear nothing of his heirs being the owners of that railroad system.

4. **C. P. Huntingdon** has been the reputed owner of the Chesapeake and Ohio Railroad and connections. Where did he make the money to buy it?

(1) At the time the Central Pacific Railroad was projected, Huntingdon was a grocer with limited means in San Francisco. He and his coadjutors built the Central Pacific Railroad. Many facts indicate that they were merely the agents of the Money Power in that enterprise. The United States government aid was only paid when a stipulated number of miles of railway had been completed: the men in the construction company had not the means to do so much work before receiving the government subsidy. All Americans who have a grand enterprise in hand go to London to get the money to accomplish it. Now, the Money Kings would not have suffered Huntingdon and company to remain principals in the ownership of the road for the construction of which the Money Kings furnished the money. They would certainly demand, as the only condition on which they would

furnish the money for construction, that the franchise should be transferred to them, and that Huntingdon and his friends should become their agents to build and operate the road.

(2) When Huntingdon appeared before a Congressional Committee, he insisted that the Central Pacific road was in very straitened circumstances. When a member of the Committee asked him if he shared the depressed financial condition of the road, he paused for a considerable time before replying; and finally answered with extreme caution,—"No: *I am said* to be rich."—He insisted that he had made no money out of the Central Pacific; but that everything he was worth had been realized from other enterprises.

I take all this to be a reserved statement of the actual truth. The Money Kings would get the lion's share of the profits of constructing and operating the Central Pacific; to Huntingdon and the others would be allowed the jackal's portion.

(3) But, if Huntingdon made no money out of the Central Pacific Railroad, where did he get the money to buy the Chesapeake and Ohio, and the other railroads of the system? We are forced to the conclusion that Huntingdon does not own those railroads at all—that he is the agent of the Money Kings, and holds his roads, as Gould does his system, in trust for the real owners.

His answer to the Congressional Committee indicates such a state of facts. He said "*I am said* to be rich." Such would be the cautious language of a man who was thought to be the owner of a great railroad system, when he knew himself to be the agent of the Money Power.

5. **In the case of Garrett,** the facts fully comport with the idea that he is the agent of the Money Kings; but not at all with the idea of a man owning a vast railroad system in his own right. But as it would be necessary to

comment on his personal misfortunes, in order to make out the case, it is passed without further notice. It is sufficient to say that the Baltimore and Ohio Railroad is fully mortgaged to London bond holders.

The whole question of the ownership of the American railroads is veiled in mystery. But, however carefully it is hidden, the Money Kings have the property securely in their hands.

Everything proves that the Money Kings are the owners of our railroads. The author of a pamphlet given me in London, in 1864, told the truth when he said of the Money Kings, as will be hereafter quoted,—"We are the railway builders of the world, and the actual owners of the greater part of the railways." They have had plenty of time since then, to have purchased what they did not then own; and they have been very busy in Wall street, during the entire interval.

CHAPTER VI.

DEVOURINGS OF THE MONEY POWER IN THE UNITED STATES, CONTINUED.

V. THE MONEY POWER DEVOURS OUR OIL INDUSTRY.

Upon the discovery of oil in Pennsylvania, many Americans embarked in the new enterprise; spending millions in prospecting for oil, and millions more in operating successful wells, engaged in active and healthy competition in the oil market. The aggregate profits of the business attracted the attention of the Money Power, which promptly took steps to crush the American well owners, and monopolize the business.

The measures adopted were as quiet, as sudden, as effectual, as the coil of the boa constrictor about its victim. A railroad was built to the oil regions;—but it was not built to the oil wells, so that all the well owners might ship by it, but its terminus was fifteen miles away on one side. A few wells were purchased, to start the business; and a pipe line company was organized, and a pipe line was laid from the wells purchased, out to the railroad, with steam engines stationed at intervals, to force onward the sluggish flow of oil.

At that time, six thousand wagons were hauling oil over corduroy roads out to the railroad. Of course, the well owners, hauling on wagons, could not compete with the pipe line, after it went into operation. The profits of oil were put down to a point that barely covered expenses, with the best facilities. The individual well owners had to plug up their wells, waiting for another railroad to be built into the oil regions, over which they might ship. But these Money Kings never jostle each other. No other railroad was built. The oil well owners, in despair, had to sell out to the Money Kings, at any price they chose to offer.

The Great Standard Oil Company, operating with a capital of $90,000,000 in the United States, has now, by a long course of oppression crushing all competitors, taken possession of the entire oil industry of the country, and established a mighty monopoly.

A number of striking facts point out the Standard Oil Company as one of the monopolies of the London Money Power:—

1. The monopoly of the oil industry is part of a grand system. We find the Money Kings engaged in establishing monopolies all over the world, and especially in our country. We naturally conclude that the oil monopoly is also a part of their system.

2. A detective can identify a burglar by his method. This oil monopoly was established in perfect accordance with the method of the Money Power. The combination of cunning, secretiveness and the deadly coil of omnipotent capital is unmistakable.

3. No American capitalists were powerful enough to break down the oil well owners by dint of unlimited capital.

4. No American capitalists would have engaged in such an enterprise, when the oil well owners might have foiled the attempt by obtaining English capital to counterwork them. Only the Money Kings would have engaged in an attempt that required such an immense outlay; for only they could be sure of being able to carry out the design without interference from other capitalists. They are thoroughly organized, and never interfere with each other.

5. It is manifest that the Standard Oil Company is not an American corporation. The method and the extent of its operations show that it is an enterprise of the Money Kings. For the Standard Oil Company is operating in Russia as largely as in the United States. It owns hundreds of millions of acres of Russian oil lands, and is supplying the neighboring markets from those oil wells, just as it is supplying the American markets from the oil wells of Pennsylvania. The Standard Oil Company, like all the monopolies of the Money Kings, is world-wide in its operations. Unlimited capital behind it enables it to construct facilities for carrying on its business,—a grand pipe line from the oil wells to the seaboard—grand refineries—tank cars for transportation of refined oil,—these and other things gave it such advantages as enabled it to put down all competition and maintain a monopoly of the bnsiness. It evidently aims to secure a monopoly of the oil trade for centuries to come.

Unlimited capital has enabled the Money Power to crush in its coil the original proprietors of the oil wells without the possibility of resistance. The same unlimited capital enables the Money Power to crush competition in every line of business, and thus to devour every business interest in the country. And it has been successively devouring one branch of business after another, until its grand imperialism now covers our land throughout its whole extent.

VI. THE MONEY POWER DEVOURS CHICAGO.

The Money Power, owning the railroads, and seeking to get into its clutches all our industries, as we shall see it has done, needed to have a great city, upon which to center the railroads and the trade controlled by it.

In 1870, Chicago was rapidly becoming a railroad and business center for the Northwest. It was the city hest adapted to become the trade center of the country, except perhaps, St. Louis. But St. Louis was out of the question, its business being operated by home capital well established. In order that the Money Kings might be able to centralize the trade of the country in their hands, it was necessary for them to get a secure clutch upon Chicago.

The great fire of 1871 afforded them their opportunity. Nobody ever knew how it originated. A high wind prevailing at the time swept the flames through the heart of the city, leaving a path of desolation three-fourths of a mile wide. The business center of Chicago was reduced to ashes.

The business community had been doing business in cheap two-story houses. In rebuilding, they would, no doubt, have preferred to erect cheap two-story buildings again; for the lower stories furnished all the room needed for business purposes.

But there has never been any money to be obtained for building, in this country, public improvements on a large scale, except in London. Chicago could only be rebuilt with London capital. The Money lenders could dictate the style of buildings to be erected,—splendid structures, from six to ten stories high, the upper stories of which could only be rented for offices or lodgings. Before the rebuilding was completed, the hard times of 1873 came on; the crisis being engineered, as we shall see, by the London Money Power. The panic caught the Chicago business men in the trough of the sea. Business was prostrate: renters were lacking for the upper stories: payments could not be made: mortgages were foreclosed; and the most of the grand Chicago business blocks became the property of the Money King mortgagees.

It was said that Chicago was rebuilt by loans of Eastern capital. We have learned, of late years, that Eastern capital means London capital. London is the point from which we have always had to get money for all improvements. At the time of the Chicago fire, the Money Kings had established many loan agencies in the Eastern states, as a part of their policy for concealing their money-loaning operations. And these loan agencies were the source whence the money was obtained to rebuild Chicago.

The railroads of the West and South are now concentrated upon Chicago in such a way as to center upon it in a wonderful manner the trade of those sections. Pushed forward with the might of the unlimited capital of the Money Kings, Chicago is growing at an unprecedented rate. It is now the second city in the country, and it is confidently declared that, in a few years, it will surpass New York. And it is very probable; for railroads now bring to it the trade of Canada and the Northwest, to Puget Sound; of the West, to San Francisco; of the Southwest, to the Gulf of Mexico and San Diego; of the

South, to New Orleans and Mobile; of the Southeast, to Atlanta, Savannah and St. Augustine. Chicago is the great center of the traffic of the London Money Kings in this country.

Kansas City was planted as the outpost of Chicago, to take away the trade of the Southwest from St. Louis and carry it to Chicago. And Kansas City is springing up like a giant, with its growth pushed with all the might of London capital. Like New York it has an elevated railroad; in cable roads it is not surpassed by any city in the country. It is not suffered to lack anything for its growth that capital can give it.

If anyone wishes to see *how these grand capitalists build up cities* by the might of capital, such curiosity will be gratified by observations in Chicago and Kansas City. Every suburb is planted, not by pioneers, as in other new towns, but by capitalists, who spend millions before they invite a settler. A railroad is first built to the prospective town; then the streets are graded: gas and water pipes are put down: the sidewalks are laid:—and then, settlers are invited to make their homes in the new suburb.—Nobody can lay out towns in such a style of princely expense but the London Money Kings.

VII. THE MONEY POWER CRUSHES ALL OUR INDUSTRIES, BY INDUCING THE CRASH OF 1873.

We have now come in the order of time to the crash of 1873, which ruined many thousands of our business men throughout the country.

The crash of 1873 was brought on by the failure of the House of Jay Cooke & Co. Jay Cooke was a London banker, and the agent of the Money Kings for building the Northern Pacific Railroad. The failure was arranged in such a manner that it did not involve the London house of Jay Cooke & Co. at all. But the failure of the American house accomplished its purpose. It started a crash whose influence lasted five years, prostrating all our industries, and sweeping the country with a deluge of bankruptcy; enabling the Money Kings to hold carnival in the purchase of our produce at low prices, and in buying up property cheap at bankrupt sales.

All prices went down so low that, though we had $900,000,000 of currency in the country, it only needed $300,000,000 to carry on all the business of the country, and the other $600,000,000 was locked up and retired from circulation.

The London Money Kings certainly prepared and engineered the panic of 1873, just as they did the crash of 1837 and 1857. We find their motive in the fact that it gave them an excuse for locking up $600,000,000, and thus causing the ruin that followed, with the hard times and low prices, in which they reaped a rich harvest of profit to themselves.

They Can Make Good Times or Hard Times whenever they please; so completely have they gotten our country in their hands. They hold our prosperity completely in their grasp. We are become entirely dependent upon them. When they wish to make good times, they put out their money freely, in building railroads, in making city improvements, in establishing new enterprises all over the country, and in lending money to everybody who wishes to borrow and has property to mortgage as security. Then we have flush times for several years; and everybody, under their leading, rushes into speculation, and everybody gets into debt.

Then, in Order to Make Hard Times, the Money Kings have only to lock up the money they make as profits out of their various enterprises in the country. They stop building railroads: they stop all outlays for city improvements: they stop all investments in new enterprises; and they stop loans to borrowers. They simply lock up their profits, and let the money lie idle.—And at once business is at a stand still: the improvements which had given activity to business cease: established businesses, such as farming, manufacturing, railroading go on: everything else stops. There is universal stagnation: prices fall: a flood of bankruptcy sweeps over the land: thousands are ruined:—and the Money Kings revel in low prices of produce, and cheap purchases of bankrupt property.

This was the way in which the Money Kings operated the hard times of 1873, and several years afterwards. But they had to have a visible cause that would account for the hard times to the public, on accepted business principles. The failure of Jay Cooke did this. It destroyed confidence, and in the eyes of the public justified the locking up of the money, with all the subsequent ruin. They thus made our people believe that the crash was an unavoidable disaster, due to regular business causes, and not to their own malignant intention.

But it was done on purpose, with malicious intent to bring about the very result that followed. That it was the work of the London Money Kings is demonstrable.—They were building the Northern Pacific Railroad. Jay Cooke was their agent in doing that work. They had engaged to build the Northern Pacific Railroad, and had started the work. Jay Cooke failed, and his failure brought on the panic. The failure was a trick, a sham. Does anybody believe that the London Money Kings who had undertaken to build the Northern Pacific Railroad were unable to carry out their contract?—that they had not money enough to complete the work, if they chose? The idea is too absurd to be entertained for a moment. They let the enterprise drop, because they chose to do so: they had their agent, Jay Cooke, to fail, because they knew that his failure would bring on a crash which they were resolved to produce, and in whose ruin they desired to glut their avarice.

They stand convicted before the eyes of the world, of an atrocious crime against the country, and against humanity. They did not even have the grace to let the London house of Jay Cook share in the failure. They sent him to America as a dynamite bomb, to explode and destroy the prosperity of the United States. And they sent him carefully disconnected from his London house, so that the ruin he wrought would not effect the London house with which he was connected. Jay Cooke may have been an innocent victim of their purpose. They do not inform their agents of their designs.

The time may come when all the particulars of this infamous plot will be revealed to the world. They may hide their tracks as carefully as they can; but the eye of history may, in the future, be able to gather many facts now hidden, and make the plot stand out, as St. Bartholomew stands, revealed to the loathing of mankind.

It is a dreadful thought that the Money Kings have our industries so completely in their power that they can cause another panic such as that of 1873, whenever they choose. They could start one to-morrow far worse than that, as their control of our industries is far more complete now than then. Our prosperity is entirely at their mercy.

VIII. THE MONEY KINGS DEVOUR OUR NEW ENGLAND MILLS.

Having brought on the hard times of 1873, and caused a broad wave of bankruptcy to oversweep our country, the Money Kings prepared to reap their harvest. Everything was so arranged that ruin, however wide-spread, would attract no special attention, but would be regarded as the natural consequence of the hard times. The time was ripe, and Money Power began at once a grand campaign against the New England Mills.

It was in its devouring the mills of New England that I first came upon the track of the Money Power, after 1873. I knew that the Money Kings had brought on the panic of 1873, by the failure of Jay Cooke, and I was sure that they were engineering it to suit their own interests. But such was their prudence and skill that for two years I looked in vain. I first came upon their track in 1875. I then found that the New York merchants were putting down cotton goods to an extremely low price,—one-tenth of a cent a yard below the cost of production. Drummers were everywhere urging merchants through the country to buy, on account of the low price, which they said would not last very long.

I at first wondered how, with the protection of a high tariff, the price of cotton goods could be so very low. I knew it was not accidental, for the fixed price,—one-tenth of a cent a yard below the cost of production in New England,—showed that it was done by design. I began to think out the cause of the remarkable fact. In finding it, I found the trail of the Money Kings. Being familiar with the operations of our tariff system, I soon made the discovery of

Their Method of Attack

upon the New England mills. They had discovered a flaw in our tariff system, which enabled them, owning the English factories, and warehouses and shipping, to crush the mills of New England, despite the protection of the tariff.

In the old days of Democratic rule, before the war, Congress, in order to accommodate the import merchants of New York City, so arranged the tariff that duties were payable, not when the goods were placed in the warehouse, but when they were taken out for sale. The London merchants, under our warehouse system, could store their goods in the New York warehouse, free of charge, and let them lie there for any length of time; and might then, if they chose, withdraw them without payment of duty, and ship them to any other market. It was cheaper for them to store their goods in the New York Custom House than in their own warehouses in London. For they had to build their own warehouses, at considerable cost; while the United States government was so accommodating as to build the warehouse and offer them free use of it for the storage of their goods.

The Money Kings availed themselves of the privilege given them by our warehouse system. They stored millions of dollars worth of goods, not really for sale, but to be offered at a nominal price, for the purpose of "bearing" down the price of goods in the New York market. The New England Mill owners would have to sell their goods as cheap as the English goods were offered in the custom house,—at one-tenth of a cent a yard below the cost of production. They had to keep on running, even at a loss; for the delicate machinery, if suffered to lie idle for six months, would become lobsided and worthless. They continued to run on at a loss until they failed. Sprague, of Rhode Island, was the richest of the mill owners of New England. When he failed for ten million dollars, the tide of bankruptcy swept over New England. The newspapers at the time were filled, not with business advertisements but, with bankrupt notices. Amid the thousands of bankruptcies throughout the country the ruin of the New England mills attracted but little attention.

But the mills did not cease operations. New companies were organized, of which capitalists from abroad had control: the mills were set in operation again: prices were stiffened up to a point that yielded a fair profit; and the manufactories resumed their prosperity.

Nobody in this country wished to break down the New England mills. And nobody on earth was powerful enough to do it but these London Money Kings. When the mills had broke their former owners, no American capitalists would have embarked in a losing business. But these Money Kings knew how they had broken them down, and how easy it would be to make them profitable.

The system of the Money Kings is not known to the public. When they break a man, or a company, they do not always set the head of the business aside. They do not wish to make a commotion in business circles by many changes; and they need the experience of the old business managers. Their system is, not to destroy, but to subordinate. Their method is the method of the Romans in extending their conquests: the Romans always left a subjugated state with a modicum of power, until the time came to reduce it to a province. The Money Kings can always kick out their allies whenever they wish, the companies being under their complete control; and they can afford to be seemingly generous for a while, till the time comes to take entire possession. In the present era of the growth of the Money Power, the Money Kings keep in partnership with their Gentile agents: in the next era, they will kick out the Gentile agencies, and put the business in the hands of their countrymen, the Jews.

IX. THE MONEY POWER DEVOURED OUR IRON INDUSTRY.

Our iron industry, like the other manufactures of the country, is protected by our tariff, so that whatever iron is sold usually brings a remunerative price. The Money Power could only crush our iron industry by so crushing the prosperity of the whole country that there would be no building, and no demand for iron. Even in hard times, people must have clothing and fuel; so that textile manufactures and the coal industry continue to maintain some degree of activity. But iron products are chiefly used in construction,—building houses and factories and railroads. Hard times which put a stop to improvements close up iron mines, and foundries and machine shops.

The Money Power, by the crash of 1873, prostrated the whole country. For years, all improvements stopped. Mechanics were thrown out of employment by the hundred thousand, in cities, in mines, in shops, and roamed as tramps over the country. The repairing of railroads was almost the only use for iron; and, as the Money Kings owned the railroads, they could send iron from England at any price; for, selling to themselves, the price made no difference. For railroad iron, the protection of the tariff was ineffectual.

For five years after 1873, all business was crushed and lifeless.—But it was the harvest of the Money Kings. They bought our products at extremely low prices, and made unusually large profits: as iron works failed, they bought their plants: as lumber companies broke from the long stagnation of business, they bought mills aud forests; and they had a grand harvest foreclosing mortgages, and taking possession of mortgaged property.

When the harvest was reaped,—when the Money Power had devoured all the weak iron and lumber companies, and had gathered in all mortgaged property, the Boa loosed its coil. By beginning to build railroads and to make city improvements, and by loans to start new enterprises, the Money Power, about 1879–80 started the country upon a new cycle of prosperity.

Possessed of boundless capital--possessed of our railroads—possessed of the great trade centers of the country—the Money Power has imperial control over our industry, and has monopolized the traffic in all the great products of the country.

X. THE MONEY POWER HAS DEVOURED THE COTTON TRADE.

The agencies of the Money Power in the Cotton States have been reduced to a perfect system. Agents have been established in every district, who make full semi-weekly or weekly reports as to the condition of the cotton crop in each district. The reports begin with the plowing season, and go on through the entire year, giving every fact having any bearing upon the condition of the crop. They report the number of acres plowed—the weather—the number of acres planted—any blight; army worm, excessive rains, drought—the prospect of crops—bolling of the cotton—the quantity picked—the amount of yield. And *every morning, the telegraph brings from Liverpool*, to all the agents, *the price to be paid for cotton that day*.

A general agent told a gentleman who was my informant, that his business was so mean and arbitrary and despotic, he hated it. He said the planters frequently struggled against the low prices which were ruining them. "But," said he, "they had just as well fight against the course of the seasons." They have no alternative but submission to the prices offered by the Money Kings. And those prices mean poverty to the planter, and penury to the colored laborers who barely subsist upon their share of the crop.

XI. THE MONEY POWER HAS DEVOURED THE WHEAT AND GRAIN TRADE.

The construction of elevators has given to the railroads complete possession of the wheat and grain trade. At first, there was a pretense of individual purchase of grain. The Money Kings perhaps feared that the open monopoly by them of the wheat trade of the country might cause discontent and murmuring, and they at first tried to hide their monopoly of the trade. The former custom was for some man to build an elevator at a depot, and figure as its owner, buying up the wheat of the surrounding country on his own account. But those agents frequently illlustrated the proverb of a beggar on horseback. Beginning to drink, they had to be removed; thus showing that they were only agents of the railroads. This plan failing, the railroads adopted the plan of granting to some wealthy individual the exclusive right to build elevators along the line, with of course the exclusive right to buy and ship grain over the railroads. This man, who is, of course, the agent of the railroad, appoints his agents at each depot, and has a monopoly of the wheat and grain trade along the line.

In this way, a few men buy all the wheat of the country. There is no competition; the railroads fix the price of wheat and grains to suit themselves, and grind the farmers down into absolute poverty. And they not only plunder the farmer in the price, but they cheat in the measurement which fixes the quality of the wheat. For instance, several years ago, No. 1 wheat was 90 cents a bushel, No. 2, 75 cents, and No. 3, 60 cents a bushel. The wheat was so graded by the buyers, that all wheat weighing 60 lbs. and over to the bushel was rated No. 1; all wheat weighing 56 lbs. and over, No. 2; and all wheat weighing 52 lbs. and over, No. 3. Now, if the wheat were measured in the good old fashioned way in an honest half bushel measure, most of the wheat would weigh 60 lbs. to the bushel, and be rated as No. 1. But these monopolists cheat systematically in the measure. They use an oval gallon measure, easily battered, by accident, to diminish its capacity. Into such a small measure the wheat will not pack close, when poured very gently out of a pitcher into it. They then weigh the gallon and multiply by 8 to find the weight of a bushel. By this system of measurement little of the wheat rates as No. 1; and very much of it is rated as No. 3. In this way, when No. 1 wheat was selling at 90 cents a bushel, this system of measuring caused much of it to be rated as No. 3, which brought only 60 cents a bushel.

But afterwards, when these monopolists sold the wheat out of the elevators, where it was under pressure, all of it would weigh 60 lbs. to the bushel, and was sold as No. 1!

The monopolists have now progressed so far with their system of oppression, that they at present only pay the farmer for wheat about 60 cents a bushel. And the farmers have to endure this system of cheating and oppression, because there is no competition, and the railroads arrange matters to suit themselves.

XII. THE MONEY POWER HAS DEVOURED THE LIVE STOCK TRADE IN CATTLE.

Ten years ago, there were in Chicago fifty buyers purchasing cattle for the Eastern markets on their own account. Two years ago, I was informed that four buyers were doing practically all the business. The live stock trade in cattle is in the hands of the Money Kings. No individuals can compete with them. They have broke down all the cattle buyers engaged in the business, and have either driven them out of the business, or forced them to become the agents of the Money Power. In the cattle trade, the Money Power reigns supreme, having crushed all competition and established a complete monopoly.

XIII. THE MONEY POWER HAS DEVOURED THE TRADE IN HOGS AND PORK AND BACON.

Thirteen years ago, there were pork packing firms in all the great cities of the West, doing an independent and profitable business. But in the hard times following 1873, pork packing became a losing business. For several years, hogs were high at the time the packers in St. Louis, Louisville and Cincinnati were buying and killing; but when the bacon was put upon the market, immense capitalists put down the market, and the packers lost money. This continued for several years, until the individual packing companies, buying hogs high and having to sell bacon in the market depressed by dominating capitalists, broke.

The King of All the Pork Packers of America is Armour of Chicago. His has been an extraordinary career. A few years ago, he was a poor butcher, doing an ordinary business like many others of his fellows. But suddenly he became rich. In a year or two after his packing house was built in Chicago, he was killing six thousand hogs a day, and operating his business with a capital of $120,000,000. These sudden fortunes, as we have seen in the case of the Railroad Kings, are suspicious. Where did Armour get his money? He could not have made it in the ordinary way of business. It was impossible.

His sudden wealth is easily explained on the hypothesis that he is the chosen agent of the Money Kings to take possession of a grand line of American production for them. This explains his immense business, which sprung up like a creation of Aladdin's lamp. This explains the hundred and twenty million dollars so suddenly embarked in his business!

Besides the business in Chicago, Armour has packing houses in Kansas City and Omaha almost as extensive as the Chicago establishment. And, in Kansas City, he has a bank with such immense resources that, in a time of stringency in the money market, other banks in the city were compelled to lean upon it for support. All this unlimited capital is fully explained, if Armour is an Agent of the London Money Kings.

It also explains another singular fact: when the other packers, in St. Louis, Cincinnati and Louisville, lost money by their operations year after year till they broke, Armour made money all the time. As they grew poorer and poorer till they failed, Armour grew grander and grander, till he became a very colossus between whose legs pigmies creep. Indeed, Armour was the storm king who ruled the storm which swept down the other packing houses.

The position of Armour in the Board of Trade, controlling prices, not only of pork and bacon and beef, but also of wheat and grain, is such as would be assumed by a chief and trusted agent of the Money Kings.

When we know that it is in accordance with the method of the Money Kings to employ such agents, and when we see a colossal American house which sprung up from nothing, like a mush-room in a night—which grew when all others broke—which thrived amid the disasters which prostrated other houses in the same line of business—the mind which seeks a cause for every effect is driven to the conclusion that Armour is a grand agent of the London Money Kings.

Another Fact shows that the London Money Kings are now controlling our pork and bacon trade through a system of agencies:—Some of the packing houses in Louisville, Cincinnati and St. Louis which broke, continued the business. Where did they get the Money? They had, after their failure, no money with which to continue the business. Friends would not furnish them money to continue a business in which they had lost their own wealth.

But they got the money somewhere, and kept on in business. Did they get their capital from the London Money Kings? Did those imperial capitalists, when they had broken down the packing houses, subordinate them, and use their skill and energy, subsidizing them as agents? If such was the fact, it will explain the state of things in the business world, otherwise inexplicable.

XIV. THE MONEY KINGS DEVOURED THE DRESSED BEEF TRAFFIC.

There are many men in Chicago and other cities engaged in the fresh meat business who, ten years ago, were worth $10,000, and who are fortunate if they are now worth $50,000. But all the great dressed Beef companies have had phenomenal success—success so remarkable as to be truly phenomenal.

1. Swift Brothers—one of the firms engaged in the dressed beef trade, when they started in the business were worth only $8,000. Three years after, they were running seven hundred refrigerator cars costing $700,000, and were operating their business with a capital of $3,000,000. Another house started on nothing, and, in ten years, was operating with a capital of $3,000,000.

We can not account for this phenomenal accumulation of fortune by any natural business laws. But if such firms are agents of the London Money Kings for monopolizing the dressed beef trade, it accounts for it all, and nothing else will.

2. Their being agents also accounts for the fact that these gigantic firms do not jostle one another—have no feeling of rivalry—do not cut one another in prices—nor seek, as individual competitors do, to gain superior advantages over each other for carrying on their business.

3. It also accounts for the dressed beef trade gaining no greater advantages over the live stock trade in the

Eastern markets. Within a few years after it was started, the dressed beef trade had taken entire possession of the New England markets, and entered the markets of the Middle states. But it has made but little progress since its first success. Private enterprise that had succeeded to such an extent and with such rapidity, would have pushed on to complete possession of all the Eastern markets. But the various corporations of the Money Kings never destroy each other. They pool their interests, and compromise their differences. This looks as though there had been an understanding between the dressed beef companies and the railroad companies shipping live stock to the Eastern markets, that the dressed beef companies might proceed to a certain extent with their industry, but should not press their competition to the full control of the Eastern markets.

XV. THE MONEY POWER HAS DEVOURED OUR WHISKEY TRADE.

The whiskey ring is a grand monopoly, involving many millions of capital. Many Americans went into distilling after the War, and for a time made a great deal of money. But about the time that the Money Power was crushing out the other industries of the country, the distillers almost all broke. Of course the thing could be explained as the result of ordinary business causes: The Money Kings always produce their results through the operation of natural causes: they have the capital to set any cause in operation they wish, for the accomplishment of any object. Soon after the distillers broke, the distilleries were set in operation on a greater scale than before.

The Grand Whiskey Ring was formed, strong enough to influence national legislation, and by increasing the tax on the whiskey, to add several cents a gallon to the value of the whiskey in stock, amounting in the aggregate to many millions of dollars.

In the breaking of the old distillers we see the method of the Money Power; we see its method in the organization of the vast whiskey ring: in the reorganization of the distilleries; and in the control of national legislation. There is no monopoly in the country that shows plainer marks of the methods of the Money Kings than the grand whiskey ring.

XVI. THE MONEY POWER HAS DEVOURED OUR EXPORT TRADE.

The Money Kings have possession of every branch of traffic in the products of the country: of the railroads: of the ocean transportation. They have the export trade so hemmed in on every side that they can not fail to have possession of it. It necessarily follows from their buying up our cotton, our wheat, our pork, our bacon, our beef, that they export all these articles that are sent to the foreign markets. And, of course, they have established export houses through which they export the products they have purchased.

XVII. THE MONEY POWER DEVOURS OUR CURRENCY.

It follows from the facts already stated that the Money Power has possession of the great bulk of our currency.

1. **It is a Money Power.** Its magnates are MONEY KINGS. One of the English writers calls the quarter in London where these operators have their places of business, "a city of money dealers." It is by their possession of money that the Money Kings control trade. Most of these Money Kings are Jews: the Jews have been money dealers for centuries. They take possession of the money of a country, first: then by means of their monied capital they devour everything else.

2. **All Banks, have Immense Deposits.** There are two classes of depositors,—individuals who have a moderate surplus of cash over the requirements of their business; and the Money Kings and their agents, who are buying all our produce and doing almost all the business of the country. These Money Kings are too shrewd to allow other people to bank on their deposits. It is a vast gain to own the banks, and make the profit of banking on their deposits themselves. Thus Armour has his bank in Kansas City. No doubt the other great trading and manufacturing corporations which are paying out many millions of dollars every year, also own the banks where the capital is held with which they do their business.

3. When the facts are known, it will be discovered that a large number of our National Banks, especially in the East, are owned by the Money Kings.

It is certain that they have our currency in their grasp. The profits of the immense business they do are realized in money. And they are constantly loaning these cash profits to our people on mortgage. *They own all our money.* Our people only get it from them in exchange—the farmer for crops: the employee for labor; and the borrower for a mortgage on property.

Owning our money, these capitalists can make hard times and low prices whenever they please, by withdrawing the money from circulation. They only need to hold their cash profits in their possession, and stop lending them back, and stop making improvements, and then stop the manufactures of iron and lumber for which the demand will have ceased:—and, at once, all business will be paralized, and millions of people will be out of employment. The Boa has its folds around us, and can tighten them for our destruction whenever it may choose, just as it did in 1873.

Thus the Money Power has advanced step by step in this country, until it has devoured almost every branch of our national industry:—

1. For years it has kept our currency constricted; and it has devoured thousands of millions of dollars worth of our produce at half price, by maintaining panic prices through scarcity of money.

2. It has thus kept us constantly in debt through an adverse balance of trade, and has devoured our gold and silver as fast as produced from the mines.

3. The Money Power has devoured all our mercantile shipping;

4. Our import trade;

5. Our railroads;

6. Our oil production and trade;

7. Our New England Mills;

8. Our iron industry;

9. Much property in Chicago and other cities;

10. Our cotton trade;

11. Our wheat and grain trade;

12. Our live stock trade in cattle;

13. Our trade in hogs, pork and bacon;

14. Our dressed beef trade;

15, Our currency;

And it has, throughout all its operations, conducted its encroachments with such cunning, craft, stealth, and subtlety, that its amazing course of ravage has not been known or even suspected by the outside public.

Chapter VII.

DEVOURINGS OF THE MONEY POWER IN THE U. S., Continued.—INDUSTRIES NOW BEING DEVOURED BY THE MONEY POWER.

The Money Power, as we have seen, has already devoured many of our great lines of industry. It is now enveloping every industry it has not already devoured, and is crushing them in the folds of its capital, preparatory to devouring them.

I. THE MONEY POWER IS CRUSHING OUR COAL MINES.

By their monopoly of transportation, the railroads are securing a monopoly of the coal supply for mines owned by them. In some instances, before the passage of the Interstate Commerce Law, they refused transportation to coal of other companies. They usually form a separate company which owns the coal mines, and they have given special rates to such companies.

Even under the "Interstate Law" regulating railroad traffic, their monopoly of coal mines is not hindered; for even if they made equal charges for their own coal and that of other companies, yet the charge for themselves is simply paid to themselves; so that they can still undersell all competitors. This state of things must give to mines owned by railroads the monopoly of the coal trade, and all other mines must be sold to them, or closed.

II. THE MONEY POWER IS DEVOURING OUR GOLD AND SILVER MINES.

As a rule, persons having gold or silver mines to develop always go to the Money Kings or their agents for the capital to develop them. And the Money Kings never put any money into a mine without having a majority of the stock given them, so as to secure to them its absolute control. They must have the lion's share in any enterprise before they will invest in it. They usually put in one of the original stockholders as their agent and manager; and generally the mine is so managed as to freeze out the other stockholders.

A shaft is sunk down upon the "lead;" if it proves to be rich, only the poorer levels nearer the surface are worked, till the outside stockholders become discouraged and sell out their stock cheap: then the mine is worked efficiently. But if, on the other hand, the mine proves to be a pocket, like the Emma Mine in Utah, it is puffed in the papers until outsiders have bought the stock; then the true state of things is revealed. Having full control of the mine, they are able, with their agent, to manipulate it as they please; and finally they thus get control of all valuable mines.

III. THE MONEY POWER IS DEVOURING OUR LUMBER TRADE.

It is evident that the Money Power has not yet gotten possession of all our lumber forests and lumber mills; for, where it has gotten possession of an industry, it stiffens up prices to a uniform and profitable rate. The fluctuation in the price of lumber, and the cuts in prices between different dealers are evidence of the war of the Money Power upon all independent lumber men. The war can have but one issue. The ownership of the railroads gives such an advantage to the Money Kings in shipping their lumber to market, that, in the end, competitors must be crushed. The Money Power will get possession of the coal mines and the lumber trade, as it has gotten possession of the mercantile trade of New York City, of the oil wells of Pennsylvania, and of the great lines of traffic.

IV. THE MONEY POWER IS DEVOURING OUR FLOUR MANUFACTURES.

Having full control of the wheat market, it would be the policy of the Money Power to make all possible profit out of the wheat before it reaches the consumer. To this end, the Money Power must manufacture the wheat into flour.

The high price of flour in comparison with wheat shows that the agents of the Money Power have a large number of flouring mills in their possession. The occasional sharp falls in the flour market, crushing mill owners of small capital, and the occasional purchase of mills by the Money Kings, as in a recent deal in Minneapolis, show that the Money Power has not yet gotten full possession of the flour mills.

The possession of the railroad transportation gives such an advantage to the Money Kings in the flour market as must, ere long, with the further advantage of their immense capital, give them entire possession of the flour manufacture. Their recent purchase of flour mills in Minneapolis shows their desire to obtain such advantageous ground in the business as will enable them to crush all competitors and get possession of the entire business.

V. THE MONEY POWER IS DEVOURING THE CATTLE RANCHES OF THE WESTERN PLAINS.

The London Money Kings are resolved to possess not only the trade in beef, but also the production of cattle. They laid their plans years ago, for monopolizing the cattle production of the Plains. It was they who killed off the buffalo. The destruction of the buffalo was thus effected: A high price was offered for buffalo hides in whatever quantity they were offered. All men who wished to hunt buffalo could get an outfit on credit and pay for it in buffalo hides. On these terms, an army of buffalo hunters was organized. Hunters lined the banks of the streams where the buffaloes came to drink, and by shooting them down, drove the herds away; and thus continued to shoot them as, parched with thirst, they came to the streams to drink. Some shot the buffaloes: some skinned the carcasses: some hauled off hides. In two or three years, the buffaloes numbering many millions were exterminated.

Nobody but the London Money Kings could have thus effected the extermination of the buffalo. None but they look so far ahead. Only they had money enough to equip such an army of slaughterers. Only they, in their immense world-wide commerce, had a market for such a vast number of hides. They had been obtaining hides for their trade in leather, shoes, and other leather products, from Buenos Ayres, in South America. It was only necessary to substitute buffalo hides for South American, for two or three years, to secure the extermination of the Buffalo.

The Money Kings saw a grand enterprise in devoting the Western Plains to the production of beef. As soon as the buffaloes were exterminated, they began to buy cattle in Texas, and cows and calves and young cattle in all the states, to start ranches on the Plains. This caused a boom in cattle all over the country; and multitudes of enterprising Americans organized cattle companies, and started cattle ranches all over the West, from Texas to Montana, mortgaging their property, and taking money out of their business, in order to take stock in the cattle companies. The boom in prices was kept up until the Plains were fully occupied with ranches; for the Money

Kings had entire control of the cattle market; and they offered high prices as long as it was their interest to induce Americans to invest in the beef production. In a few years, the Western Plains were fully stocked with cattle ranches.

When the ranches were established, it was time for the Constrictor to tighten its folds. The agents of the Money Power were the only buyers in the cattle market. The Money Kings themselves owned many cattle ranches in the West. They could always have a supply of their own cattle in the Market to be offered to their agents, the cattle buyers, at a very low price, so as to force down the market on other cattle owners. It would make no difference to them how low the price of their cattle—for they were selling to themselves: It was money out of one pocket into the other. They thus kept down the market for cattle, until almost all American cattle companies are now broke.

A gentleman largely interested in cattle companies told me, two years ago, that, at that time, fifty-seven per cent. of the cattle companies were broke. When we remember that many of the remaining forty-seven per cent. of the cattle companies are owned by the Money Kings, it is evident that almost all the American cattle companies have failed, and that the Money Power has now almost completed its devouring of the cattle companies.

In order to destroy these American cattle companies, and also to crush the farmers raising cattle, the Money Kings have forced down the price of cattle, in defiance of the law of supply and demand. The market for beef is active, and growing with the growth of our population. The supply of beef has greatly diminished in the last few years; two winters ago, a million cattle perished upon the Plains, from Texas to the Canada line: four hundred thousand perished in Montana alone. The cattle market is never glutted. Beef is consumed as fast as it is offered. Prices ought to be good in the presence of an increasing demand and a decreasing supply.

Furthermore, the consumer pays as high for beef as he formerly paid when beef cattle brought a fair price. There is no reason why beef cattle should not now command a fair price. There is demand enough; and the retail price is high enough. In view of the circumstances of the case, the pressing down of beef cattle to less than half price is an outrage upon our people. Beef cattle down to half price, with an active demand for beef, and a high retail price in the meat store: It is a shame!

It shows conclusively that the Money Power should no longer be allowed to control our prices.

The Money Power is now crushing and devouring the cattle companies, as it, a few years ago, crushed and devoured the other business interests of our country. It put down the price of cotton goods until it broke the New England Mills, and then put up the price again when it had gotten possession of the mills: It put down the price of oil until it broke the oil men of Pennsylvania, and then, when it had gotten possession of the business, it put up the price of oil: It put down the price of iron wares until it got possession of the iron mills, and then it put up the price of iron.—So now, the Money Kings are putting down the price of beef cattle, until they get possession of the cattle ranches, and the farms of our farmers, and then, when they themselves have entire possession of the cattle production, they will put up the price of cattle fast enough.

VI. THE MONEY POWER IS DEVOURING ALL BRANCHES OF PRODUCTION AND TRADE IN OUR COUNTRY.

A new era of the growth of the Money Power has recently arisen.

It is originating vast Trusts which take possession of an entire branch of production or trade, and crush out all competition by the might of capital. A trust is a device for concentrating the investments of several Money Kings in a single line of business under a single head. For instance: where many Money Kings have invested in a line of trade, by organizing a trust, they put all their business houses in that line and their stocks of goods into a single company, and place them under one management. The trust is thus able to control the amount of production, and all prices in that line of business; and it can destroy all outside companies that are not in the trust. Thus, two years ago, a coffee trust was originated, which at once set to work to destroy all the coffee merchants not in the ring. It put down the price of coffee so low as to break down the competitors of the trust; and no sooner was this accomplished, than the trust put up the price of coffee to more than double.

These trusts are, in effect, corporations without a charter—without any authority from the state; and they are thus above governmental control. It is a new step the Imperialism of Capital is taking. Through these trusts, the Money Kings purpose to do as they choose, and crush out all competition with a high hand. They used to conceal their track, and hide their meanness as far as possible from the public eye. But now, emboldened by success, and intoxicated with the pride of imperial power, they unmask their aims, confident of their ability to over-ride all opposition.

1. The Standard Oil Company is a great trust operating with many millions of capital, and throttling all competition in the petroleum market.

2. Many Americans invested their means in the manufacture of cotton seed oil. But the Money Kings wanted the oil for the manufacture of their bogus lard and butter.

And they organized a "Cotton Seed Oil Trust" with millions of capital, and are taking possession of the entire industry.

3. A "Sugar Trust" has been organized, to take possession of the sugar production and traffic.

4. A "Whiskey Trust" is monopolizing the manufacture and sale of distilled liquors.

5. Recently, a "Cattle Trust" has been organized, to take entire possession of all cattle ranches, and the raising of cattle and production of beef.

6. Grand Trusts, each with millions of capital, are monopolizing production and traffic in salt, lead, cordage, nails, coke, lumber, sheet zinc, copper, crucible steel, and other products. Well did the English writer of the pamphlet soon to be quoted, say, "Nothing is too large, and nothing too small for English capital, and English enterprise."

All these Trusts, like the Coffee Trust, will put down prices till competition is destroyed, and then they will double the price of the article they monopolize. Individual competition against these grand monopolies is hopeless. If an outside company goes into the Trust, they stop its business, and give to it a part of the profits; till other establishments have been started sufficient to supply the market without it, and then the idle establishment, with its trade and its business connection all gone, is kicked out in the cold to die. On thē other hand, if individual enterprises do not go into the Trust, goods are put down in the markets which they supply, and their business is taken away. In the Trust, or out of it, outside enterprises are bound to be destroyed.

But Trusts do not merely war upon individual competitors. There is another aspect of their operations, in which they especially war upon our national prosperity.

Trusts are of two kinds,—1) Those which operate in

industrial products which are protected by our tariff; and 2) Those which operate in branches of production in which we fully supply our own market and export a portion of the product. To the latter class belong the Standard Oil Company, and the Cotton Seed Oil Trust, and the Whiskey Trust. To the former, belong the Crucible Steel Trust, the Cordage Trust, and other various manufactures.

In the manufactures which fully supply our own markets, we ought very soon to take possession of the markets of the world. And we would soon do so, if production went on unobstructed. But the Trusts come in and arrest production, and keep us limited to the supply of our own markets, in order to maintain high prices, for their own profit. The Trusts do not merely injure the public by putting up prices;—but in order to put up the price, they commit a crime against the nation, by arresting our prosperity, and preventing us from supplying the markets of the world.

The Money Kings who are at the head of the Trusts are the London Jews who want to keep possession of the markets of the world for their English manufactures; and the only way in which they can do this, is to arrest our growth by means of these Trusts. Such a crime against the national prosperity ought to be punished by the heaviest penalty.

Of a like tendency is the work of the Trusts which operate in those products, to which, not supplying our own markets, we afford protection by the tariff. The object of the Trusts is, to continue to obtain the high price derived from the tariff. And in order to effect this, they arrest production, so as to prevent our production from fully supplying our own markets and thus cheapening the price by home competition. They do this, in the first place, in order to get the high price of tariff protection.

But they have another object which they desire especially to accomplish,—to prevent us from fully supplying our own market, and thus save it, in part, to their English manufactures. They know that, with unimpeded manufactures, we would in a few years fully supply our own market, and then, with our great advantages, would soon drive English manufactures out of the markets of the world. They wish especially to prevent this; and, as the only means of doing it, they organize these trusts, to limit our production, and keep us continually dependent upon English manufactures.

These trusts are really a conspiracy against the nation; and they ought to be treated as such. They are worse than murder; for they destroy many individuals by the slow torture of financial ruin. And they also strike at the national prosperity and the national life. They ought to be suppressed.

VII. THE MONEY POWER IS DEVOURING THE RETAIL TRADE.

The Money Power long since engrossed the great wholesale trade of the Eastern cities, and much of the wholesale trade in the West. It is now making rapid strides toward the monopoly of the retail trade of our cities and country towns.

1st. The First Stroke of the Money Power at the Retail Trade

of the country was the establishment of the great house of A. T. Stewart & Co., in New York City. A. T. Stewart was a Scotchman who, for years, occupied a little narrow place on Broadway a few feet wide, where he peddled needles, and thread and tape. He suddenly bloomed out in a palatial building, with a thousand clerks behind his counters, and twenty million dollars worth of goods upon his shelves. At the same time, there was a branch house of A. T. Stewart & Co., in Glasgow, Scotland, and another in Germany; besides establishments in Belfast, Ireland, and in Paris. The peculiarity of his style of business was, that he had in his House a number of departments; and, in the various departments, goods of every variety, of the best quality, and at the cheapest wholesale prices.

1. Many stories have been told to deceive the public, as to the means by which Stewart could sell such excellent goods so cheap. One story was that he bought his goods at auction, and very cheap, because they were the tail end of stocks, and damaged; and that Mrs. Stewart renovated them, and thus enabled him to fool the ladies of New York, and make them believe them new goods. The story is absurd. A. T. Stewart could not have kept up his stock by auction purchases; nor could he have obtained such goods at auction. It is only a clumsy attempt to account for a fact inexplicable by all the laws of business.

2. A. T. Stewart could not have accumulated in any regular business the immense fortune of one hundred million dollars which he was credited with possessing at the time of his death. His colossal business, so suddenly established, and the excellent quality and low price of his goods, can only be accounted for on the hypothesis that the London Money Kings appointed him head agent and Manager of a great retail house which they established in New York, and supplied with goods, in order to strike the first blow for the monopoly of the retail trade of New York City. This accounts for the immense establishment which sprung up like Jonah's gourd, in a night, and the colossal business: it also accounts for the superior quality of the goods; and it explains how, supplied from the manu-

factory direct, he could retail his goods at wholesale prices.

3. **The events following his death** show conclusively that *A. T. Stewart was an agent of the Money Kings.*

1) He was closely watched by Judge Hilton, who dined with him every Sunday on pretext of friendship, but really, no doubt, to talk over business and compare notes. At his death, Stewart left his business in Hilton's hands. And the American people were soon afterward shocked by the intelligence that Judge Hilton had cheated poor Mrs. Stewart out of all her husband's property, giving her only one million dollars for the entire estate of which Stewart died possessed.

Now, this is absurd. Mrs. Stewart was a very sensible woman. She had a perfect knowledge of the value of her husband's estate. Judge Hilton could not cheat her out of one hundred million dollars worth of property, giving her only one million dollars for it. But if he showed her papers that proved Stewart to be the agent of the London Money Kings, she would sign the transfer conveying to Judge Hilton the property that belonged to the Money Kings, and say nothing about it.

2) The heirs of A. T. Stewart afterwards brought suit against Hilton for the property, alleging that he had obtained it from Mrs. Stewart by fraud, and the whole matter was investigated in court. It was there proved under oath, by Hilton and the book-keeper of the House, that A. T. Stewart was only worth about $8,000,000—that he owned no interest in any real estate—that he had no interest in the palatial building in which the business was done—that he had no interest in the grand buildings erected by A. T. Stewart & Co. at Saratoga—no interest in the house of A. T. Stewart & Co. in Glasgow, Scotland, nor in the German house. It was sworn that he had no interest in the business, except a commission on sales. In

other words, he was simply the agent of the London Money Kings, who were the "Co." that owned the business.

3) The arrangement Hilton made of the business showed that *he* was only an agent in the matter. If the business had been really Hilton's, he would have continued to carry it on and make millions out of it every year, as Stewart had done. But instead, he closed out the business in a short time, attempting to deceive the public as to the cause of failure, by the farce of giving offense to the Jews, by excluding them from the hotel built by Stewart, at Saratoga.

2nd. These Mammoth Retail Stores Everywhere.

1. Three immense establishments were started in New York City on the model of Stewart's, keeping in the various departments everything, the goods excellent, and retailed at wholesale prices. And these stores were avowedly in the hands of agents.

2. And now, in all large cities, are to be found these immense retail establishments on the plan of the house of A. T. Stewart, and each with an agent at its head, managing the business for a per centage of the profits. There are several such stores in Kansas City. One of them does such an immense business that, as I was informed, the commissions of the manager amount to over sixty thousand dollars a year. The Money Kings pay their agents well.

3rd. These Stores Are Breaking Down All Other Merchants.

The House of A. T. Stewart broke down one thousand retail merchants in New York City, many of whom became his clerks. In all our cities, these grand agency retail stores are monopolizing the retail trade. I found such stores in many of our country towns. They always keep immense stocks of goods of all kinds in their various departments, which they sell at retail at wholesale prices: —and their counters are swarming with customers. The old merchants are being driven from business.

I have found these stores in different towns in Missouri, and Iowa and Kansas, where I have lectured. The American merchants are driven from business, and have to leave town. All who live by the merchants are also thrown out of employment. The towns are slowly dying. I recollect, in a town in Iowa, where I delivered the lecture on the Money Power, on the next morning as I walked along the street, a man came out of his grocery store and invited me to enter. When I went in, he wrung my hand with tears in his eyes, and said:

"Ah Sir, one of those Jew stores you told about last night is established here in town. They make a specialty of groceries, they say, and profess to sell them at cost. My business is ruined, and the business of the dry goods merchants also. The people are swarming into the Jew store to get things cheap. And I do not know what we are going to do."

What can they do but get out? How can a man with only a moderate individual capital compete with people who have the capital of the world at their back? They can afford to sell at a loss for a time, till they get possession of the trade. The American merchants can only give up the struggle and retire from business. If things go on as they are, in a few years more, the Money Power will have monopolized the retail traffic, as it has monopolized and is now monopolizing all the other branches of business in the country.

The Money Kings never carry any business by storm. Their approaches are always quiet and stealthy, their methods secret and tortuous. But they never yet have failed of accomplishing their end. A few years more will put them in possession of all the mercantile business of the country.

4TH. A NEW DISCOVERY: A NEW METHOD OF ATTACK BY THE MONEY KINGS.

While this work has been passing through the press, I have heard of a new method of attack upon the stores of our country towns. It is like every thing else that the Money Power originates,—very effective, and sure of success if not arrested; and it has all the traits of secretiveness, cunning, craft and slyness, that mark every thing that emanates from that source.

The * * * * Store System, as stated by one who knows, is based upon the following plan:—If a person has a small capital to engage in the business,—$500 or more,—the promoters of the plan will furnish him goods at a very low price to that amount, and as much more *without interest*, to be paid out of the business. On the other hand, the party binds himself to purchase a certain amount of goods every month—not large; and to sell the goods for cash, and at a *fixed* price, from thirty to fifty per cent. lower than any other merchant can afford to sell them. He will thus inevitably bankrupt all competitors.

This System has purchasing agents all over the country, to buy up bankrupt stocks as fast as the old merchants are broke. This system, of course, must be furnished with goods from New York, at first; but after the merchants begin to break rapidly, the bankrupt stocks, purchased very cheap, will keep up the supply of goods, until the new stores are in full possession of all the business.

A list is made out of all the states and territories, with the available towns still unoccupied—one store to be started at a place.

This System is already widely established over the country, and, as my informant says, is making the merchants "open their eyes wide." The Money Power is resolved to root out our country town merchants, and themselves take possession of the business.

VIII. THE MONEY POWER IS DEVOURING OUR FARMS.

So vast is the income of the Money Power from its various sources of wealth, that it can no longer find investment for it in its immense loans to the nations of the old world—in its loans to states and counties and cities and municipalities and corporations—in building new warehouses and ships for its ever extending commerce—in erecting new factories—in building new railroads—in opening new mines—in starting new mercantile establishments. All these vast branches of enterprise can not afford the Money Power sufficient investment for its enormous and constantly increasing income.

It can only find investment in mortgages of city property and improved farms, and in the purchase of new and grand branches of business.

1st. Farms Mortgaged.

Until I began to lecture on the Money Power, I had no idea of the extent to which our farms have been mortgaged to the Money Kings. I thought that perhaps one-twentieth of the farms were mortgaged. I knew that Dakota was shingled over with mortgages; but I supposed that the condition of Dakota was exceptional. I was astonished upon reading an article in a New York paper, evidently intended to soothe the public mind, stating that the public need feel no uneasiness about Dakota—that statistics proved that there are more land mortgages in the state of New York in proportion to area and value, than in Dakota! I was astounded at the statement. The Lord have mercy on New York!!

I thought that, in Missouri, the people surely are out

of debt. I knew that they are economical, and not over-venturesome and enterprising. What was my surprise when, in the first place where I delivered my lecture on the Money Power, a good citizen said to me:—

"I don't know much about prophecy. But I do know that what you say about these foreign capitalists is true. To my certain knowledge, at least two-thirds of the farms in this community are mortgaged to foreign capital."

I traveled widely through Missouri, and everwhere I found statements that two-thirds to three-fourths of the farms are under mortgage!!—In Iowa, the same state of fact exists. In some counties of that state, where farms used to sell for twenty-five dollars per acre, the farms were mortgaged for one-third of their value; and after a number of farms were bought in by the mortgagee for eight dollars an acre, the amount of the mortgage, all the lands receded to that price.—A gentlemen told me that, in one of the counties of Iowa where he had investigated the state of things, the property valuation of the county was $3,000,000, and there are $2,000,000 worth of property mortgaged. Perhaps this is an average of the condition of things in the state.

In Kansas, a very large proportion of the farms are mortgaged—a much larger proportion than in Iowa or Missouri.

In Nebraska, as I am informed, the agents of the Money lenders are to be found in every neighborhood. They go through the country like lightning-rod agents, urging the farmers to borrow money on five years time, secured by mortgage on their farms.

2ND. LAND LOAN AGENCIES.

In any of the large cities, if you go into the office of one of the Farm Loan Agencies which has agents all over the state, and ask for a loan on your farm, the agent will ask where it lies: tell him the county, and he will ask the township; and as soon as you tell him, he will step to the wall and, after a moment, will draw down the map of your township and will show you your farm. They are prepared to mortgage and buy every farm in the whole country.

A banker said to me:—"The money line of these Land Loan Companies always has three points,—the agent in the West, who loans the money; the intermediary in the East, from whom he gets it;—but the third point in the line is always London. There is where the money comes from."

How the Money for the loans is obtained was told me by an agent who loans large amounts every year, through a large number of subagents. He sent his mortgages to a little bank in an Eastern state; from which the money was sent to him. That bank transferred the mortgage to the third party from which the money came originally. And this third party is the Money Power of London, or some of its immediate agents.

The Money Kings hide their trail in these loan transactions without difficulty. They need only to buy up the stock of a bank or an insurance company, in some Eastern state; and then, through such an agency, they can loan millions of dollars:—and the American people think it is simply Eastern American capital! Thus, a little bank in Connecticut can loan millions of dollars every year, when it is only making in its regular business some twenty thousand dollars a year.

The Money is London Capital, as is evident from the vast amount of it loaned in this country. Billions of dollars have been loaned upon farm mortgages, to say nothing of the vast amounts loaned on city property. No American banks or insurance companies could loan such immense amounts of money.

The London Money Kings have, in this country, an income of many hundred millions of dollars, every year, derived from interest on loans—from the profits of their various lines of investment—from the various industries they have monopolized—and from the various lines of traffic they have taken possession of. They invest in the United States all the income derived from their investments in this country; and statistics prove that, besides this, they are sending to this country, annually, a large amount of specie for investment, being a portion of their profits derived from their vast trade with the outside world. It is manifest that the Money Power is loaning in the United States many hundred million dollars every year.

We have about reached the end of our tether. About two-thirds of the farms of the country are now mortgaged for one-third of their value, on five years time. In the ten great states of the West and Northwest,—Ohio, Illinois, Indiana, Michigan, Wisconsin, Minnesota, Iowa, Nebraska, Missouri and Kansas, the valuation of farm property, according to the census of 1880, making a liberal allowance for the increase of value, amounts to $7,000,000,000. It is estimated that the farm mortgages in those states amount to $3,400,000,000. The farms are usually mortgaged for one-third of their value on five years time. The amount of farm mortgages given above is probably excessive. One-half the estimate is most probably nearer to a correct statement. We may perhaps safely say that, in the above ten states, two-thirds of the farms are now under mortgage for one-third of their value on five years time.

How much of the other one-third of the farms is now owned by the Money Power it is impossible to say. Thousands of agents have been loaning money all over the country for more than twenty years, on improved farms and plantations. Down South, in Mississippi or Alabama, ask in any neighborhood about the grand plantations of the past, and they will tell you those plantations are under mortgage or owned, as the phrase is, "by foreign capital." The Southern plantations passed into the hands of the Money Power in the hard years following the war: the Western farms are passing to them now. Many of the plantations of the South and many of the improved farms of the West have had the mortgages on them foreclosed, and now belong to the Money Power. If we include the farms on which mortgages have been foreclosed together with those now mortgaged, we can see what an immense area of our country the Money Power will own, when the mortgages they now hold shall have been foreclosed.

3RD. THE MONEY POWER IS CRUSHING THE FARMERS,

so that they can not pay their mortgages and save their farms. Having two-thirds of the farms of the country mortgaged to them, the Money Kings are putting down the price of all farming products, so that it is impossible for the farmers to pay off their mortgages. The Money Kings are the only purchasers of produce, and by establishing Boards of Trade which are absolutely subject to their control, they are able, through them, to fix prices to suit themselves. By the agency of the Boards of Trade, and by their monopoly of the traffic in all farming products, they have put down the price of farming products, until it is impossible for the farmers to pay off the mortgages on their farms.

1. THE MONEY POWER HAS PUT DOWN THE PRICE OF BEEF.

We have already seen how the Money Kings have put down the price of Beef, in defiance of the laws that regulate business prices, wholly setting aside and annulling the law of supply and demand.

2. The Money Power Has Broken Down the Wheat Market.

Two years ago, our wheat crop was fifty million bushels short. It was naturally expected that the price of wheat would rise. I saw a quotation from a Liverpool paper, at the time, stating that it was expected that the price of wheat would be high, owing to the short American crop and the active demand, and expressing surprise at the low price of wheat that prevailed in America. The price was put down by the imperial power of the Money Power over the American markets.

When it was known that the wheat crop was fifty million bushels short, the price of wheat was seventy cents a bushel. It was naturally supposed that the price would go up. A syndicate of Cincinnati capitalists, acting on this business probability, organized with a capital of $12,000,000, to operate in the Chicago market; not to put up the price of wheat to ninety cents or a dollar a bushel, which the condition of things would have warranted, but merely to keep the price up to the existing rate of seventy cents a bushel. They had capital enough to make their operations a sure success under the rules of the Chicago Board of Trade, which only allowed wheat to be sold as it was delivered into the elevator. The regular average amount of delivery was about three hundred car-loads a day, and they had money enough to purchase this amount of daily delivery, until they could make their operation a success.

But the wheat operators of Chicago had the elevators all over the Northwest full of wheat: they ordered the Chicago Board of Trade to rescind the rule which prohibited the sale of wheat except as delivered into the elevators, and allow it to be sold out of the cars; and when their order was obeyed, they rushed down to Chicago from all over the Northwest three thousand car loads of wheat a day! They sold the Cincinnati syndicate wheat at seventy cents a bushel, till their $12,000,000 was gone; and then, when they had broken the syndicate, they at once put down the price of wheat to sixty cents a bushel!

It was a great outrage! When the wheat crop was fifty million bushels short, and the supply was inadequate to meet the demand, wheat, according to all the laws that regulate prices, ought to have gone up to at least one dollar a bushel. To put down the price, under such circumstances, lower than it had ever been before, was an outrage—a violation of all the laws of trade—a revolutionary overthrow of the law of supply and demand.

In the same way, and at the same time,

3. The Money Power Broke Down the Cotton Market.

Two years ago, a Southern syndicate was formed, to sustain the cotton market at the low price at which cotton was then held. A capitalist at Houston, Texas, headed the movement, with $15,000,000 at his back.—But the Money Kings now own many of the cotton plantations of the South; and they delivered cotton to the syndicate at the price offered, till the $15,000,000 were gone; and then, when they had broken the syndicate, they immediately put down the price of cotton one and one-half cents a pound!

The Money Kings have the cotton market completely in their grasp. As one of their agents said, "the planters had as well struggle against the course of the seasons as against the prices fixed by the Money Power." They have put down the price of cotton, until it will not pay wages to the laborers who produce it. It could not be grown at all at the present price, if the negro laborers did not take their pay in a part of the crop, so that they share the oppression and poverty of the planters. The negro laborers are barely able to subsist, by raising their own provisions; but they are brought down to the condition of the Hindoo peasant.

4TH. TWO YEARS AGO WAS AN ERA

in the history of American prices. That was the time when the Money Power boldly and openly went into the Boards of Trade and crushed all opposition, and put down prices to suit themselves, in open defiance of the law of supply and demand, and all the laws that regulate prices. Before that time, other persons dared to operate in Boards of Trade, on the indication of the markets under the Law of Supply and Demand. But the Cincinnati and Southern syndicates were so completely crushed, that no man will ever again dare to interfere with the Money Kings in their manipulation of prices in Boards of Trade. The Money Kings then made so terrible an example of their opponents as to deter all others from repeating the offense.

The Cincinnati syndicate was so sure that, with a short supply of wheat and an active demand, they could sustain their move in the Chicago Board of Trade, that some of them were tempted, when hard pressed, to use other people's money in their possession. For this offense they were prosecuted, and sent to state prison.—After such terrible examples, no one will ever dare again to interfere with the Money Kings in their regulation of prices.

Boards of Trade are instruments controlled at will by the London Money Kings, *and may be made to register their will.* Under the rule of the Chicago Board of Trade the Cincinnati syndicate was perfectly safe in its operation: they had enough money to pay for all the wheat that could be offered them under the rule of the Board of Trade. When Armour went into the Board of Trade, and demanded that the rule should be changed, so as to enable the agents of the Money Kings to break down the Cincinnati syndicate, and the Board of Trade at once complied with the demand, the fact was thereby established that Boards of Trade are conquered by the London Money Kings, and made agencies by which to regulate prices as they see best, and that all persons are to be broken down who attempt to sustain against them the law of supply and demand. That was a practical announcement of the fact that

The old law of supply and demand is wholly abrogated, *and the will of the Money Kings is put in its place, as the sole regulator of prices in our modern age.*

The law of supply and demand can only regulate prices when there is a free market, *and the free competition of buyers and sellers operates to regulate prices.* But there is no such competition now: the agents of the Money Power are the only buyers of all produce. Boards of Trade are subdued by them, and answer to their manipulations. By the might of Capital, they can regulate prices in any Board of Trade. They control absolutely the Chicago Board of Trade, and Chicago regulates the price of produce for the whole country. They can fix all prices to suit themselves by their imperial power over the markets, in utter disregard of the law of supply and demand, and in utter violation of all the laws that regulate prices.

The time has come for the public to consider this question of prices, *and find out some new way in which we may regulate prices, and keep them at a proper and uniform standard. We can never suffer the Money Kings to regulate prices and ruin our farmers by their arbitrary exercise of imperial power, thus subverting all the legitimate laws of trade.*

As long as it is left to them, they will do as they have

been doing: they will put down the prices of all produce while it is in the hands of the farmers, so as to buy it cheap; and then, when it is in their own hands, they will put up the price, so as to sell it high!! This has been their regular habit for years. How long are the American people going to stand it? How long will they suffer themselves to be plundered by these capitalists? When the old method of regulating prices by the law of supply and demand is no longer operative,

We Must Find Some Other Way

by which to regulate prices.

And it will not be difficult to find a much better way. One method will be presented in this work, later on. Either it, or some other method will have to be adopted, if we do not intend for the Money Kings to freeze out all our farmers, and get possession of their farms.

5th. The Money Power Determined To Have the Farms.

No farm product, except hogs, brings a fair price. And the price of hogs is owing to hog cholera. With the danger of cholera, the farmers would not raise hogs at all, but for the inducement of a fair price. No Western farmer, at present prices of grain, and beef, and other produce, can pay wages, pay taxes, and support his family in comfort—much less pay off his mortgage. Some of the newspapers, setting forth the views of the Money Power, are already saying that the farm laborer of the Northwest must submit to a reduction of wages. And other newspapers declare that our farmers must lose their farms, and let us have the Tenant Farm System that prevails in Europe.

The wages of the farm laborer may be reduced, but this will not save the farmers. At the present price of produce, no mortgage can be paid off.

A distinguished gentleman of Iowa told me that he, not long since, traveled in the same seat with a general agent for farm loans who has many subagents in different counties of the state; and, in the course of conversation, he asked him if the farmers could pay off their mortgages? The agent laughed at the idea. He said it was impossible—that he had orders not to foreclose, except as a last resort.—The Money Power means to have the farms;—but it wishes to appear indulgent.

Conversing with a banker in Kansas, a very clever gentleman, I spoke to him of the great evils that would follow the loss of the farms. He laughed pleasantly, and said, "I think the farmers will have to lose their farms."—From present appearances that must be the result. If things continue in their present grooves, in a few years more, the Money Power will have foreclosed its mortgages, and will own in fee simple two-thirds or three-fourths, or even a larger proportion, of the farms of the country.

And then, when the farms have been devoured, it will be an easy matter to finish the merchants and grocers of the country towns. When the Money Kings own the farms of the Northwest, as they do many of the cotton plantations of the South, they will pay off their peasant farm laborers, as they now pay off the negro laborers on their Southern cotton plantations, with orders to their own stores. Then all the outside merchants who are not already broke by the stores established by the Money Power, will have to give up business. The merchants will have the sad grace accorded to them which the Cyclops accorded to Ulysses, of being the last to be devoured.

Then the Money Kings will have accomplished their aim. They will have everything in the country. America will be the Ireland of the New World—its people peasants, groaning under the yoke of foreign landlordism.

CHAPTER VIII.

DEMONSTRATION OF THE WORK OF THE MONEY POWER IN THIS COUNTRY.

That it is the London Money Power which is thus crushing our industry is proved by evidence that is a scientific demonstration. I make no assertion without proof. The demonstration has been necessarily delayed till the facts were all presented. But the proof is absolute, and overwhelming. It is, indeed, a scientific demonstration, based upon the application of the fixed laws of industry.

The evidence is cumulative. Each point of evidence strengthens the others, until the conclusion is demonstrated beyond the possibility of doubt.

I. FIRST PROOF:—BRITISH TESTIMONY TO THE EXISTENCE OF THE MONEY POWER, IN 1864 A. D.

The year 1864 was an era in the growth of the Money Power. The English public then first realized its growing greatness, and the idea produced a powerful impression upon the English mind. The English are reticent on the subject of the growth of the Money Power. Not a word is ever said of it in Parliament. The papers never publish a line that would enable the foreign world to know of the centralization of all wealth and property in Britain. It is their national secret.

But when they first learned of it in 1864, in the first flush of joy and pride they forgot reserve for a moment, and gave utterance to their self-gratulation. Some of these outbursts fell under the eye of the author of this work. The English writers speak in glowing terms of the rising Imperialism of commerce and wealth, then building up by the Money Kings; but they couch their thoughts in enigmatical phrase, which would be understood by the initiated, but would not expose their national secret to the outside world.

I quote two of these press statements published in 1864, in the beginning of this grandest era of the growth of the Money Power. They fully bear out all I have stated in describing the Imperialism of capital, industry and wealth established by these Jew Money Kings.

1st. First British Statement.

I will first quote some statements from a brilliant writer in one of the English reviews, who gives a grapic outline sketch of the Imperialism attained, at that time, by the Money Kings. He says:

"London, as every one knows, contains a city within a city; and within this inner city there is yet another [the Money Quarter], the very heart of the metropolis. It is a small place. In a couple of minutes, you may walk across it, from side to side, from end to end. Yet it [the Money Quarter] is the center and citadel of our greatness—the heart whose pulsations are felt to the farthest extremities of the empire. The occupants of the precinct [the Money Kings] have dealings with all the world. The railways which accompany the ceaseless advance of the white race into the prairies of the Far West, in America [our North-western States]—the [mining] companies which explore and develop the [mineral] resources of California and Australia—the iron roads and irrigating canals which are maturing the prosperity of India—the enterprise which covers with tea plantations the valleys and slopes of the Himalayas, and which carries our countrymen [the agents of the Money Kings] into new regions everywhere,—are created or sustained by the outgoings [of capital] of this little spot in London.

"The wastes of Hudson Bay—trading companies for the Nile—the cotton planting which is invading Africa—ocean lines of steamships—submarine telegraphs connecting dissevered continents—water works for Berlin—gas for Bombay—these and a hundred other matters and projects engage the thoughts and EMPLOY THE CAPITAL which is at the command of this busy hive of operators [the Money Kings]. *Almost every country is included in their operations.*

"And ALMOST EVERY STATE IS INDEBTED TO THEM. From gigantic Russia to petty Ecuador and Venezuela *they hold the bonds of every government*, those of Persia and Japan excepted. Prosaic as their operations are in detail, taken in the mass, they constitute a grand work. DAILY AND HOURLY, *it is their business to scan in detail the condition of the world.* They weigh the influence of the seasons—they know the condition of every mine—the prospects of every railway—the dividends of every Company.

"It [the Money Quarter of London] is a city of Money Dealers—a Sanctuary of Plutus.—Blot out that inner heart of London, and the whole world would feel the shock." (!!!) (Capitals and italics mine).

His calm style and intimate acquaintance with facts and commercial principles place this writer above the charge of exaggeration. Indeed, there is reticence throughout the article; allusion instead of statement, suggestion rather than fact. And yet, what a picture does he draw of the imperialism over industry, trade and wealth attained by the Money Kings of London.

2ND. SECOND BRITISH STATEMENT.

I next quote from an article in Blackwood, for 1864, in which the writer speaks of the Money Quarter of London as a Temple of Mammon, in which the Money Kings are storing up the wealth of the world. He says:—

"There [in the Money Quarter of London] they are ceaselessly storing up the the wealth that flows to them from the rest of the world. Men in strange climes, and in strange dresses, and speaking all manner of tongues, are seen preparing produce and luxuries of all kinds for the Temple, which flow thither in long streams across land and sea. And still the work of storing goes on: gold, silver, and all precious things, [bonds, stocks, etc.], —the delights of life—the cream of the earth's good things—accumulate higher and higher in the chambers of the Temple [the Money Quarter]."

3RD. THIRD BRITISH STATEMENT: THE PAMPHLET.

I do not think that any one can still doubt the fact that the Money Kings of London have established a grand imperialism of industry, trade and wealth, extending all over the world. If a shadow of doubt remain in any mind, it will be dispelled by the utterances of a pamphlet given me, in London, in 1864. The pamphlet was intended for private circulation only, and therefore speaks out frankly with regard to this grand English Imperialism of Capital. In a discussion with the author of this work, the writer of the pamphlet lost his temper and coolness of judgment, and gave him a copy of this remarkable publication.

The author of the pamphlet speaks of the wealth of the Money Kings as national wealth, and of their capital as English capital. Where he speaks of England, therefore, he means the Money Power of London; and when he speaks of the English, he means the Money Kings. The writer shows but little literary skill, either in his style, or in the grouping of his facts; but his statements are true, and his facts authentic. The following extracts from the pamphlet present a picture of the monopoly of industry, commerce and wealth, attained by the Money Power, in 1864, that will startle mankind. The writer says:—

"It is a remarkable position England occupies in the world. A little point amid the Northern seas, almost invisible to the school boy as he seeks for it on his globe, and which he may hide with his finger point as he turns the colored sphere, the British Isles are nevertheless the heart of the world—the center to which the thoughts and acts of men most generally tend—and to and from which the streams of material life are ever flowing.

"If we draw on a map the great lines of commerce, we will see what a large proportion of them converge to our shores. It was once a proverb that "all roads lead to Rome;" and England, commercially, holds in *the world* [italics his] the same predominant position which the Eternal City held in the restricted era of the Roman empire. Our country is the chief goal of the highways of commerce. Caravans, with their long strings of laden camels and horses, are ceaselessly crossing the plains and deserts of Asia—railway trains drawn by the rapid fire car rush across Europe and America with their freights of goods—and ships in thousands bring to us, from all parts of the world, the staple supplies of our food and industry."

* * * * "China sends raw silk, and tea; India sends cotton, indigo and rice. We get our spices from the Phillipine Islands; almost all our coffee from Ceylon; a portion of our cotton from Egypt; hides, chiefly from the pampas of Buenos Ayres; wool, chiefly from Australia and the Cape; wood, from the Northern countries of America and Europe; flax and tallow, from Russia; corn, chiefly from the United States and Russia; and the precious metals from Australia, California, Mexico and the Andes of Peru. * * * * England [i. e. the Money Power of London] furnishes employment to tens of millions of people in the uttermost parts of the earth, —the Chinaman in his tea plantations and mulberry gardens—the Hindoo in his rice and cotton fields—the poor Indian miner in the Andes—the Guacho, as he follows his herds in the Pampas—even the Negro of Africa, and the natives of the far and fair Islands of the Pacific."

"Of our exports, we send beer to India and Australia; coal, to many places, to supply coaling stations for steam vessels, but chiefly to France. We send cotton yarn for manufacture to India, Holland and Germany; cotton piece goods to the United States and Brazil. Our hardwares and cutlery go chiefly to Australia, India and the United States; and our woolen and worsted goods to the United States, India, and China, Germany, British North America and Australia."

* * * * "The trade of England is ubiquitous. It penetrates to every part of the earth. Fully three-fourths of the exportable produce of every country is sent direct to England, and of the remaining one-fourth, the greater part is carried by English enterprise, and at English risk to the port of consumption. In like manner, almost every spot on the earth receives its foreign supplies from this country, or by the hands of English traders [agents of the Money Kings]; and by means of English capital. * * * * We are the great general merchants of the world." * * * *

"We [the Money Kings] are the manufacturers for the world. Every nation in the world except England may be called an agricultural country; each no doubt, has some few manufactures more or less rough; but the manufactures of every one are trifling in the extreme in proportion to the raw products which it grows. Consequently, few countries export much except raw produce; and the direct trade between the various countries of the world is very small. All trade through England; for what little goes direct from one country to another is generally on English [Money King] account, carried by English [Money King] enterprise, and with English [Money King] capital."

"We [the Money Kings] are the great carriers for the world. Thirty thousand ships sailing under the flag, or bearing the cargoes of [the Money Kings of] England, are ever on the seas going and coming from all parts of the globe. * * * * * From the Thames, the Mersey, the Tyne, and the Clyde argosies and commercial armadas are ever leaving, and jostle in our estuaries with similar squadrons making to port.

"We [the Money Kings] are the ship-builders for the world; *and own or have mortgages on every vessel afloat. The shipping in every foreign port either belong to England* [the Money Power,] *or are employed by England* [the Money Power,] *with the exception of a few coasters.*"

"The shores of our estuaries, lined with miles of docks and building yards, ring with the clang of hammers; and vast ribs of wood and iron, curving upward from still vaster keels, show where leviathan vessels are being got ready for their adventurous career. * * * * * Both classes of our ships, both steam and sailing, are regularly increasing in numbers. In both kind of vessels, too, there is a steady increase of size. Comparing the present amount of our shipping [in 1864,] with what it was in 1850, we find that we have 11 per cent. more ships, 40 per cent. more tonnage, and 15 per cent. more men."

Filled with enthusiasm at the picture presented to his mind, the writer exclaims :—

"Our little islands no longer suffice for us. Our energies have far overpassed their limits. There is room for us to live and work here—that is all. *These islands are our house and garden, but our farm is detached.* * * * *We live upon the world.*"

The writer goes on :—

"We [Money Kings] are the railway makers of the world: *and the actual owners of the greater proportion of foreign railways.*

"We [Money Kings] carry the mails for the whole world. Strange as it may appear, even the letters from South America to North America have always passed through the London post-office.

"No one can go from one part of the world to another without passing through England; so completely do we [Money Kings] monopolize the whole passenger traffic."

"We [Money Kings] *are the bankers of the whole world.* If the North sends money to the South, or the East to the West, the money must be sent through London—there is no other way.

"We [Money Kings] are the bullion dealers of the world: all gold and silver is brought direct to England [to the Money Kings,] in payment of debts due to us [Money Kings,] *and then is redistributed by us in the shape of public and private loans.*"

"We [Money Kings] have the lion's share in every mine."

"We [Money Kings] are the great capitalists of the world. * * * * * It may be truly said that there is not at any time any corner of the world in which Englishmen [the Money Kings] have not more or less pecuniary interest. Without English [Money King] capital, and English [Money King] enterprise, the tallow of Russia could not be brought from the interior to St. Petersburg; nor the timber of Norway and Sweden and Poland be brought to the ports of embarkation; nor the cotton of Egypt to Alexandria. *English* [Money King] *capital performs the internal traffic of every country, and largely supplies the means of interior production.*"

"We [Money Kings] are the annuitants of the world. *We have loaned money to every government, and almost to every municipality.* Every country has to pay large sums to the English [Money Kings] as interest upon loans, amounting to many hundreds of millions [pounds]."

"Nothing is too large and nothing is too small for English [Money King] capital, and English [Money King] enterprise. We [Money Kings] even pave, light, watch, and drain numerous foreign cities. The very water-works of Berlin were constructed by the English [Money Kings], and are owned in England [by them]. So endless are the ramifications of Brittish [Money King] trade and enterprise, that the slightest misfortune to any country or people seriously affects [the Money Power of] England. A severe drought in the most remote spot on earth leaves England [the Money Power] a serious loser. A deluge in any country fills our [Money King] ledgers with bad debts. An earthquake in any quarter of the globe largely reduces English [Money King] profits. Every flood washes away English [Money King] dividends, English [Money King] exports, English [Money King] imports, and sweeps away English [Money King] capital, and ruins English [Money King] future expectations."

"IN FACT MORE THAN HALF THE WORLD IS MORTGAGED TO ENGLAND [the Money Kings]."* (Capitals and italics in the forgoing are mine.)

The foregoing statements make it evident that, in 1864, the Money Kings of London had already established a grand empire over industry, manufactures, commerce and wealth, which was then dominating all the countries of the globe. The Money Kings were the only great capitalists of the earth. No country had sufficient capital to

---

* The author will have occasion to quote further from this remarkable publication, later on.

build its own railroads, or make its own public improvements, or even raise and market its own products. All gold and silver was sent direct to London as soon as taken out of the mines, in part payment of debt, and then was redistributed by the Money Kings in loans to nations,—to states—to counties—to municipalities and to individuals. The Money Kings were then "the actual owners of the greater proportion of all the railways of the world." They "owned or had mortgages on every vessel afloat." The ocean commerce of the world was in their hands. Their "capital performed the internal traffic of every country." The world was even dependent upon them for "money to supply the means of interior production." Even at that date, this writer says, "More than half the world is mortgaged to [the Money Kings of] England."

No one can doubt that, in 1864, the great capitalists of London had established an Imperialism of Capital that was then dominating the earth, and monopolizing industry and commerce.

If its capital was so great at that time, to what gigantic proportions must it have attained *in the twenty-five years that have since elapsed.* Its capital has at least quadrupled since then. No wonder they are everywhere seeking farm loans, and are buying up property all over the earth.

The above declarations of English writers, if there were no other proof, would alone establish all that I have said about the operations of the Money Power in this country.

II. SECOND PROOF:—SCIENTIFIC DEMONSTRATION, DEDUCED FROM THE LAWS OF POLITICAL ECONOMY, APPLIED TO INDUSTRIAL CONDITION OF U. S.

In a natural state of things, industry moves forward in accordance with the laws of Political Economy which regulate business and trade. When we perceive that the present condition of things in the business World is utterly contrary to what the natural laws of industry would bring about, we know that some mighty influence is at work, powerful enough to override all the laws of Political Economy, and bring about the abnormal condition of things, by the might of irresistible capital. Such is the state of fact at the present time.

The Law of Scientific Demonstration has not been generally comprehended. Any Hypothesis respecting the facts of a case is scientifically demonstrated to be true, when it harmonizes and explains all the facts of the case. It is not necessary to have any outside evidence: the harmonizing and explaining all the facts of the case is, without any outside evidence, a Scientific Demonstration of the truth of the Hypothesis.

It is by such evidence that the Copernican System is demonstrated to be true. In the era before Copernicus, while the Ptolemaic theory, that the Earth is the center of the universe, was held, Astronomy was not a science. When Copernicus promulgated the view that the Sun is the center of the Solar System, and that the Earth and all the Planets move around it, the theory was held to be scientifically demonstrated to be true, by the fact of its harmonizing and explaining all the phenomena of the Solar System.

So, I now present the Theory that all these grand corporations that are overshadowing this country are run by Money King capital; and I demonstrate its truth, by showing that it harmonizes and explains all the facts, which, on any other supposition, are a jumble of discordant incidents utterly contradictory of all the principles of Political Economy.

1st. The Laws of Political Economy Which Are Violated.

The laws of Political Economy are as fixed as the stars in their course. They are the Laws of the Business World, which are as immoveable and unalterable as the Laws of Nature. Let us note some of these Laws of the Business World :—

Principle I. *In a normal state of things, all prices are regulated by two things,—1) The amount of currency; and 2) The law of supply and demand.*

Principle II. *A large capital in business operations is a great advantage, and gives to its possessors a marked superiority over competitors having small capital.*

Principle III. *Persons established in business have an advantage over those just starting in the same business, other things equal.*

Principle IV. *From the above principles, it follows that a New Man who starts in business poor, is at a great disadvantage in competition with Rieh Men who are already established.*

Principle V. *A New Man who is Poor, if he starts in business in antagonism with Rich Men who are already established, will be at such a disadvantage that he will be almost certain to fail.*

Principle VI. *In Business Crises, men of large capital who are already established in business, have a great advantage over New Men just starting in the business with small capital.*

Principle VII. *In Business Crises, men of small capital, who are overtrading, and have to borrow money, are at such disadvantage that they are usually the first to break.*

Principle VIII. *It follows from the above principles, that New Men of small capital can not, as a rule, enter into competition with Rich Men already established, and drive them* *out of business; but in such cases of antagonistic competition, the New Men of small capital will be the first to fail.*

Principle IX. *And especially in Business Crises, New Men of small capital can not, as a rule, successfully enter into competition wich Rich Men already established, and take their business from them; but, in such antagonistic competition, the Rich Men already established will be able to sustain themselves, and the New Men of small capital will fail.*

Principle X. *The superiority of a large capital is equally apparent in all operations in stocks and produce, in Boards of Trade.*—For

Principle XI. *The Laws of Chance have their variations only within certain limits, and in the long run conform to regular law: so that, in gambling operations, the longest purse will win, in the long run.*

Principle XII. *In operations in Boards of Trade, New Men with smaller capital can not, as a rule, break down richer men, and reduce them to bankruptcy;—but the New Men will, in the long run, fail in such operations.*

Principle XIII. *From the above principles it follows that, in the Business World, a man can only make a reasonable amount of money in a given time.*

Principle XIV. *The wealth of a country, under the operation of the natural laws of Political Economy, will increase most rapidly in times of prosperity, and will increase more slowly in eras of industrial depression.*

The above Principles are Industrial Axioms. Their truth is recognized as soon as they are stated. They are Laws of the Business World, which are as fixed as the course of the Planets in their orbits. The Planets have their perturbations: and there may be occasional exceptions to the Laws of Industry laid down in these Principles. But the exception proves the rule. There can not be any general departure from these Principles.

2ND. THESE FIXED PRINCIPLES OF POLITICAL ECONOMY ARE NOW VIOLATED IN EVERY PARTICULAR

by the facts of the business world, in our time. We call attention especially to four points:—

THE PRINCIPLES OF POLITICAL ECONOMY ARE VIOLATED:—

1. **In the abnormal condition of prices**; which are no longer regulated by the amount of currency, and by the law of supply and demand;

2. **In the abnormal condition of business**; in which New Men who started poor have taken possession of everything;

3. **In the unheard of aggregation of wealth in the hands of New Men**, who have sprung up from poverty into unprecedented wealth; and

4. **In the anomalous fact** that the wealth of our country has increased most rapidly when the general prosperity was at the lowest ebb.

---

1. THE PRINCIPLES OF POLITICAL ECONOMY VIOLATED, BY PRICES BEING NO LONGER REGULATED BY THE AMOUNT OF CURRENCY, AND THE LAW OF SUPPLY AND DEMAND.

The Amount of Currency and the Law of Supply and Demand would, at present, give us good prices. And the fact that prices are now broken down is evidence that there is an active and powerful agency at work subverting the laws of Political Economy that regulate prices.

We live in an age of wonderful industrial movement. But it is one of the most striking facts of our time, that all prices are in an anomalous condition, not to be explained by the ordinary laws of industry and trade. All prices, especially those of farming produce, are extremely low.

The depression of the farming interest has depressed every other interest of the country. The farmers are compelled to economize closely, and buy as little as possible from the merchants and other tradesmen of our towns. Consequently, business in our towns is dull. The wave of enforced economy has spread from the farmers to the people of the towns. This general pressure, with its necessitated economy, affects our manufactures, in diminishing the ability of our people to consume manufactured products.

The question that stares us in the face and calls for an answer, is

WHAT IS THE CAUSE OF THE LOW PRICE OF FARMING PRODUCTS?

Heretofore, two causes have regulated prices,—the volume of currency, and the law of supply and demand. If, at any time, prices were very low, we could see the cause, either in a scarcity of money, or in production carried beyond consumption, and a consequent glut of the market.

In the hard times, from 1837 to 1850, there was a great lack of currency; there being, in 1842, only $64,000,000 of currency in the whole country. In such a state of fact, we see an adequate cause for the low scale of prices then prevailing.

Scarcity of money is not now the cause of our low prices. Money is now abundant in the country. We have much more money than can be used in carrying on the business of the country, at the rate of prices now prevailing. The men who purchase our farming products have such abundance of means that they are able to pay cash for all our products, without needing bank accommodations. At our great money centers, money is abundant, and the rate of interest is low. Money is so abundant in the country, that any man can get a loan, for any amount, provided he has property to mortgage as security. Hundreds of millions are for loan, constantly, on farms and real estate. Money is so abundant, that its holders are seeking in every direction for opportunities of investment.

The low prices of farming produce now prevailing can not be caused by a scarcity of money.

Nor are the low prices caused by overproduction. We have not an oversupply of wheat, or cotton, or pork, or beef, or any of the great staples of the country. The growth of population keeps pace with the growth of production, and the increased supply is merely sufficient to meet the increased demand. The crop of each year is always consumed by the time the next crop is ready for market. At no time has the market been oversupplied.

The present low prices can not be attributed to a glut of the market. On the contrary, prices have gone down, especially, at times when the supply was inadequate to meet the demand. The present condition of prices is anomalous. So far as as money and the law of supply and demand go, we have the conditions for fair prices.

There is now as much money in the country, and we have as good a market for produce, as in 1870, and in 1881 and 1882, when prices were much higher than now.— Prices are no longer regulated by the amount of currency and the law of supply and demand.

Prices are now regulated by a Titanic Imperialism of Capital. Facts already mentioned, and which it is unnecessary to repeat here, prove this demonstrably. The prices of farming produce are low, because the Imperialism of Capital is the only buyer of our produce, and there is no competition: because prices are manipulated by an Imperialism of Capital, in Boards of Trade, and fixed according to the will of the Money

Power: because the Money Power so dominates the markets of the world that it makes the Liverpool price the standard for all countries; while it keeps down the Liverpool price, by keeping on hand shipments of India produce, raised on plantations owned by the Money Kings, with Hindoo *Ryot* labor, at five cents a day.

---

2. THE PRINCIPLES OF POLITICAL ECONOMY VIOLATED, IN THE FACT THAT NEW POOR MEN HAVE TAKEN POSSESSION OF EVERYTHING, IN ALL DEPARTMENTS OF BUSINESS.

A multitude of New Men have grown up from poverty into sudden wealth, dispossessing richer men of business in which they were well established, thus throwing all the business of the country into new channels.

New Men are at the head of the import and export trade of the country—of the trade in all lines of produce—in the oil business—in manufactures—in the great wholesale trade—in the packing business—in all the great lines of business in the country.

In New York City, New Men bankrupted the old merchants, and took away the business from them.

These New York merchants—English branch houses—afterwards put down the price of goods, and broke down the New England Mills. They were evidently in collusion with their London principals; and their ability to break down the New England Mills is another proof of the mighty capital behind them.

New Men went into Wall Street, and broke the old operators, and acquired immense fortunes; a positive proof that the New Operators were backed by the unlimited capital of London, which made their operations a certainty.

New Men went into the oil regions, broke down the old operators, monopolized all the wells, and secured a grand monopoly of oil; manifest proof that they had behind them the power of an immense capital.

In pork packing, the old Louisville and Cincinnati packers were all broke, while a New Man sprung up in Chicago from poverty into sudden and immense wealth; a demonstration that the New Man who rode the storm before which the others went down, and who put $120,000,000 into his business in a few years, is not a principal in his business, but is an agent of the Money Kings, who gave him unlimited capital for his operations.

This is an age of New Men. In all the great branches of business, the old business men have gone down, and New Men have taken their place. New Men who started poor, have, all over the country, broken down and displaced the former operators who were rich, and well established in business.

The fact is capable of Scientific Demonstration that those Americans who have thus suddenly grown up into wealth and power, are

The Agents of the London Money Power.

It is impossible, under the regular laws of business, that these New Men could be independent operators, conducting business on their own account. To suppose them independent operators makes the business life of the age an anomaly,—full of facts utterly contradictory of all the laws of the business world.—Our age is moving onward, with the facts it presents in utter antagonism to all Law. Its facts are a jumble of irreconcilable contradictions to the past experience of the world, and to the fixed and immutable laws of Political Economy. Enlightened Reason revolts against the idea that these men are engaged in independent business, and rejects it as utterly absurd.

When, in all lines of business, we see New Men who were poor break down the rich men who were in the business before them, and drive them out of the business and take possession of it themselves, *we may know that the New Men have, from some source, not known to the public, supplies of capital greater than is at the command of the men whom they break down.*

All the facts are explained, if we suppose that the New Men, who started poor a few years ago, are the agents of the Money Power, and are using its capital. *But to suppose that they have, unaided, by their own narrow means, supplanted and driven from business richer men, is the rankest absurdity.*

The absurdity of the idea is manifest. It is impossible for poor young men to go into business, and bankrupt the rich men already established, and take their business from them, unless the Poor Young Men were secretly the agents of the London Money Power, and were supplied with funds by the Money Kings, so as to enable them to break down all opposition.

Napoleon said, Providence always favors the strongest battalions, in war. In business, as in war, God does not choose to work miracles by setting aside the regular laws of nature, but leaves natural laws to work out their natural results; and men of smaller capital who launch out boldly into business in antagonistic competition with rich men already established, will, as a rule, come to ruin. In business, the longest purse wins, as the strongest battalions, in war.

Whenever we see a multitude of poor men growing rich, and bankrupting rich men already established in business, we may be sure that, from some source,

THE VICTORS HAVE THE HEAVIEST CAPITAL.

This is Law—*Law fixed as the course of the planets.* As has been said, the planets have their perturbations; and there may be occasional exceptions to these business laws, where a poor man may grow rich in such a manner. But when a multitude of such cases occur—when, indeed, it is the rule for Poor Young Men to get rich, and rapidly supplant their predecessors in trade—so that all business changes hands—in such cases, it is certain that *the poor men whō thus get rich have behind them the backing of a mighty capital.* This is Law. By the opēration of the Law of Cause and Effect, *the heaviest Capital carries with it power to crush smaller operators; as surely as a thunder cloud carries rain, or the North Wind cold.*

LOOK OVER TO LONDON,

and all is plain. We have seen that in 1864, the London Money Kings were carrying on business all over the earth. In 1865, Mr. Gladstone stated in the House of Commons that the United States was the best place for investment, and advised British capitalists to make investments here. What is more natural than that they should concentrate their capital upon this country?

The Drift of Gold to the United States, proves that London capitalists have not only been reinvesting here all their profits derived from their business in this country, but that they are sending profits of their world-wide commerce over here for investment.

Where is the Money that has been coming in a constant stream for investment? We can not find it, unless it is the money these New Men have been investing in their own name. If the capital these New Men have been investing is London capital, it makes all plain.

There is More Evidence to prove that the London Money Power has been extending its Imperialism over our country by breaking down our business men, and thus conquering and taking possession of our business, than there is to prove the truth of the Copernican Theory of the Solar System. It establishes the fact of the work of the London Money Power in this country beyond the possibility of doubt.

This evidence is enough. But it is not all:

3. The Principles of Political Economy Violated, in the Sudden Acquisition of Inordinate Wealth by a Multitude of Poor Men, in a Very Short Time.

It is needless to mention the names of the multitude of the newly and immensely rich. All know them. That they have the wealth is evident: they have the property to show for it.

The Important Question is, Whose wealth is it? Is it theirs? and did they make it out of their own resources? Or is it the wealth of the London Money Kings, which they are holding in trust, and managing on commission?

All is Plain if they are the agents of the Money Kings;—but to suppose them to have made all the money themselves, in so short a time, and under such conditions, is a contradiction of all the fixed laws of Political Economy.

Let Us Note Some of the Facts. We have a vast number of facts in the industry of our times which, if we leave out of view the London Money Power, are the strangest anomaly in the history of the world. There are a multitude of facts in the history of our age, which, as they are commonly regarded, transcend the vivid imagination of the Romancer, or the wild dreams of Oriental fable.

When Eugene Sue needed a Collosal Fortune as the basis of that strange work of fiction, *The Wandering Jew*, he constructed a fortune of $42,000,000, as the result of the accumulation of several generations. But, in our times, we have the Vanderbilts credited with $200,000,000, acquired in a little over twenty years. And Armour was operating his business, in a year or two after starting it, with a capital of $120,000,000.

If Eugene Sue had stated such a thing as this in his novel, it would have been scouted as perfectly ridiculous. If the author of the Arabian Nights, in narrating the adventures of Sinbad the Sailor, had made him acquire such a fortune, the credulity of his readers would have been too severely taxed. Such a Collossal Fortune would have overtaxed the powers of the Genii of Aladdin's Ring and Lamp;—and yet, we believe all that is told us about the mushroon fortunes that are said to be made in our time. Without consulting probabilities at all, we take it for granted that the natural laws of industry are wholly suspended, and that MIRACLES of accumulation are being wrought around us.

We believe that Com. Vanderbilt made $100,000,000, in twelve years!—that Jay Gould made $200,000,000, in ten years!—that Rockafeller has made $150,000,000, in fifteen years!—and that Armour made $120,000,000, in three years!!! Is there anything the American people will not believe, if the newspapers tell them it is so?!! Had those men possessed Aladdin's lamp, and diligently rubbed it all the while from Monday morning to Saturday night, they could not have made so much money, in the time!

The Gambling Argument Refuted.

It may be said that these men made their money dealing in stocks,—that they were gamblers; and luck was in their favor! But the mutations of chance correct their variations in the long run, and return to some regular order, by a series of changes which may be calculated. The gambler at the roulette table may win for a time on the turn of the wheel; but as surely as he continues to tempt Fortune, he will have a turn of luck, and will lose all, at last.—So these gamblers in stocks.

They would long since have lost all they had gained, if it were mere luck; as so many others have done, who trusted to fortune entirely, without any great unlimited capital at their back. But these men uniformly win.

Their success is the result of Capital, which enabled them to insure success. Commodore Vanderbilt went into Wall street with only a million dollars. He was constantly opposed by Daniel Drew, who was worth $15,000,000; and he frequently had the whole street against him. And yet he wâs able to carry out all his plans successfully. It is known that he had command of unlimited capital—more than could be brought against him in all North America. The operations of Vanderbilt, and Gould and others in Wall street can only be accounted for by the fact that they were the agents of the London Money Kings, and were supplied with sufficient capital to make their operations an assured success.

THE FACTS OF THE OUTSIDE WORLD,

make it apparent how impossible it is that so many Americans should have made such colossal fortunes in a few years.

An article has recently appeared which shows the concentration of wealth in a few hands in the United States, from which it appears that there is greater concentration of wealth here than in any other country. There are about seventy persons who average over $37,000,000 each, most of them having made it within the last thirty years. This makes these persons,—these Newly Rich,—wealthier than the richest capitalists of Europe, whose fortunes have been growing up for generations. It is said that "The richest dukes of England fall below the average wealth of a dozen American citizens; while the greatest bankers, merchants and railway magnates of England can not compare in wealth with many Americans."

The average annual income of the wealthiest one hundred Englishmen is about $400,000; while the average annual income of the richest one hundred Americans largely exceeds $1,000,000!

Even the richest of the Rothschilds left only about $17,000,000, the result of the accumulation of several generations.*—Earl Dudley, the owner of the richest iron mines, was worth at his death but $20,000,000.—The Duke of Buccleuch left about $30,000,000.—The Marquis of Bute is now estimated to be worth $40,000,000; the Duke of Norfolk, about the same; and the Duke of Westminster about $50,000,000.

It is perfectly evident by comparison with these grand fortunes abroad, which have been actually made, and under the most favorable circumstances, how impossible it is that these Americans should have amassed these fabulous fortunes, in a day. It is impossible.

The idea is contradicted by all the history of the past: it is contradicted by the actual facts known to exist in other countries, in our time: it is contradicted by the laws of Political Economy which govern the business world: it is contradicted by the certainties which limit the possibilities of business accumulation.

The Absurdity of the Idea is too gross for belief. The men have not made these fortunes. It is impossible

---

* This proves that the Rothschilds are the head of a syndicate. For that House loaned over $500,000,000 to national governments in the ten years from 1854 to 1864; besides all its other immense operations in the same time; and all its previous loans. The House of Rothschild has loaned several billions of dollars. And yet the richest of the Rothschilds was worth only $17,000,000. The House is evidently a syndicate loaning much money not owned by the Rothschild family.

that they should have made them. They are the agents of the London Money Kings—have been using their capital—and are holding their property in trust for them.

---

4. The Principles of Political Economy Violated, in the Enormous Growth of Wealth in the United States, from 1870 to 1880.

A Remarkable Fact Fully Corroborates the conclusions drawn from the foregoing testimony, and proves positively the workings of the Money Power in this country. From 1870 to 1880, the wealth of this country increased from $30,068,000,000 to $43,642,000,000; an increase of $13,574,000,000. That is, the wealth of the country increased in these ten years of disaster over two-fifths of the whole amount!

This Immense Growth of Wealth would indicate that our country was then enjoying an unprecedented prosperity,—that our merchants, and manufacturers and farmers were growing rich with unprecedented rapidity. But the fact is, that those were ten years of overwhelming and universal financial ruin. Business was dull during the whole ten years: and five years out of the ten were years of such general prostration of business, and such overwhelming ruin, as no country ever before suffered in time of peace. Prices were never so low—business was never so prostrate—bankruptcies, never so numerous.

Our people were all growing poorer: farmers were getting in debt: there were from nine thousand to ten thousand great business failures every year; besides the multitude of small bankruptcies of which no account was kept. The American people were poorer, in 1880, than in 1870;—and yet the wealth of the coontry vastly increased,—increased beyond precedent,—during the interval.

How do We Account for the Anomaly? The people getting poorer, and the country two-fifths richer during the ten years? It is easily accounted for. The accumulation of wealth was not the wealth of our people; but the wealth of the corporations established in America by the Money Kings.

Those Were the Ten Years when Armour was building up his gigantic business, while American packers were being broken down: when the Money Kings were getting possession of property in Chicago and other cities: when the Money Kings were taking possession of the great lines of trade, buying up our cotton and wheat and pork and bacon and whiskey, and breaking those engaged in the business before: when the Money Kings were taking possession of our manufacturing interests in the North, and planting the beginnings of a grand manufacturing system in the New South: when Jay Gould was buying up his grand railroad system: when other railroads were being purchased; and when lumber forests and lumber mills and hundreds of other branches of American industry were purchased cheap by the Money Kings at bankrupt prices.

All These Purchases Required a Vast Outlay of Foreign Capital in the country; and they account for the strange anomaly that the wealth of the country increased so vastly, while the American people, suffering from hard times and low prices, were getting poorer, and suffered one hundred thousand great bankruptcies.

There was indeed the opening up of new farms;—but the great increase of wealth in the country was the growth of the wealth of the Money Power in America. It was the growth of grubs in the head of the sheep—of worms grown from the eggs of the ox-fly in the back of the ox. The wealth was not our wealth, but the wealth of the Money Power. It did not belong to our people, or our nation, but to the horde of predacious vermin—PARASITES—that are preying upon us.

SYNOPSIS OF THE ARGUMENT.

As has been said, the evidence here adduced proceeds on the same scientific basis as the Scientific Demonstration that proves the truth of the Copernican Theory. As that Scientific Theory is demonstrated to be true by its harmonizing all the phenomena of the Solar System, so the Theory that it is the Money Power which is devouring all our industries is proved to be true by its harmonizing and explaining all the facts of the Business World that have been so perplexing to all observers.

Everybody knows that the times are out of joint. The most startling business developments are constantly occurring;—but no one has been able to account for them. Our business system is like Astronomy under the old Ptolemaic System: it is a jumble of incongruous facts, wholly unaccountable by all the ordinary laws of industry, and indeed in antagonism with them.

The Hypothesis, that all the facts are caused by the work of the Money Kings through a system of agencies in this country, makes all plain.

1. We have the existence of the Money Power set forth by English writers, who declare that it is constantly piling up the wealth of the whole world higher and higher in its Temple, the Money Quarter of London: that its capital is carrying on the business of all countries, and generally supplying to them the means of interior home production: that, twenty-four years ago, it owned almost all the railroads of the world; and that it is carrying on its operations, all over the earth. The existence of the grand world-wide Imperialism of Capital is a demonstrated fact.

Furthermore, this Money Power always operates through

joint stock corporations: it always systematically conceals its operations: thoroughly organized, it proceeds in the accomplishment of its aims of conquest in accordance with a regular method.

2. Hence, when we see in this country grand corporations monopolizing all business, thoroughly organized, proceeding in their breaking down of independent business men with regular uniform method—carefully concealing their wrecking operations from the public—working always by secret underhanded methods:—these facts create a strong presumption that these corporations are the agents of the London Money Power.

And when we see a multitude of other facts, all pointing in the same direction, it becomes a certainty.

3. We find a multitude of New Men, who started poor, going into business without capital of their own, and breaking down Rich Men already established in business, and taking the business from them.

4. We find New Men, starting poor, in a few years ostensibly having possession of vast fortunes, greater than the wealth of the Rothschilds, or the richest Plutocrats of Europe.

5. We find our country vastly increasing in wealth in the decade when business was dullest, times hardest; and when the whole country was swept by an overwhelming tide of ruin.

6. We find business drifting into new channels—being monopolized by a few great capitalists—the multitude of small business operators being ruined, while grand companies with overwhelming capital are taking possession of all kinds of business.

7. We see times hard, while money is plenty: we see business dull in the ordinary business channels, while the railroads are pressed beyond their capacity by the constantly expanding industry of the country.

8. **We have more business than ever before;** but it is gone out of the hands of the many small operators, and has gone into the hands of a few great business companies.

9. We see money abundant, and demand for produce steady and active; and yet prices of produce as low as in old days of the 40's, when money was so scarce that we had only $64,000,000, of currency in the country. * * *

The people have seen these and other anomalies already mentioned, and have been asking the reason. The reason for this state of things is sought in vain in ordinary business causes. The action of ordinary business causes would, in a normal state of things, give us general prosperity. There is great business activity—plenty of money lying idle—an abundant market and an active demand:—there are all the elements of prosperous times, high prices and general prosperity;—and yet, notwithstanding, we have low prices, hard times, everybody in debt, and great masses of our people on the verge of ruin. The state of things is unaccountable by all ordinary business principles.

Some Great Cause for these Effects.

These uniform violations of the principles of Political Economy can not be fortuitous. In all these great lines of facts the principles of Political Economy are violated; and the facts are too numerous, and too varied, to have occurred by chance. There is some great cause, of which all the facts are the effects.

Without the presence in our Country of a grand Imperialism of Capital, these facts, numerous, and on varied business lines, and all in utter violation of the principles of Political Economy, and wholly contrary to the results that would have followed the regular operation of natural business laws, could not have occurred. They are the natural effects which the capital of the Money Power, invested in vast amounts, would produce. And they could not have originated from any other cause.

The facts of our Industrial System are wholly inexplicable, unless we adopt the Hypothesis that the London Money Kings own all these great enterprises, ostensibly owned by Americans; and that their capital is producing all the anomalies apparent in our Industry.

This Hypothesis harmonizes and explains all the facts of our Industrial System; and this harmonizing and explaining the facts demonstrates the truth of the Hypothesis on the strictest Scientific principles. It is A SCIENTIFIC DEMONSTRATION.

The reasoning is without a flaw. It is the same kind of evidence as that by which the Copernican System is proved to be true. And it is even more conclusive.

And yet this is not all the proof. There are other facts, which strongly corroborate the proofs already offered, and which make the conclusion doubly sure.

III. THIRD PROOF: CORROBORATING FACTS, PROVING THAT THE CAPITAL OF THESE NEW MEN IS THE CAPITAL OF THE MONEY POWER.

If there were no other evidence, that which has been adduced is amply sufficient to prove the work of the Money Power in this country. But the last shadow of doubt is dispelled when we see so many facts in corroboration of it.

Jim Fisk dies, and at his death it becomes evident that the firm of Fisk & Gould were not the owners of the Erie Railroad, but were only agents.—Jay Gould's railroad system breaks down, and proves that he did not own the railroads he was believed to possess, but was only an agent of the Money Kings.—Commodore Vanderbilt dies, and only divides up three and one-half millions among his children.—Wm. H. Vanderbilt sells out a controlling interest in the Vanderbilt system for $50,000,000, and places the money in a London bank.—And, at his death, he leaves his property, so that it can be easily controlled by a single will.—A. T. Stewart dies, and it is proved that he was only an agent of the London Money Kings:— These and many other similar facts make it certain that these grand corporations in our country are the agencies of the London Money Power.

2. If any agent wants to deny that the Money Kings are his principals, it is very easy to prove the denial to be true.

Let him show the stock books of his corporation, and show who the stockholders are; and let him show that his corporation is not mortgaged to the London Money Kings. *No man who is afraid to show his stock books, can deny that he is the agent of the London Money Kings.*

3. **The necessity for concealment** shows why employees of those corporations, when testifying in court, and before committees of Congress, can not be induced to to state who are the stockholders of the corporations they serve. That is their secret—a secret that is never divulged.

One of them, after answering frankly the questions that were asked him about the management of his company, begged to be permitted not to tell who were the stockholders. He said he had come prepared to answer truly all the questions that might be asked him concerning the management of the business, but he had no right to tell who were the stockholders of the corporation. He was excused by the Committee; and the American people do not know who are the stockholders of the Standard Oil Company.

They do not wish Americans to know that all these grand corporations are owned by the London Money Kings! They guard this precious secret with the greatest care.—The books of a corporation were once taken out of a New York court by force, and carried off to Canada, to prevent it from being discovered who were the stockholders.

They never will permit the public to see their books,—unless indeed, hereafter, they should divise a new system, in which the agents might be allowed to hold the stock under trust bonds, and carry it upon the books in their own name, in order to deceive the American people. They will do it, if necessary. Anything to keep their secret!

IV. FOURTH PROOF: THE JEWS TAKING POSSESSION OF PROPERTY, IN EUROPE, AS IN THIS COUNTRY.

What the Money Power has been doing in this country, it has been doing all over the world. All over the earth it is extending its empire over industry, commerce and wealth. The national debts of the world now amount to about $26,000,000,000. It is estimated that the entire indebtedness of the world, national, state, county, municipal, corporate, and individual, amounts to over $75,000,000,000. If three-fourths of this indebtedness is owed to the Money Power—and this is a moderate estimate—then at four per cent., the income from interest alone, amounts to $2,150,000,000 a year. Beside this, it has the profits derived from its manufactures—from its ocean commerce—from its city rents—from its mines of coal and lead and silver and gold and copper and tin—from its petroleum—from its freights and passenger traffic on its railroads and ocean vessels—from the profits of its farms and plantations—from the profits of its merchandizing—from its trade in all the productions of our country, and of the whole world. From all these sources, the Money Power have an annual revenue vast beyond computation.

In the United States, the Money Power is Making Almost All the Money that is made. Our people used to get the Liverpool price for our produce; the profits being divided between the producer, the merchant who shipped, and the ship-owner who carried it. But after the Money Power bought our ships, we only made the profits received at the sea board. And now, the Money Power has devoured our import and export sea board trade—our railroads—our mines—our manufactures, and the traffic in all our products; and all that our people now get is, what the Money Power pays our farmers for produce, at the railroad depots. All the profits, from that point, are realized by the Money Power and its agents. And it is the same in all other countries. From these facts, we can form an idea of the immense profits the Money Power is realizing from its imperialism over industry, commerce and wealth, all over the earth.

Though the fact that the Jew Capitalists are the London Money Power, a grand Imperialism of Capital, has never been thought of before, yet thoughtful observers have noticed the rapid rise of the Jews into astonishing wealth.

Since this work was written, a thoughtful book, entitled *The Jews*, by Samuel H. Kellogg, D. D., has fallen under my eye, from which I take some very startling facts that are new to the public. The statements are more striking in their bearing upon the Imperialism of Capital attained by the London Jews, from the fact that the author of the work has no idea of the Jewish London Money Power. It shows that the Jews have done, and are doing, in Europe, all I have shown that they are doing in the United States.

1st. Jewish Power and Influence.

Dr. Kellogg says:—"Everywhere in Europe is noted the extraordinary tendency of capital to concentrate in Jewish hands."

A writer in the *Nineteenth Century* makes the following statements:—

"**The Influence of the Jews** at the present time is more noticable than ever. That they are at the head of European Capitalists, we are all well aware. * * * * The Jews are, beyond dispute, the leaders of the Plutocracy of Europe. * * * * In all the vast financial schemes of recent years, the hand of the Jews has been felt, both for good and evil. The Rothschilds are but the leading name among the whole series of capitalists, which include the great monetary chiefs of Berlin, Amsterdam, Paris and Frankfort. During the ten years, 1854 to 1864, the Rothschilds furnished in loans, $200,000,000 to England, $50,000,000 to Austria, $40,000,000 to Prussia, $130,000,000 to France, $50,000,000 to Russia, $12,000,000 to Brazil, in all $482,000,000.—This, besides many millions loaned to small states."

And this was twenty-four years ago, when these capitalists were comparatively feeble! How many millions have they loaned in the last twenty-four years?!!

In Prussia, where the Jews are only two per cent. of the population, in 1871, out of six hundred and forty two bankers, five hundred and fifty were Jews; *i. e.* about six-sevenths of the whole number.—And this was seventeen years ago. How great has been the growth of Jewish capital in the interval!!

In Austria, a similar state of things exists. One of the religious papers of Berlin makes the statement that "The Bourse of Vienna actually lies wholly in Jewish hands."

The petition of the Anti-Semites, circulated in Germany, in 1880, complains:—"The fruits of Christian labor are harvested by the Jews. Capital is concentrated in Jewish hands."

2ND. THESE JEW CAPITALISTS ARE TAKING POSSESSION OF THE BUSINESS OF EUROPE.

So long ago as 1861, according to the Prussian official returns, out of seventy-one thousand Jews in Prussia, capable of work, thirty eight thousand, or more than half, were engaged in commerce; while, at the same time, only one Jew in five hundred and eighty six was a day laborer.

In Berlin,—where the Jews were five per cent. of the population,—in 1871, while, out of every hundred Protestants, thirty nine were returned as "employers," out of every hundred Jews, seventy-one were engaged in commercial life. It is evident that the Jew merchants make at least five times as much profit as the Protestant "employers" engaged in various lines of business.

In Lower Austria, out of 59,122 merchants, 30,012 are returned in the last census as Jews.—Over half the merchants Jews, while the Jews are less than five per cent. of the population! And we know that the Jew stores are always extensive establishments; while the native merchants have the small stores.—When the Jews are half in number of the merchants of *our* towns, what will have become of our merchants? Where will they be?

In Algiers, even a worse state of things exists. According to *Le Telegraphe*, "Constantina, Algiers and Oran belong almost completely to the Jews. The whole trade of Algiers is in their hands; and, in consequence of high and usurious rates of interest, a large proportion of the natives are fallen into the power of the Jews." The writer adds, "Here is a dark point, full of danger for the future."

3RD. THESE JEW CAPITALISTS ARE DEVOURING THE LANDS OF EUROPE.

The Jews have become to a vast extent the owners of the soil of Europe, and are rapidly becoming the owners of Europe in fee simple, as they are of the United States.

In a debate in the German Reichstag, on the famine of 1880, in Upper Silesia and Posen, it was said that one of the causes of the starvation of the people was the fact, that the lands of those countries had passed, by mortgage foreclosure, to a vast extent, out of the hands of the German Proprietors into the hands of the Jews. So far had this foreclosure of mortgages gone that, as it was stated, the German population were so stripped and impoverished that they were "almost incapable of raising themselves again."—So will it be in this country, in a few years more. Thank God that it is not so yet.

A Berlin paper asserts, "It is a fact which can no longer be denied, that the population of the remote districts of Russia, Austria, Hungary and Roumania, are only the nominal possessors of the soil, and for the most part cultivate the land for the Jews, to whom they have mortgaged all the estates."—One would almost suppose this writer to be speaking of farmers of Iowa and Kansas!

In Galicia, mortgages have, for several years past, increased at the rate of about eight million florins per annum; and it is stated that one-third of the total amount has already passed, by foreclosure, into the hands of the Jews. The sheriff's sales of peasant land were one hundred and sixty-four in 1867; but, in 1879, these sales had risen to 3,164; "and it was almost exclusively the Jews who brought about these foreclosures, and acquired thereby the property."

In the province of Berkowina, of the private mortgages registered in 1877, eighty-two per cent.,—according to the official returns,—were owned by the Jews.—In 1881, it was stated that already one-half of the real estate of that province, in town and country, had been taken possession of by the Jews, under foreclosure of mortgages. And Dr. Thaddeus Pilat, the Director of the Bureau of Statistics, expressed the opinion that "the remainder would, very shortly, go the same way."

From Hungary, similar facts are reported. In that country, in 1878, there were sixteen thousand sheriff's sales of property, far the greater part of which passed over to the Jews. The London *Spectator* stated, a few years ago, that the Jews had obtained posession of so many of the old estates of Hungary, "as to make a change in the constitution a necessity."

In Roumania, the same authority says the gravest apprehensions were entertained that the Jews "would gradually oust the peasantry, till they possessed the whole land."

In Russia it is said that, as early as 1869, seventy-three per cent. of the real estate of certain provinces in the West, where the Jews are the most numerous, had passed from the Russians into the hands of the Jews.

The Money Power is in a fair way to devour all the property of Asia Minor. Several years ago the New York *Nation* made the following statements:—

"Capital has fixed its eye on the magnificent region known as Asia Minor, and found it full to overflowing of material for handsome returns, which nothing prevents it from getting at, but insecurity and oppressive taxation. * * * * * * The Money markets of London and Paris, now that they will not lend the Sultan any more money, are beginning to insist, with a subtle, silent, but always in the end irresistible persistence, which unemployed capital knows so well how to exert, that he must at least give them a chance at his mines, and his minerals, and his wheat fields, olive yards and vineyards, must let them carry their own police with them, and fix their own taxation. * * * * From this," the editor significantly remarks, "the Ottomans are probably in greater danger at this moment, than they have ever been from the armies of the Czar."

In this dreadful state of things, can we wonder that the Jews are about, in every way, to dominate Europe?

4TH. THE JEW MONEY KINGS ARE MENACING EUROPE, AS WELL AS AMERICA, WITH DOMINATION.

M. De Lavileye, the eminent publicist of Belgium, has expressed the general uneasiness that prevails on this subject, in these words:—"The rapid rise of the Jewish element is a fact which may be observed all over Europe. If this upward movement continues, the Israelites, a century hence, will be the masters of Europe."

The London *Spectator* says:—"The Jews display a talent for accumulation with which Christians can not compete, and which tends to make of them an ascendant caste."

The New York *Tribune* quotes one of the German papers as saying, "The rapid rise of the Jewish nation to leadership is a great problem of the future for East Germany." And the writer states in justification of this opinion that "All the lower forms of labor, in the work shops, the fields, and ditches and swamps, fall to the lot of the German element, while the constantly increasing Jewish element obtains enormous possessions in capital and land, and raises itself to power and influence in every department of public life."

In view of all these things, the London *Spectator* gives utterance to the prevailing feeling of anxiety in the following editorial, which appeared some years ago:—

"The nations feel insecure, as if they had no defense; the working population are distressed till their irritability shakes the governments; there is deep unrest everywhere, a sense as of over-fatigue; a popular looking forward, not for a millennium, but for some colossal catastrophe in which all prosperity shall be submerged; a tension which half makes statesmen wish that the cataclysm would come and be over. And we see ahead no prospect of amelioration, no gleam of hope in the sky."

5TH. THE JEW MONEY KINGS HAVE LATELY SECURED A MOST EXTENSIVE CONTROL OF THE PRESS.

Dr. Kellogg says: "The increase of Jewish influence is further illustrated in the extensive *control of the press* [italics his] which the Jews have lately acquired. This is much insisted on, and with good reason greatly lamented, by many of the most eminent Christian men in Europe. *The fact is to be observed in every country where the Jews exist in any number.*" [Italics his.]

In Dresden, in a gathering of the representatives of the press, twenty-nine out of forty-three were Jews.

Out of twenty-three Liberal and Progressive papers of the Berlin daily press, *there are only two which are not, in one way or another, under Jewish control.*

In Italy, the Jews have control of the *Liberal Press.*

The most influential paper in Spain is under Jewish control.

It is well known that the Jews have control of a great portion of the Metropolitan Press of the United States. They are always open to give the gloss to events, inspired by the Money Power.

It is a part of the astute policy of the Money Power, *to have Jews in control of the Liberal Press in Europe.* There are two advantages they derive from this:—

1.) **They keep up the agitation**—keep it boiling all the while—*but keep it within limits fixed by themselves.*

2.) **The great advantage the Money Kings derive from the agitation** of so-called Liberals and Progressives, is this: they are afraid the nations will rise against their own outrageous monopolies. They are destroying the business men of all countries; and they are afraid the business class may rise up against them, and check their atrocious outrages in the business world. To prevent this, it is their policy to keep up an agitation of the working class, aiming at projects to which the business men are utterly opposed.

It is their policy to keep up a hot agitation for Communism and Socialism in the great cities; so that the business men, in their antagonism to those ideas, will keep on the side of the Money Power. It is a significant fact that most of the agitators for Socialism are Jews, who are most probably the agents of the Money Power, to keep up this agitation for their own purposes.

Thus, most of the Nihilists in Russia are Jews. Prof. Wassiljew of the Imperial University of St. Petersburg, in his testimony, given in the London *Times*, says, "It is an open secret that the Jews are among the leaders of the Nihilistic agitation."

The London *Spectator*, in a review of Victor Tissot's *Russians and Germans*, says: "M. Tissot calls attention to the notable fact that the Nihilist ranks are largely recruited by Jews. * * * * * There are ten times as many Jews as there are Russians, Poles, or Germans."

This shows that the Nihilist movement is largely an agitation against the Russian Government, started up by the Money Power through its Jewish agents. The Russian property class, in their horror of the Nihilists, keep in sympathy with the Money Power.

So, in this country, it is the interest of the Money Power to keep up the agitation of Socialism; *so that the businees class, in their abhorrence of Communism, may keep* *in sympathy with the railroads, and the other corporations of the Money Power.* It is a part of the consummate craft of these Money Kings.

No one can any longer doubt that these grand corporations are the agencies of the Money Power. The Scientific Proof is positive: and the Money Kings are doing in Europe what they are doing in the United States. Their movement in Europe, for the possession of all business and all lands, is even more advanced than it is in our own country.

V. FIFTH PROOF: ANTICIPATION OF THE EVILS THE MONEY POWER HAS CAUSED IN THIS COUNTRY.

There is no stronger evidence of the existence of a cause, than the fact that it has been traced to its effects before the effects were wrought out.

The Author of this work, twenty-three years ago, traced out in a published work the evils British capital has since wrought out in this country, and predicted its monopoly of our industry, and its devouring of our property. In that work, he gave two chapters to the subject: one headed "*British Centralization of Commerce,*" the other "*British Centralization of Wealth.*"

Want of space forbids any extended quotations from the work. One passage must suffice, quoted from memory, as the work is not beside me:—

"The English cuckoo has no nest of its own, but lays its eggs in the nest of the hedge-sparrow and the robin. When the young birds hatch, the intruder, by its larger growth, soon needs the whole nest; and it throws out the young sparrows, one by one, upon the ground to die, while the stranger consumes all the food brought by the parent birds.—England is laying a cuckoo's egg in every nation's nest. It will not be long before the foreign egg will hatch, and, in its gigantic development, will need for its growth all the nation's wealth. Then, one by one, it will cast out of their nest the nation's young, to perish, while the intruder will devour all the nation's wealth." * * * * * * "It is the prosperity of England against the world: one or the other must go down."

The Author, in that work, represents the American people as a prodigal heir, mortgaging his possessions to Moneybags. And he says that all would be pleasant, while Moneybags was accommodating; but ruin would come when he insisted on having his own. Then the bankrupt prodigal would bewail his folly, too late.

All this has come upon us; and worse than the Author anticipated. The Cuckoo's egg has hatched; and the foreign intruder has already thrown most of the nation's young out of the nest, to perish. Manufacturers, wholesale merchants, oil men, dealers in wheat, cotton, hogs, beef, and all the products of the country have been remorselessly pitched out of the nest, to perish, while the intruder takes their place.

But the Author did not dream of the impudence of the Money Power, in daring to commit the ravages it has perpetrated in devouring the business of our country, step by step. He did not dream of its entering the country, and making Americans its agents to aid it in devouring their countrymen. He expected oppression, but he did not anticipate such mastery as it has achieved. He was expecting the money lender's harassments; he did not realize the grasp of the mighty Imperialism, now throttling our country, and the world. He supposed they were merely English capitalists. He did not know that this Knot of Capitalists are the Great Red Dragon, the Seventh Head of the Beast, the mightiest Imperialism that has ever risen upon the earth; which is now controlling all governments, devouring all property, and threatening to destroy all national life.*

* Some may object that the Jews can not be the great Money Kings of London, because the great banking houses of Lombard street are not Jewish, but English banking houses—that the Jews are not on Lombard street, but on Threadneedle street, and others in the vicinity.

But this fact is merely a specimen of the habitual craft of the Jews. They habitually hide their operations behind other parties. Nothing is more in keeping with their policy than to hide their operations behind English banking houses.

Wherever the Money Kings break down a bank, or a business, it is their habit to reorganize the establishment, take into their own hands a majority of the stock, give the original bankers, or business managers, the minority of the stock, and continue the business under the name of the old firm. They have done this repeatedly in this country.

In some of the many business crises of the past, the Jews may have driven these English banking houses to the wall, and subordinated them to themselves. Or, they may have entered into some business arrangement with them, and made them their agents. The fact is known that *the Jews are at the head of the capitalists of England, and of the world.* There is nothing that militates against their imperial position in the fact that a large part of the foreign business of London capital is done through English banking houses.

PART II.

THE GREAT RED DRAGON A SYMBOL OF THE LONDON MONEY POWER.

CHAPTER I.

THE SEVEN HEADS AND TEN HORNS.

The Seven Heads and Ten Horns appear three times in the book of Revelation: 1) In the 12th chapter, upon the body of the Great Red Dragon; 2) In the 13th chapter, upon the body of the Beast like a leopard, that rises up out of the Sea; and 3) In the 17th chapter, on the body of the Scarlet-colored Beast, that has a Woman upon its back, called the Beast from the Pit.

In all cases, the seven heads have the same signification.

The following is the text of the passage where the Seven Heads and Ten Horns appear upon the body of the Dragon:—

"And there appeared another wonder in heaven; and behold a great red dragon, having seven heads and ten horns, and seven crowns upon his heads." *Rev.* xii: 3.

The following is the text of the passage where these Seven Heads and Ten Horns appear upon the body of the Beast from the Sea:—

"And I stood upon the sand of the sea, and saw a beast rise up out of the sea having seven heads and ten horns, and upon his horns ten crowns, and upon his heads the name of blasphemy." *Rev.* xiii: 1.

In the 17th chapter of Revelation, where the Seven Heads and Ten Horns appear upon the body of the Beast from the Pit, they are elaborately described by the angel to John. The following is the text of the passage:—

"So he carried me away in the spirit into the wilderness: and I saw a woman sit upon a scarlet-colored beast, full of names of blasphemy, having seven heads and ten horns.

"And the woman was arrayed in purple and scarlet color, and decked with gold and precious stones and pearls, having a golden cup in her hand full of abomination and filthiness of her fornication: and upon her forehead was a name written, MYSTERY, BABYLON THE GREAT, THE MOTHER OF HARLOTS AND ABOMINATIONS OF THE EARTH.

"And I saw the woman drunken with the blood of the saints, and with the blood of the martyrs of Jesus: and when I saw her, I wondered with great admiration.

"And the angel said unto me, Wherefore didst thou marvel? I will tell thee the mystery of the woman, and of the beast that carrieth her, which hath the seven heads and ten horns.

"The beast that thou sawest was;

"And is not;

"and shall ascend out of the bottomless pit;

"and go into perdition:

"and they that dwell on the earth shall wonder, (whose names are not written in the book of life from the foundation of the world) when they behold the beast that was, and is not, and yet is.

"And here is the mind which hath wisdom.

"The seven heads are seven mountains on which the woman sitteth.

"And there are seven kings:

"five are fallen;

"and one is;

"and the other is not yet come; and when he cometh, he must continue a short space.

"And the beast that was, and is not, even he is the eighth, and is of the seven, and goeth into perdition.

"And the ten horns which thou sawest are ten kings

which have received no kingdom as yet; but receive power as kings one hour with the beast.

"These have one mind, and shall give their power and strength unto the beast. * * * * *

* * * * * "And the woman which thou sawest is that great city which reigneth over the kings of the earth." *Rev.* xvii: 3–13, and 18.

In each of the above instances, while they appear upon different bodies, the Seven Heads and Ten Horns are the same, and symbolize the same powers. In the 17th Chapter, the angel explains to John that the Seven Heads and Ten Horns symbolize "seven kings," prophetic phrase for seven kingdoms or empires. The angel says "five are fallen; and one is; and the other is not yet come, and when he cometh he must continue a short space."

From this explanation, we are able to understand

The Appearance of the Seven Heads and Ten Horns,

as they appear on the body of the Dragon. As the Dragon stands uplifted before the woman, five heads hang down dead, underneath its neck, symbolizing the five empires which had fallen at the time the Revelation was given. The Sixth Head is on the end of the Serpent's neck, and on it are ten horns. The Seventh Head is the Serpent's head, jutting out through the top of the Sixth Head, and dominating all. Such is the appearance of the Dragon, with its Seven heads and Ten horns.

What is the symbolic signification of the Seven Heads and Ten Horns? What powers do they symbolize?

Before giving the true exposition, it will be best to notice

I. THE ERRONEOUS INTERPRETATION FORMERLY GIVEN OF THE SEVEN HEADS.

In former interpretations, the Seven Headed Beast was interpreted as symbolizing the Roman empire, exclusively. This interpretation could be made, only by an entire misapplication of the facts of history. The Five Heads that had fallen at the time of the vision, have been interpreted as symbolizing the five forms of administration that existed under the Roman Republic,—Kings, Consuls, Decemvirs, Military Tribunes, and Dictators.

1st. I Object To This,

1. **That there were only two forms of government in Rome** that had fallen at the time the vision was given,—the Kings; and the Republic.

The Republic was always a government of the Senate and the People, throughout its entire existence. And, during its entire existence, the Executive of the Republic was in the hands of the Consuls, except during brief intervals.

2. Again, I Object to the Interpretation, that

It is a violation of all the facts of history to call the Decemvirate, the Military Tribunes, and the Dictators, such forms of the Roman government as would be symbolized by "heads."

1) **The Decemvirate** was a brief rule of ten persons who had been sent to Greece, to obtain new institutions, and who ruled about a year, while they put the institutions in operation. They were overthrown in a popular uprising against the crime of one of their number.

2) **The Military Tribunes** were a temporary arrangement, that lasted only a few years. It was only another name for the Consuls; and it was adopted, in order that one of the officers might be a Plebeian. It was merely a temporary expedient for a special purpose, and was soon set aside.

3) **The Dictatorship** only existed in times of great public danger, when a Dictator was appointed, whose authority only lasted six months. It is absurd to call the

Dictatorship a "head" of the Beast. What sort of a head is that, which comes on and falls off constantly? Such a symbol is ridiculous.

4) **These forms of administration can not be called "heads."** The government of the Roman Republic was continuous all the while; and these changes of administration did not affect its identity in the least.

France, since the Revolution of 1789–93, has had nine different forms of executive administration,—the Monarchy, the Convention, the Directory, the Consulate, the Empire, the Monarchy again, the Republic, the Empire, and the Republic. All these were much more fundamental than those changes of the Roman executive. And yet, France has been the same power all the while.—Who would think of saying that any prophecy would represent France, during the last hundred years, by a beast with nine heads? The idea is absurd. The French nation has been the same, all the while.

3. I OBJECT TO THIS APPLICATION OF THE SYMBOL THAT,

If the Different Forms of the Roman Administration Are to be Continued as Heads, then the Triumvirate of Octavius, Antony and Lepidus must be counted also; and it will make six heads that had lived, instead of five!!

4. I OBJECT TO THIS INTERPRETATION, THAT

A Head, in Prophecy, is Never the Symbol of a Mere Form of Administration. A head, in prophecy, always symbolizes a kingdom, or an empire. The four heads of the Macedonian Leopard, in the second vision of Daniel, symbolize the four kingdoms into which the Mecedonian empire was divided.—And these seven heads, in like manner, represent seven empires that have risen in the earth.

2nd. But the Greatest Absurdity of This Exposition

remains to be stated.—By making the "Seven Heads" symbolize the seven forms of Roman administration, former expositors had to find fulfillment for the Seventh Head in some form of Roman power; and they found it in the Heathen Roman empire.

1. But the Dragon is a Power of the Latter Days.

This is certain.

1) It is contemporary with the Beast from the Pit; and all expositors agree that the Beast from the Pit is a power that has not yet risen.

2) In the Great Final War of the Earth, just before the Millennium, the Dragon is engaged in the war, in alliance with the Beast from the Pit and the False Prophet.

3) And all the facts respecting the Dragon, in the Apocalypse, prove that it is a power of the Latter Days.

The idea of making the Dragon symbolize the Heathen Roman empire is perfectly absurd. It is this kind of interpretation,—such a straining of all the facts of history—such a jumble of symbolism and imagery,—that has made of this grand symbol, the Beast with Seven Heads and Ten Horns, an epithet of contempt and derision, hurled by the scoffer against all prophecy.

II. THE TRUE INTERPRETATION OF THE SEVEN HEADS AND TEN HORNS.

The Beast with Seven Heads and Ten Horns is a most remarkable symbol. It is so peculiar, so complex, and yet so simple, that it will not fit any powers but those it was intended to set forth.

As the four heads of the Macedonian Leopard, in the second vision of Daniel, symbolize the four kingdoms into which the Macedonian empire was divided, so here, the

Seven Heads symbolize seven empires. But, as we might suppose, from the analogy of the vision of Daniel, that the seven empires were contemporary like those of the Macedonian Beast, it is expressly stated that they are consecutive.

The Seven Heads Symbolize Seven Empires having relations with the people of God, and existing from the earliest times down to a time yet future. Of these empires, five had fallen at the time of the vision.

1st. Exposition of the First Five Heads.

The first Five Dead Heads hanging down under the neck of the Dragon symbolize five empires that had fallen at the time the Revelation was given: "five are fallen."

1. The First Dead Head Hanging Down

under the neck of the Serpent, symbolizes the Egyptian empire; which, under the Eighteenth Dynasty, as we learn from the records of the Egyptian monuments, recently deciphered, extended over Western Asia beyond the Euphrates and the Tigris. It was the Nineteenth Dynasty which persecuted Israel. The Pharaoh of the Persecution, under whom Moses was born, was the second king of the Nineteenth Dynasty. The Pharaoh of the Exodus died at Memphis, some twenty years after that event, with his Asiatic empire all lost, and with Egypt divided between himself and two rival kings, who reigned in the Delta. The great Egyptian empire fell before the judgments of God, visited upon Egypt for the deliverance of His people.

2. The Second Dead Head Hanging Down

beneath the neck of the Dragon is a Lion's head, and symbolizes the Assyrian empire, which carried away the Ten Tribes into captivity in Media.

3. THE THIRD DEAD HEAD HANGING DOWN

is also a Lion's head, and symbolizes the Babylonian empire, which carried Judah away captive to Babylon.

4. THE FOURTH DEAD HEAD HANGING DOWN

is a Bear's head, and symbolizes the Persian empire, which restored the Jews to their own land, and always treated them kindly.

5. THE FIFTH DEAD HEAD HANGING DOWN

beneath the neck of the Dragon is a Leopard's head, and symbolizes the Macedonian empire, which, under Alexander the Great, overthrew the Persian empire, and which, under Antiochus Epiphanes, afflicted the Jews with a grievous persecution.

These five empires had fallen, when the vision of Revelation was given.

2ND. EXPOSITION OF THE SIXTH HEAD, WITH ITS TEN HORNS.

The Sixth Head was the Roman Empire, which was then in existence, and of which the angel said "One now is." The Sixth Head, the Roman empire, was slain by the "sword" of the Northern Barbarians, in the year 476, A. D., at which time historians date the fall of the Western Roman empire.

The Northern Barbarians Planted Their Kingdoms in the territories of the Roman empire. In the year 476, A. D.,—the very year of the fall of the Western Roman empire,—we find, for the first time, Ten Kingdoms within its boundaries.

In the eye of prophecy, the Babylonian, the Persian, and Macedonian empires continued to *exist geographically, after their fall as political powers;* just as Ireland and Poland are still recognized as having a geographical existence, after they have ceased to be political powers. According to prophecy, the Roman territory was that part of the Roman empire which was not covered by the Babylonian, Persian and Macedonian empires,—the territory extending from the head of the Adriatic to the Danube, and thence westward, within the Rhine and the Danube, to the Atlantic and the Mediterranean, and including England and a part of Scotland.

Within This Territory, We Find Ten Barbarian Kingdoms in the year 476, A. D. And there have been Ten Kingdoms in the territories of the Roman empire ever since that time.

Not always the same kingdoms: sometimes, some would fall, and others would rise in their place: sometimes, in eras of transition, there have been one or two more or less than ten kingdoms. But when these eras of transition were over, and Europe returned to its normal condition, there would be Ten Kingdoms again. There have been Ten Kingdoms in Southern and Western Europe, for thirteen hundred years: there are Ten Kingdoms in Europe now, within the limits of the Roman empire.

These Ten Kingdoms are fully set forth in my work, "*Key to Prophecy*," and it is not necessary to present them further here.

These Ten Kingdoms within the territories of the Roman empire are symbolized by the Ten Horns, which grew out of the dead Sixth Head. This Sixth Head corresponds with the fourth beast of the second vision of Daniel. That beast symbolized the Roman empire: so here, the Sixth Head. That beast had ten horns; so, on the Sixth head here, are the same ten horns.

3RD. THE SEVENTH HEAD.

The Seventh Head is the Serpent head,—the empire of the Dragon. It is the subject of this work to prove that the Seventh or Dragon Head symbolizes the London Money Power—the Imperialism of Capital centered in London. We will proceed in the next chapter to give the proof. At present we will proceed to the identification of

4TH. THE BEAST FROM THE PIT.

After explaining to John the Seven Heads and Ten Horns, the angel goes on to give an explanation of the Scarlet Beast,—the Beast from the Pit. The angel says of him: "The beast that thou sawest was, and is not; and shall ascend out of the bottomless pit, and go into perdition." And he says again: "The beast that was and is not, even he is the eighth, and is one of the seven."

1. **This shows that the Beast from the Pit rises after** all the other seven empires have risen,—after the rise of the Dragon Empire, the Seventh Head. "He is the Eighth."

After the rise of the Dragon empire, another empire rises, which is the Eighth in order of time, but which is actually not a new empire, but is one of the first Seven Empires: that is, it is a new imperial power, in whose dominion one of the dead six empires comes to life again, and is re-established.

All expositors agree that the Roman empire,—the dead Sixth Head,—**is to be re-established** in the dominion of the Beast from the Pit. There are many other prophecies which foreshow this re-establishment of the Roman empire. The re-establishment of the Roman empire under the dominion of the Beast from the Pit is set forth with great clearness in the 13th chapter of Revelation, and also in the First and Second Visions of Daniel.

In the 13th chapter of Revelation, this re-establishment of the Roman empire is set forth. The context reads as follows:—

"And I stood upon the sand of the sea,

"and saw a beast rise up out of the sea, having seven heads and ten horns, and upon his horns ten crowns, and upon his heads the names of blasphemy.

"And the beast which I saw was like unto a leopard, and his feet were as the feet of a bear, and his mouth as the mouth of a lion.

"And I saw one of his heads as it had been wounded to death [or slain;] and his deadly wound was healed.

"And the Dragon gave him his power and his seat and great authority."

"And all the world wondered after the beast. And they worshiped the Dragon which gave power to the beast: and they worshiped the beast, saying, Who like unto the beast? Who is able to make war with him." *Rev.* xiii: 1–4.

I have, in one place, slightly transposed this passage, so as to give the proper order of sequence.

The Seven Heads here, as has been already explained, are 1) Egypt; 2) Assyria; 3) Babylon; 4) Persia; 5) Macedon; 6) Rome; 7) The Dragon head; which I expound as the symbol of the Money Power. This is the point now being established.

2. It is Important to Fix the Time

when the vision begins.

The Beast, in its first rise from the Sea, represents Medieval Europe, after the fall of the Roman empire, under the Ten Kingdoms. This is evident both from history, and from the symbolism of the Beast:—

1) **The Ten Horns represent the Kingdoms of the Northern Barbarians** who overran the Roman empire. It is Europe under the Ten Kingdoms that is here represented. That the time is during the reign of the Ten

Kingdoms is evident from the fact that the ten horns in the symbol are crowned; which shows that they are reigning in the era set forth in the vision.

2) **The Beast rises up out of "the Sea."** The "Sea" is a prophetic image frequently employed, to represent a chaotic condition of society, in which all the elements of social life are unsettled. Such was the condition of the territory of the Roman empire after the fall of the Western empire. All the institutions of Roman civilization were broken down: society was dissolved by the Barbarians who overswept the Roman empire, ravaging, destroying, burning; until the remnant of the Roman population were reduced to the condition of serfs, hoveled in the forests which grew up in the cultivated provinces that were reduced to desolation. Out of this chaos modern Europe emerged.

3) **When the Beast rose it had the Sixth or Roman head** "as it had been wounded unto death," that is, freshly slain. This was true of the Roman empire, which was just recently slain by the "sword" of the Northern Barbarians.

All the symbolism shows that the Beast represents Europe during the era of the reign of the Ten Kingdoms, after the fall of the Roman empire.

4) **The description of the Beast also** agrees perfectly with Europe under the Ten Kingdoms.

1] "*The Beast was like a leopard.*"—In the Macedonian Leopard (*Daniel* vii), the spots indicate the great number of Grecian states that entered into the Macedonian empire. The Amphyctionic Council of the Grecian states made Phillip, King of Macedon, and afterwards Alexander, the head of Greece for the war with Persia, while each state continued to maintain its independence.

So here, the spots of the Leopard indicate the Ten Kingdoms of Europe, which have maintained a sort of loose combination through their community of religion and interest, but have always maintained their independence as separate states.—They were combined during the Crusades by a common religious enthusiasm; and all through the Middle Ages, they were united in their allegiance to the Papacy.—In Modern Times, community of interest has caused them to combine against any preponderant nation, to maintain the Balance of Power. The ten crowned horns have thus been united on the head of the Beast from the Sea.

2] "*The feet were as the feet of a bear.*"—The Persian bear was slow in its conquests; and these bear feet show that the states of Europe were, like Persia, slow in their military operations. And indeed, the Ten Kingdoms of Europe have always been slow and sluggish in any military conquests, and generally close their slow wars with but little or no conquests on either side.

3] "*His mouth was as the mouth of a lion.*"—This lion mouth tears and ravages, and shows the ferocity of the European states in their furious and bloody wars.

There can be no doubt that the Beast from the Sea represents Roman Europe after the fall of the Roman empire, under the dominion of the Ten Kingdoms.

3. The Healing of the Deadly Wound.

The Seer defers the mention of the deadly wound, until he speaks of the healing of the wound. The first act which John saw was the healing of the deadly wound. This symbolizes the Restoration of the slain Roman head to life,—the re-establishment of the Roman empire.

After the healing of the dead Sixth Head, that head, when restored to life, is the Beast from the Pit. This fully explains the symbolism of the Beast from the Pit:—

1) It shows how the Beast from the Pit was the Eighth

empire in the order of time, but was not a new head, but one of the seven heads, being the Sixth Head restored to life.

2) We also perceive how the Beast from the Pit might be called "The Beast that was, and is not, and yet is." It is the Roman empire; it is not, in its new form, actually the Roman empire but the German empire; and yet, it is the Roman empire, re-established under a new form.

3) The Beast from the Pit is the Roman empire re-established, under the imperial supremacy of Prussia over the kingdoms of Southern and Western Europe. The symbolism plainly shows that the power under which the Roman empire is to be re-established is Prussia:—

1] From the nature of the symbolism, none of the ten horns can be the Beast from the Pit. For a horn can not be a head, much less can a horn be a Beast. The horns are all on the Sixth Head of the Beast: they are all accounted for; and none of them can be the Beast from the Pit.

This shows that none of the Ten Kingdoms of Western and Southern Europe can be the Beast from the Pit. This excludes all the kingdoms in the territories of the Roman empire, within the Rhine and the Danube, from the head of the Adriatic westward to the Atlantic, including England and part of Scotland. Neither France, nor Austria, nor Italy, nor Spain, nor Britain, can be the Beast from the Pit; *for they are horns on the head of the Beast.*—A common sense analysis of the symbol would have prevented all the blunders that have been made in expounding the Beast from the Pit as the symbol of the French empire.

2] The Beast from the Pit must, from the nature of the symbol, be some power in Europe outside of the Rhine and the Danube. It must be either Prussia or Russia.

But it is not Russia; because, in prophecy, Russia is

called by name as at the head of Europe, at an era after the Beast from the Pit has fallen.*

Hence, as the Beast from the Pit can not be any of the ten kingdoms of Europe within the Rhine and the Danube, on the one hand, and, on the other hand, can not be Russia, it must be Prussia.

The very nature of the symbolism demonstrates the fact that Prussia is the Beast from the Pit.

We will find that identifying Prussia as the Beast from the Pit is a strong point of the evidence in proving the Dragon to be the symbol of the London Money Power.

Chapter II.

MODE OF IDENTIFYING SYMBOLS WITH THE POWERS THEY SYMBOLIZE.

As I wish to set forth the evidence that the Dragon is the symbol of the London Money Power in regular order, I desire, in the first place, to show the method by which expositors of prophecy prove that the symbols of prophecy symbolize the powers which they set forth. This can best be done by means of illustrations.

To illustrate the laws of prophetic symbolism, I will take, as examples, the first two beasts of the second vision of Daniel.

In Prophecy, objects in the *natural world* are employed to symbolize or represent objects *which they resemble* in the *political world.*—Thus, an earthquake, which breaks down and destroys objects in the world of nature, is made the symbol of a revolution which breaks down and de-

---

*This will be fully explained in my work on "*The United States in Prophecy.*"

stroys political institutions.—A storm of lightning and thunder, the effect of conflicting winds and opposite electrical conditions, in the natural world, is made the symbol of a great war arising out of furious opposing elements in the political world.—Thus also, a wild beast, cruel, sanguinary, is a proper symbol of a political empire.

Thus, in the second vision of Daniel, four beasts which rise one after another, are made the symbols of the successive empires of Babylon, Persia, Macedon, and Rome. Upon this expositors are agreed.

1. In identifying these beasts with the powers they symbolize, the first thing to notice is the historical order of succession. The first Beast that rises, of course symbolizes the empire that rises first in the order of time. No one would make the first Beast symbolize Persia, the second empire, or make the second Beast symbolize Babylon, the first empire.

Hence, any facts mentioned which enable us to determine the historical order of events may be very important elements in identifying the symbol with the power it symbolizes.—These identifying facts, for want of a better name, I term *Historical Marks.*

2. Furthermore, in prophetic symbolism, symbols are chosen which resemble, *in character*, the power symbolized. Thus, a lion is made the symbol of the Babylonian empire, and a bear, of the Persian empire; because those wild beasts resemble, in character, the empires they symbolize. These resemblances in character between the symbol and the power symbolized, I term *Parallelisms of Character.*

But Historical Marks and Parallelisms of Character do not always sufficiently designate the power represented by the symbol.—And hence, in symbolic prophecy, another means of identity is also employed: certain facts are stated respecting the symbol, which represent corresponding facts that are true of the power symbolized. These points of resemblance in respect of facts, I term *Coincidences of Fact.*

Let us now observe the manner in which the Lion is identified with the Babylonian empire,—by Historical Marks—by Parallelisms of Character—and by Coincidences of Fact.

I. THE LION WITH EAGLE'S WINGS.

The following is the text:

"And four beasts came up from the Sea, diverse from one another.

"The first was like a lion, and had eagle's wings.

"I beheld till the wings thereof were plucked;

"and it was lifted up from the earth, and made to stand upon its feet like a man, and a man's heart was given to it."

Daniel vii: 3, 4.

All expositors are agreed that the Lion is the symbol of the Babylonian empire. We will, by way of illustration, identify it by Marks, by Parallelisms of Character, and by Coincidences of Fact.

1st. Historical Marks.

First Mark:—There is only one important Mark which aids the expositor in identifying the Lion with Babylon. But it alone is sufficient. Babylon was the first of the four great empires which arose in succession; and we would naturally expect the first of the four beasts to be the symbol of Babylon.

It is apparent that this Mark alone would not be sufficient to identify Babylon as the power symbolized by the Lion. The evidence is cumulative. The Marks, the Parallelisms and the Coincidences, all go to establish the identity. And when all four of the beasts are thus identified with the powers they symbolize, the force of the Historical Mark becomes intensified. For we know that, if the other beasts symbolize respectively Persia, Macedon and Rome, then, most certainly, the first beast symbolizes Babylon.

In some of the symbols of prophecy, however, the Historical Marks are quite numerous.

2ND. PARALLELISMS OF CHARACTER.

There are several Parallelisms of Character between the Lion with Eagle's wings and the Babylonian empire:

First Parallelism of Character:—*The Lion is a ferocious carnivorous wild beast.*—The Babylonian empire, under its founder Nebuchadnezzar, was a sanguinary conquering empire, ravening and destroying among the nations, like a lion among flocks and herds.

Second Parallelism of Character:—*The Lion is a magnanimous wild beast.*—Unlike the tiger and the leopard, which raven with the mere lust of slaughter, it only destroys to appease hunger.—The Babylonian empire only assailed and conquered the countries which resisted its possession of the great trade between the East and the West, leaving all other nations in peace. And Nebuchadnezzar sought, first, to treat the subject nations of the West with leniency, and was only provoked to severity by repeated revolts.

Third Parallelism of Character:—*The Lion had Eagle's wings.*—The lion lies in wait for its prey, and springs upon it from ambush. To indicate that this was not the case with this symbolic Lion, it was furnished with Eagle's wings.—These Eagle's wings show the rapidity of the conquests of Nebuchadnezzar. At the head of his Chaldean horsemen, the conquerer overran in a few campaigns Syria, Palestine, Egypt, and North Africa as far as the Straits of Gibraltar.

3RD. COINCIDENCES OF FACT.

Besides the above Parallelisms of Character, there are mentioned two Coincidences of Fact respecting the Lion with Eagle's Wings, which represent corresponding facts in the history of the Babylonian empire.

First Coincidence of Fact:—"*I beheld till the Eagle's wings were plucked.*"—The plucking of the Eagle's wings, of course prevented the Lion from sweeping on any longer in its career of conquest. Deprived of the Eagle's wings, the Lion henceforth would be like other lions, and lurk in its habitat, lying in wait for prey. The plucking of the Eagle's wings indicates a sudden event which stopped, once for all, the Babylonian career of conquest. The conquering career of Babylon was terminated by the madness of Nebuchadnezzar. That event plucked the wings of the lion; and henceforth, Babylon remained content in the enjoyment of the wealth and grandeur derived from its possession of the grand commerce between the Indian Ocean and the Mediterranean, which flowed through the city.

Second Coincidence of Fact:—"*It was made to stand on its feet like a man, and a man's heart was given to it.*"—In some of the *bas reliefs* from Nineveh, we see the hunted lion rearing upon its hind feet, confronting the hunters, whose spears are transfixing it.—In its fall, Babylon was like the hunted lion. For years, it held the conqueror at bay behind its city walls, standing like a lion upreared against the hunters. During all the siege, Babylon had the man's heart, afraid to meet the foe in the open field. But it fell fighting, and hopeful of victory to the end.

Now, by this one Historical Mark, these three Parallelisms of Character, and these two Coincidences of Fact, all expositors agree that the Lion with Eagle's Wings is sufficiently proved to be the symbol of the Babylonian empire.

II. THE PERSIAN BEAR.

In the same way, the Bear is proved to be the symbol of the Persian empire.

The following is the text:

"And behold another beast, a second, like unto a bear.
"And it raised up itself upon one side.
"And it had three ribs in its mouth between its teeth.
"And they said thus unto it, 'Arise, devour much flesh.'" *Daniel* vii: 5.

1st. Historical Marks.

There is one Historical Mark which aids in identifying the Bear with the Persian empire:

Historical Mark:—As the Persian empire was the second empire in the order of succession, we naturally are led to expect that the second beast is its symbol.

2nd. Parallelisms of Character.

There are two Parallelisms of Character between the Bear and the Persian empire;—

First Parallelism of Character:—*The Bear is not an exclusively carnivorous animal:* it subsists largely on vegetables and fruits.—This shows the bear to be less ferocious than the lion and other carnivorous animals.—And the Persian empire was the mildest of all the empires of ancient times. It treated the conquered nations with greater leniency. It suffered the people carried into captivity by Babylon, to return to their own countries. It allowed the Phœnicians to resume their trade by way of the Red Sea. The countries desolated by Babylon resumed their prosperity under Persian rule.

Second Parallelism of Character:—*The Bear is a clumsy, slow moving animal.*—So, the Persian empire was slow and clumsy in its military movements. Great numbers of women and children accompanied its armies; and the officers carried with them all the appliances of luxury. All military movements were impeded by the vast quantities of baggage which were carried with the armies.

3rd. Coincidences of Fact.

The Bear is also identified with the Persian empire by three Coincidences of Fact.

First Coincidence of Fact:—"*The bear raised up itself on one side.*"—Persia was on the Eastern side of the empire, and all the conquests of the Persians, in founding the empire, were made toward the West. The Persian empire, like the bear, "raised up itself on one side."

Second Coincidence of Fact:—*The Bear "had three ribs in its mouth between its teeth.*"—These ribs indicate three victims fallen prey to the Bear.—The Persian empire, in its rise, overthrew three powers,—Lydia, Babylon and Egypt.

Third Coincidence of Fact:—"*It was said unto it, Arise, devour much flesh.*"—The bear was thus indicated to be an animal very destructive of human life.—The Persian empire conquered many countries not under the Babylonian yoke. It extended its conquests far to the North, and East and South; it subdued all Asia Minor; and its invading armies penetrated into Greece, and the plains of Southern Russia.—And, during its entire existence, the Persian empire was convulsed with frequent revolts. The conquests and the revolts occasioned very destructive wars.

By this Historical Mark, these two Parallelisms of Character, and these three Coincidences of Fact all expositors agree that the Bear is proved to be the symbol of the Persian empire.

CHAPTER III.

PROOF THAT THE DRAGON IS THE SYMBOL OF THE LONDON MONEY POWER.

By the illustrations given in the last chapter, the reader can perceive the method by which the symbols of prophecy are identified with the powers they symbolize. We are now ready to proceed to identify the Dragon as the symbol of the London Money Power.

And here, I wish to say that, if there were not more evidence to prove that the Dragon is the symbol of the London Money Power, than there is to prove the identity of the other symbols of prophecy with the powers they symbolize, I should not venture to advance the idea at all, in this age of general scoffing of prophecy.

But there is about eight times as much evidence to prove that the Dragon is the symbol of the London Money Power, as there is to prove the identity of any other prophetic symbol with the power it symbolizes.—There is one Historical Mark, three Parallelisms of Character, and two Coincidences of Fact, to prove that the Lion with Eagle's Wings is the symbol of the Babylonian empire; and one Historical Mark, two Parallelisms of Character, and three Coincidences of Fact, to prove that the Bear is the symbol of the Persian empire.—But, on the other hand, there are no less than six Historical Marks, twenty Parallelisms of Character, and twenty-two Coincidences of Fact, to prove that the Dragon is the symbol of the London Money Power. It seems as though divine inspiration had purposed to give such an array of evidence to establish the fact that the Dragon is the symbol of the Money Power, as would force conviction upon the most incredulous.

The Marks, the Parallelisms of Character, and the Coincidences of Fact, which prove that the Lion with Eagle's Wings is the symbol of the Babylonian empire, and the Bear, of the Persian, are not very striking;—but the Historical Marks, the Parallelisms of Character, and the Coincidences of Fact, which prove that the Dragon is the symbol of the London Money Power, are, all of them, striking, and some of them very remarkable—so remarkable, indeed, that no idea of a chance resemblance can be entertained for a moment. They prove that Divine inspiration intended thus to mark the Dragon unmistakably as the symbol of the London Money Power. It is evident that Divine Providence wished to make the proof of the identity of the Dragon with the Money Power so certain that none can doubt; but that, as it is said in another prophecy of the Dragon in the Old Testament, "He who runs may read." The proof dispels all doubt, and compels belief.

As the world may be slow to accept the fact that the Dragon is the symbol of the Money Power, I shall array the evidence in regular order, even at the risk of seeming tedious.

I. FIRST PROOF THAT THE DRAGON IS THE SYMBOL OF THE LONDON MONEY POWER: HISTORICAL MARKS.

1st. Recapitulation.

Let us now briefly review the facts respecting the Seven Heads and Ten Horns:

1. **The angel says of the seven heads,** "*There are seven kings*," that is, kingdoms or empires. Of these seven empires he says, "five are fallen."—These are the Egyptian, the Assyrian, the Babylonian, the Persian, and the Macedonian empires, which had all fallen at the time the vision was given.

2. **The angel continues,** "*And one is.*" This was the Roman empire, which was in existence at the time when the Revelation was given.

1) Immediately after the fall of the Roman empire, ten Barbarian kingdoms were planted in its territories, which have been in existence ever since. These Ten Kingdoms are symbolized by the Ten Horns which grew upon the dead Sixth Head of the Beast.

3. **The angel continues,** "*And the other*, [the Seventh Head] *is not yet come; and when he cometh he must continue a short space.*"—This is the Dragon head; and, as I shall prove, it symbolizes the London Money Power.

4. **The angel then proceeds to explain the Beast from the Pit as an Eighth empire, but not an eighth head**, being the Sixth Head come to life again, or the Roman empire re-established.—This Eighth empire, as we have seen, is the empire of Prussia at the head of Germany, extended over Southern and Western Europe.

5. **The Dragon gives to Prussia its imperial dominion**, as we learn from the 13th Chapter of Revelation: "*The Dragon gave to the Beast his power, and his seat, and great authority.*"

6. "**And then the prophet saw that the Dragon and the Beast wielded a united imperial sway over the empire:**" *they worshiped the Dragon which gave power unto the beast: and they worshiped the beast* saying, who is like unto the beast? Who is able to make war with him?"

2nd. Six Important Historical Marks

are here found, which will go far toward enabling us to identify the Dragon empire:—

First Mark:—*The Dragon empire is the seventh empire*

in order of time.—Hence it is an empire which rises after the fall of the Roman empire, 476 A. D.

Second Mark:—*The Dragon empire, "When he cometh must continue a short space."*

1. Both of these marks prove that the Dragon empire is not the Papacy: for 1) The Papacy rose in the Pontificate of Leo the Great (440 A. D.—460 A.D.) before the fall of the Western Roman empire; and 2) The Papacy, instead of continuing "a short space," has been in existence more than 1,400 years.

Leaving the Papacy aside, what empire has risen since the fall of the Roman empire, 476 A. D.?

2. It can not be the empire of Charlemagne; nor that of Charles V; nor that of Napoleon I. For those empires were only the temporary rising into power of one of the horns; and in each instance the access of power continued only for a generation. The nature of the symbol precludes the idea that either of these empires could be the Seventh Head; for, as has been said, a horn can not become a head. The ten horns are all upon the Sixth Head: they are all accounted for: from the nature of the symbol, neither of them can be the Dragon.

3. Aside from these empires and the Papacy, no empire has risen in Europe since the fall of the Roman empire, 476 A. D., except the Money Power of London. It is the seventh empire of the earth. It is the grandest Imperialism that has ever existed in the world.—This is especially an age of industry; and it has established an empire over industry, of which it is the head. It is at the head of the mighty movement of the age in which the whole world is marching. The kingdoms of Europe are all dependent upon it for loans. They all truckle to it, and do its will. They are kingdoms: it is an empire.—Being the one empire that has risen since the fall of the

Roman empire, it is the seventh empire: and this Mark proves it to be the power symbolized by the Dragon.

That the Dragon empire is the London Money Power is corroborated by the other Historical Marks mentioned of the Dragon:—

Third Mark:—*The Dragon empire is a power of modern times.*—In the 13th Chapter of Revelation it is cotemporary with the healed head, or Beast from the Pit,—the Prussian empire. And all expositors agree that the Beast from the Pit is a power that has not yet risen. In the 13th Chapter of Revelation, the Dragon is represented as aiding in the rise of the empire of the Beast from the Pit, and as wielding with it a partnership imperial sway.—The The Dragon empire is certainly a power of modern times, existing cotemporaneously with the Beast from the Pit, a power that has not yet risen. This agrees perfectly with the Money Power, which has also risen in modsrn times.

Fourth Mark:—*The Dragon is represented, in the 13th Chapter of Revelation, as attaining its highest power at a time yet future.*—This agrees with the Money Power, which is, in our time, rapidly rising in power, and will reach its highest point of dominion at some time yet future.

Fifth Mark:—*The Dragon empire is the Seventh head: the Beast from the Pit, or Prussian empire, is the eighth,* in order of time.—Therefore it rises after the Dragon empire; the Dragon empire being in existence at the time of its rise, and aiding it to attain its imperial dominion. Hence, if the Prussian empire is about to be established in the near future, the Dragon empire is now in existence.—And as the Money Power is the only such imperial power now in existence, it must be the Dragon.

Sixth Mark:—*The Dragon empire was only to continue a short space.*—And, as it is in existence at a time yet future, according to prophecy, its rise to imperial dominion can not be very far in the past.—This agrees with the Money Power, which, as we have seen, rose to imperial dominion in the year 1757, A. D., and has now been in existence one hundred and thirty years.

The Dragon Agrees With the Money Power in all these particulars. There is no other power now in existence that agrees with these Marks in any particular. The Historical Marks of the prophecies point unmistakably to the Money Power as the imperialism symbolized by the Dragon.

This Far, the Conclusions Reached Are Sure. It is impossible to dispute them. The clear statements of prophecy are irresistible.—1) It is certain that the Roman empire is not yet re-established.—2) It is certain that the Dragon empire is in existence before the re-establishment of the Roman empire, and aids in its re-establishment.—3) It is certain that, if the Roman empire is about to be re-established at an early day, the Dragon empire is now in existence.—4) It is certain, as the Dragon empire is to "continue only a short space" that, as it is in existence at a time yet future, it has risen to imperial power in very recent times.—5) It is certain that the Dragon is a power of modern times.

On the other hand, the Money Power is the only great Imperialism that is now in existence.—The Money Power is an Imperialism that has not been long risen.—The Money Power is an Imperialism that is still rising.—The Money Power is an Imperialism which has, by its loans, enabled Prussia to crush Austria and France, and to become the first power in Europe; and which, according to present indications, will soon, by its loans, enable Prussia and her allies, Britain, Austria and Italy, to crush Russia and France, and attain to imperial dominion over Southern and Western Europe, and thus re-establish the Roman empire.—And just as the Money Power has wielded the power of Britain in the past, it will wield the power of Prussia, the Beast from the Pit, in the future.—All these Marks point unmistakably to the Money Power as the Imperialism symbolized by the Dragon.

Chapter IV.

PROOF THAT THE GREAT RED DRAGON IS THE SYMBOL OF THE MONEY POWER, Continued.

II. SECOND PROOF:—PARALLELISMS OF CHARACTER.

1st. What is a Dragon?

A great error has obtained as to the personality of a Dragon. During the ignorance and superstition of the Middle Ages, the idea of a mythical Dragon arose, which resembled a winged crocodile. But the historical dragon of antiquity, which was the universal conception of a dragon prevailing at the time the Revelation was given, was a great serpent.

A fact is mentioned in the early history of Rome which shows what was the classical and historical idea of a Dragon.—When the Roman army, under Regulus, invaded the Carthaginian territories in North Africa, a great dragon appeared in the neighborhood of the Roman camp, and devoured a number of the soldiers. The Romans were greatly terrified, but finally killed the monster by hurling stones upon it with their *balistas*. This dragon was undoubtedly a boa constrictor, which had found its way across the desert from Central Africa. The Dragon of Revelation, then, was a great red serpent.

2nd. Parallelisms of Character.

We have seen that certain things in the natural world are chosen by Divine inspiration, to symbolize the powers they set forth, on account of a resemblance in *character* between the symbol and the power symbolized.—Thus, the Great Red Dragon is chosen by Divine inspiration to symbolize the London Money Power, because, in all the realm of nature, nothing but a great serpent resembles the Money Power, in its character, and its modes of action. In its character, and all its activities and methods, the Money Power is like a snake.

The Great Red Dragon, like all great serpents, belongs to the constrictor species. We must, therefore, look to the Boa Constrictor for the points of character and action, in which the parallel is to be found. Prophecy represents the Money Power as a great Serpent, with its den in England, but its body extending in mighty coils all over the earth.

First Parallelism of Character:—*The dragon is a devourer.* The Boa Constrictor, when it has devoured a sheep or a deer, remains torpid until its meal is digested: then it lives for nothing else but to lie in wait, watching for another victim. Its whole sluggish life is absorbed in devouring.

So the Money Power is a devourer of industry, commerce, wealth and property. It lives for nothing else but to accumulate. It differs from a Boa Constrictor only in its inordinate size. A Boa Constrictor, if it swallows a sheep, is torpid for a time, till its meal is digested;—but give it a mouse, and it is still hungry and wants more. This Great Dragon, the Money Power, is so vast, that it can never be gorged to repletion. It is devouring industry, trade and property, all over the earth, and it never has enough. The inspired prophet, speaking of this Money power, says, "He enlargeth his desire as hell, and he is as death, and can not be satisfied, but gathereth unto him all nations, and heapeth unto him all people."

We have seen how the Money Power is devouring all

over the earth. It is devouring in Europe—in India, and all over Asia—in Egypt, South Africa, on the Congo, and wherever Africa is penetrated—in South America—in Mexico and Central America—in Canada—in the United States—in Australia, and the Isles of the ocean. Everywhere it is devouring the industry and wealth of the earth. It aims to devour all industry,—all manufactures—all banks—all shipping—all railroads—all commerce—all traffic, import and export, internal and foreign, wholesale and retail—all transportation—all mines, of coal and iron and silver and gold—all oil wells—all city property—all farms—and all the wild lands of the world.

Besides the fact of its being a devourer, there is a certain method in its devourings that identifies the Dragon with the Money Power. These points of similarity I point out in the several Parallelisms of Character next following:—

Second Parallelism of Character:—*Unlike the lion or the tiger, which spring upon their prey with a roar,* so that all the neighborhood knows when the victim is destroyed, *the Serpent steals secretly upon its victim, and seizes it noiselessly.*

So the Money Power is sly and secretive in its methods, and steals upon its victims secretly, and destroys them without noise or struggle. The secret sly methods of the Money Power are exemplified in every assault it has made upon our industries. Thus it stole upon the merchants of New York City—the oil well owners of Pennsylvania—the operators in beef, pork, cotton and all the various business enterprises it has devoured. So silently, so stilly is it now stealing on the cattle ranches—the coal mines—the retail merchants—the breweries—the flour mills—the farmers—and all the business interests it is now devouring.

Third Parallelism of Character:—*The serpent charms its victims, and lures them to their doom.*

So the Money Power has charmed and is charming the world, with the lure of its money. It lures people from all over the world to its London den, to get money to build railroads, and water works, and gas works—and, in the end, all that was built with the money it devours.—It lures miners after money to develop mines: and it crushes the miner and devours the mine.—By starting a boom in cattle, it lures farmers, merchants, mechanics, to borrow money on mortgaged property and put it into cattle ranches: and then it devours the mortgaged property, and the ranches in which the borrowed money was invested.—By starting booms in cities and towns, it lures all classes who have property, to borrow money on mortgage and invest it in town lots: and then it devours both the mortgaged property, and the boom investment.

Fourth Parallelism of Character:—*Unlike the lion and the tiger, and all other beasts of prey*, which rend and tear their victims in furious assault, *the Boa destroys its prey by enveloping it in its coils, and crushing it.*

So the Money Power always envelops the industry it assails in the coils of its capital, and crushes it by constriction.—Thus it enveloped the oil industry—the New England Mills—the New York merchants—and all the industries it has devoured. In every instance, it used its immense capital in such a manner as to crush the operators instantly, as the boa constrictor crushes its victim in its coil.—The method of the Money Power is identical with that of the Boa.

Fifth Parallelism of Character:—*The Boa Constrictor crushes only to devour, and devours all it crushes.*—In this it is unlike the tiger or the leopard. The tiger will destroy forty sheep, and eat only one; or will kill half a dozen bullocks, and devour only a part of a single carcass. In this they resemble political despotisms, of which such wild beasts are made the symbols. For such political powers wage grand and destructive wars, and in the end, the conquering state gains only a petty acquisition. Thus, all the grand wars of the first Napoleon ended in but small accessions of territory: Prussia, after crushing France, gained only Alsace-Lorraine.

This is unlike the Money Power which, like the serpent, attacks only to devour, and devours all it attacks. It never attacks any business interest, unless it means to devour it. It did not attack the New England Mills, or the iron interests of Pennsylvania, till the time came for them to be devoured. A caged Boa will leave the rabbits in its cage unharmed for days, till it is ready to devour them. So the Money Power will work side by side with business interests for years, without showing any hostility, till the time comes when it is ready to take possession of them; and then, it makes its attack suddenly, and crushes them inexorably. We find illustrations of this, in all the operations of the Money Power in this country. It has never assailed an American business which it did not devour. It is now assailing the cattle men—the lumber men—the wholesale merchants—the retail merchants—the farmers, and other business interests; and is crushing them; and, unless its career be arrested, it will devour them all, as it did the New York merchants and the oil well owners.

Sixth Parallelism of Character:—*The Boa always has to beslime its victims, before it can devour them.*—It pounces upon a deer and crushes it, bones, flesh and tissues, till all within its hide is perfectly soft. Then, before beginning to swallow the victim, it beslimes it from head to foot; when it begins to swallow gulp after gulp, until the entire victim is engorged in its maw.

Thus the Money Power always beslimes its victims with the slime of its capital before devouring them. Thus it beslimed our railroads with construction capital—our mines with capital, to develop and operate them—blocks of city property and broad areas of farming lands, with mortgages.—The Money Power always beslimes everything with its capital, before devouring it; and it surely devours all business, and all property, it is allowed to beslime.

Seventh Parallelism of Character:—*The Serpent's victims are paralyzed and powerless to resist.*

It is one of the most remarkable phenomena in the destructions of the Money Power, that none of its victims have ever been able to make the slightest resistence. There is always a conflict in ordinary trade contests, before one of the parties is crushed. But the victims of the Money Power never resist: they are paralyzed in the coil of the python, and submit quietly to their fate. Thus the New York merchants, the oil well owners, the mill owners of New England, the cattle companies, and all whom the Money Kings have crushed have submitted to their fate as quietly as a rabbit in the coils of a boa. This paralysis of its victims is one of the reasons why the destroying career of the Money Power has attracted so little attention.

Eighth Parallelism of Character:—*The Serpent swallows its prey whole.*—In this it is unlike all other beasts of prey. The lion, the tiger and all other beasts of prey devour their prey a mouthful at a time, and leave the bones and horns and hoofs. And they always leave a portion of the prey to the jackals and other beasts that follow their footsteps.

The Money Power is like the serpent in this regard. It always takes entire possession of every industry it seizes upon. It did not content itself with dividing the business with the New York merchants, or the oil well owners;—it devoured the entire business. So with every business: it never divides with previous competitors; it devours the whole business it takes possession of.—It never will engage in any business, unless it is put into a joint stock company; and it always demands the controlling interest in the stock, before it will invest. And then it is only a question of time when it will devour it all.

Ninth Parallelism of Character:—*The lion and the tiger gorge their prey at once: unlike them, the serpent is a long time swallowing its prey: it requires many gulps before it is finally engulfed in its maw.*

In this characteristic, the serpent strikingly resembles the Money Power. As has been said, these Money Kings always want a controlling interest in an enterprise before they will invest, and then they begin a systematic process of gulping down the remaining stock of the company. They never buy up all property in an enterprise at once. They begin with a mere start, as the serpent begins with the head of its victim; and then they keep on devouring till they have swallowed the whole.—Thus, they began with a few wells in the oil region, to start the business: afterward, they kept on devouring till they had swallowed it all.—So in a gold or silver mine, they must always have a controlling interest in the stock; and then they begin systematically to freeze out the other stockholders. —This small beginning and persistent continuance in devouring, till all is engorged, is not the least striking of the parallelisms between the Dragon and the Money Power.—Who can doubt that Divine inspiration meant by the Great Red Dragon to set forth the London Money Power?

The Serpent is chosen by Divine inspiration to be the symbol of the London Money Power, because, in all the realm of nature, the serpent alone perfectly resembles the

Money Power. In its character, as well as in its processes, and methods and modes of activity, the Money Power is like a snake.

We have seen the striking parallelisms between the Money Power and the Serpent, exhibited in its methods of devouring: let us now mark some of the parallelisms, in *disposition and intrinsic character.*

Tenth Parallelism of Character:—*The serpent is the synonim of worldly wisdom, craft and cunning: "wise as a serpent."*

The Money Power displays the wisdom of the serpent in all its policy—in its entire career. It never takes a step that is not thoroughly matured. It never alarms its victim by a premature attack. Its assaults are always made on a well considered plan, and have always been successful.—How skillful its attack on the oil wells! first building a railroad, and then constructing a pipe line to it. How thoroughly matured the plan! how skillful the execution! Like the combinations of a great military genius, the movement was irresistible!—What consummate skill in its mode of getting possession of the railroads, by first mortgage bonds for the iron! first furnishing the money to build the road bed, on city and county bonds that had to be paid; then getting possession of the railroads upon first mortgage bonds for the iron!—How wise its attack on the New York merchants! by establishing branch houses, and then starting drummers to take away their trade!—How crafty their booms! building up a city by lavish expenditure of capital, and getting multitudes to invest and make partial payments, and then stopping all investment and letting the boom collapse; so that, when prices fall, they can take back the property for the remaining payments, and have it all ready for the next boom!—Still more crafty their booms in small towns, where they buy the land around a country village, build up the town to fifteen thousand in a couple of years, and so make the world believe it will be a city of one hundred thousand inhabitants; and when the gulls have bought prairie lots at high prices, let the boom drop, pocket the money made, and take back the lots, for final payments!

But why particularize? They never make a blunder. All their acts are marked by wonderful skill and wonderful wisdom. But if there is any act showing most consummate craft and skill, it is their wonderful attack on the New England Mills. We have a saying, "Sharp as a Yankee." But these Jew Money Kings far surpass all American shrewdness. American wisdom had exhausted itself in devising measures for the protection of the New England Mills from the competition of foreign merchants. But these Money Kings found a flaw in our system of protection, through which they crept like a serpent, and enmeshed the New England Mills in the coils of their capital, and crushed and devoured them. And they did it all so skillfully, so quietly, so secretly, that, to this day, nobody knows it was done!

The serpent is wiser than all the beasts of the field; and it only, is a fit symbol of this crafty secretive devourer. The Money Power is a veritable embodiment of the wisdom of the serpent.

Eleventh Parallelism of Character:—*The serpent hides in the grass.*

So the Money Power systematically hides its operations from the eyes of mankind, in such a manner that its path can hardly be traced. It always operates through joint stock corporations, in which its identity is concealed under the agencies it establishes. The stockholders of these corporations are the London Jew Money Kings. But they elect directors and officers in the country where the corporations are established; and the people believe that the men who manage the corporations are their owners.—The Money Kings put a man at the head of a railroad system, as its ostensible owner, and the public does not suspect that the owners are in London.—They loan money by billions of dollars, on city property and improved farms, through their agencies, and make the public believe that it is American capital.—They ruin business, and own property all over the country, and yet manage to conceal their identity.

They have induced government to fix the laws of joint stock corporations, with the special purpose of concealing their identity.—All other real estate is transferred on record books open to public inspection. These joint stock corporations own real estate in railroads and city property, in business houses in which they transact their business, in improved farms, in wild lands;—and yet the stocks which represent all this real estate are treated by the law as personal property, and are transferred like a horse, or any other personal property. All transfers of stock are made on the books of the company, and the public is never allowed to know who the stockholders are. The whole system of laws regarding joint stock corporations has been devised for the special purpose of concealing the stockholders from the public.—As a snake hides in the grass, so the Money Power systematically hides its operations and its existence, behind the concealment of joint stock corporations.

Indeed, when this hiding secretive Money Power, always seeking concealment, is now presented as an Imperialism actually existent in the world, all are astonished, and wonder how such a terrible Imperialism could have risen in the earth, and mankind be kept in utter ignorance of its existence. It is now overshadowing the whole earth with its monopolies of trade and industry, and has almost ruined the world, and yet its existence is unknown. How strikingly like a serpent hiding in the grass!

The trail of a snake can never be found, except where it crosses a dusty road. So, it is only at death where evidence can usually be found that a man is the agent of the Money Power. If A. T. Stewart were still living, he would be universally believed to be worth over $100,000,000. His death revealed him as the agent of the Money Power. The track of the serpent could only be found as it ran across his grave. So, the death of Jim Fisk revealed the fact that he and his partner, Gould, instead of being the owners of the Erie railroad, were the agents of the Money Kings.—The Money Power hides all its operations under the guise of agencies.

Who can doubt that it is the crafty, secretive hiding Money Power which is symbolized by the Dragon?

Twelfth Parallelism of Character:—*The serpent crawls on his belly*. The curse of baseness was fixed upon it at the beginning.

The whole course of the Money Power is a tissue of fraud, falsehood, trickery and treachery, comparable to nothing but a serpent crawling on its belly. Its career is a living lie, as it systematically hides itself behind its agents, pretending that they are the owners of the business they control. Like the garroter, it throttles and plunders its victims in the dark. Like the gambler, it entices its victims to bet in its gambling hells, the Boards of Trade, upon the rise and fall of stocks, and the rise and fall of produce; while it holds the game in its hands, and stocks the cards for the robbery of its victims. It is a slugger, whose purse, filled with gold, is its sandbag, with which it strikes down in the dark its victims, in all the busy avenues of trade. There is honor among thieves: the robber is true to his "pal;"—but the Money Power systematically plunders its partners, freezing out minority stockholders, and all men who take part in its enterprises.

It knows that if the world knew of its system of plunder, mankind would rise up against it: it therefore robs through agencies, and makes agencies the "cribs" where it hides its plundered goods. Its whole career, from the first, has been a tissue of lying, robbery, fraud and concealment. It has acted falsehood in the past, to hide its trail: And now that it is discovered, and exposed to the eyes of the world, it will no doubt attempt to escape, like the scuttle fish, by making the waters around it inky black with falsehood, causing its minions to swear in the columns of the press, that its existence is a myth, that the discovery of it is a "mare's nest," and that this exposure of it is all imagination.—The Money Power is always a snake crawling on its belly. Its whole life is a living lie.

Thirteenth Parallelism of Character:—*The serpent is a cold blooded malignant beast.*

In this it strikingly resembles the Money Power, which is without either heart or conscience; and which, in pursuit of its selfish aims, displays a cold blooded remorselessness, without a parallel in the history of the world.

The Money Power operates entirely through vast imperial joint stock corporations; and, in such corporations, there is no place for human sympathy, or a sense of individual responsibility. Such a corporation has no conscience—no soul.—An individual is withheld from too flagrant wrong, by sympathy, by conscience, by a sense of moral responsibility; but no one connected with the management of these grand Money Power Corporations feels any sense of personal responsibility. The stockholders feel none; for they are away off in London, and do nothing but elect the directors. The directors feel no sense of personal responsibility; for they are not principals, but only agents; and they simply appoint the officers and leave the management to them. The officers feel that they have no individual responsibility, because they are under orders, like the officers of an army, and are not acting for themselves, but for the directors and the stockholders. They come to feel that their only duty is to take care of the interests of the corporation.—The management of these imperial corporations is utterly selfish, without a tinge of sympathy or generosity.

This does not apply to ordinary business corporations, where individuals incorporate themselves into a company for the transaction of business. There are many advantages in such an incorporation, and it is free from objection. In such corporations, conducted as individual enterprises, on a moderate scale, the sense of justice influences the minds of the stockholders, and pervades the management, as much as in the individual management of business.

But an imperial system of corporations, bent upon attaining a universal control of industry, and a universal monopoly of wealth and property, like an ambitious conquerer, is utterly selfish and remorseless. The cold blooded heartlessness of these Money Kings is glaringly displayed in the entire course of the Money Power. Its whole course is a black night of oppression, injury and wrong. It is as useless to attempt to particularize, as it is to seek the darkest cell in a dungeon, or the foulest corner in a lazar house. The Money Kings are bent on getting all the business, all the wealth, and all the property of the earth into their own hands: they can only do it by bankrupting all the business men in the world, and reducing the great mass of mankind to the condition of serfs, subject to their will, and dependent upon them for bread; and they are pursuing their aim of the subjugation of mankind with ruthless energy.—The Money Power is as cold blooded, pitiless and malignant as a snake.

I have now presented thirteen Parallelisms between the Dragon and the Money Power:—

1.) I have showed that, **like the Boa Constrictor, the Money Power is a devourer.**

2.) **I have showed eight points of Parallelism** between the serpent and the Money Power, in respect of the manner in which they both devour their prey.

Both steal secretly on their prey, and destroy them silently; and so secretly, that the world knows nothing of the destruction:—both charm their victims, and cause them to come to them, and place themselves in their power:—both crush their victims in their coils, the serpent, of its body, and the Money Power, of its capital which constitutes its body:—both crush only to devour, and devour all they crush:—both beslime their victims by their secretion before devouring them, the serpent with slime, the Money Power with money:—both paralyze their victims by their attack, beyond the possibility of resistance:—both swallow their prey whole, leaving nothing behind:—both swallow their prey gradually.—The devouring of the Money Power is, in all points, like the method of the serpent, and is like that of no other beast of prey on the earth.

3.) **I have showed four points of Parallelism in Character** between the Money Power and the serpent.

Both have certain personal characteristics peculiar to themselves, among all the beasts of the earth, and all the powers that have ever risen.—Both are wise, and skillful, and cunning and crafty, beyond all comparison with others of their kind:—both are secretive, and habitually hide themselves from the eyes of men, the one in the grass, the other behind its joint stock corporations:—both are despicable, false and treacherous, habitually crawling on the belly:—both are cold-blooded, and malignant and remorseless.

But these thirteen Parallelisms do not exhaust the likeness between the Serpent and the Money Power. There yet remain seven other parallelisms to be mentioned. The proof already offered is sufficient to convince the most incredulous that the Dragon is the symbol of the Money Power. But the evidence is abundant even to nausea. I proceed to mention four other parallelisms between the Dragon and the Money Power, in respect of the modes of activity.

Fourteenth Parallelism of Character:—*It was a* **"Great" Dragon.**—The great Boa, unlike other wild beasts which appear in one spot, may stretch its long body afar.

Prophecy well chooses the python as the symbol of the Money Power; which, while its head is in England, stretches its body all over the earth, embracing in its folds India, China, Africa, Australia, Europe, South America, Mexico, Canada and the United States. Everywhere, the body of the Boa appears. It is as active in Europe, and Asia and America, as in England. England is its den; but the Dragon is, indeed, a *great Dragon;* its long body encircles the earth, and it has everywhere enveloped industry in its folds.

Fifteenh Parallelism of Character:—*The Boa, as it lies along, may throw its folds around many objects.*

So, the Money Power has, in its huge length, many folds, which encoil about many objects. We call these folds of the python "Rings," or Monopolies. Each monopoly is a "Ring," formed by a fold of the serpent, thrown around a branch of industry, or a branch of trade. "The whiskey ring," "the railroad ring," "the oil ring," "the cotton ring," "the wheat ring," "the cattle ring," "the coffee ring," "the sugar ring," "the packing ring," and all the other grand monopolies are each only a fold of the serpent thrown around the industry. Woe to the man who attempts to operate inside of one of these "Rings." Instantly the coils of the Boa will be around him, and he will be crushed in its folds, and devoured.

Sixteenth Parallelism of Character:—*The grand Boa Constrictor habitually twines upon a tree*, while watching for victims which pass beneath.

So, the Money Power twines about the government, while plundering its people. The Money Power habitually twines about governments. The British government is its servile instrument: it sways India with autocratic rule: the European governments yield to its will.—In our own country, it too often controls Congress, and State Legislatures, by lobby influence. The lobby,—"the third house,"—controls all legislation that effects the interest of the Money Power; procuring legislation to suit its aims, and preventing legislation injurious to it. Not only does the government leave industry defenceless in the grasp of the Money Power: it also, by vast land grants,* by paying interest on bonds in gold that were, by law, to be paid in paper, and in various other ways, gives to it immense bonuses. Our country is hardly in a less degree than England in the grasp of the Money Power.

Seventeenth Parallelism of Character:—*The Boa Constrictor, waiting for its prey, hides in a tree, behind the green foliage.*

So, the Money Power hides its own bloated wealth under the guise of national prosperity. Thus, our people are deceived by the statement that the United States is now the richest nation in the world. The wealth consists, not so much in the wealth of the American people as, in the growth of the Money Power and its invest-

---

* Our land grants to railroads cover 159,621,000 acres, or 326,000 square miles; an area more than twice as large as Great Britain and Ireland, and about three times as large as Italy.

ments. The Money Power has built railroads, factories, and city improvements; is opening up bonanza farms; is pushing forward with its capital many branches of production and trade; but it owns them all. The American people are getting poorer: the Money Power has mortgages upon two-thirds of our farms: the Money Power alone is getting rich.

It is investing in our country the revenues it derives from its world-wide manufactures and commerce. These investments increase the amount of its wealth, located in this country. But it is not our wealth: it is not the green foliage of national prosperity. It is the body of the Boa; and, instead of helping our people, its wealth is an engine of oppression, destroying Americans engaged in independent business, crushing our farmers, and devouring our national wealth.

Two oaks, standing in the forest, are alike vigorous and flourishing. A wild ivy vine twines around and around one of the oaks, and girdles it from bottom to top in its twining folds, and wraps trunk and limbs in a mass of most luxuriant foliage.—How gloriously the oak seems to flourish.—But soon it ceases to grow:—and finally, it begins to wither.—But the ivy vine flourishes more and more luxuriantly: its twining folds around the oak grow larger and larger; until the tree is strangled in its clasp, and dies!—Our country is the oak; the Money Power is the twining ivy vine. Already our oak is pining. Limb after limb has withered and fallen. The great farming branch, with many others, is slowly dying. But the twining ivy vine,—the Money Power, with its vast possessions,—is flourishing; and it crowns our dying country with a greener foliage than in the days of our greatest and most real prosperity.—The serpent folds of the Money Power are throttling us.

Besides these Parallelisms, there are three others which show, especially, that

THE MONEY POWER IS THE ENEMY OF THE HUMAN RACE.

Eighteenth Parallelism of Character:—*The serpent is the immemorial enemy of the human race.*

So also, a necessary antagonism exists between the Money Power and the human race.

The People Can Only Prosper by Doing the Business which the Money Power is doing, and covets to monopolize entirely. If the individuals keep the business, they prosper, and their countries flourish;—but the Money Power, under such conditions, will languish. On the other hand, if the Money Power takes the business, those who had it before are reduced to poverty, just in the degree in which the Money Power flourishes. *The prosperity of the Money Power is the ruin of the human race.*

The Money Power is hostile to the well being of man beyond all despotisms that have ever existed. It is more oppressive than any national despotism. A despot rules by law, and makes specific exactions by taxation. No despot desires to break down people in business—to plunder them of their property—to reduce them to bankruptcy—and to appropriate their property to himself. No despot enters the home, to take it from the owner.—The Money Power does all this. It crushes individuals: it oppresses people *en masse*. It cheats: it swindles: it extorts: it plunders: it destroys: it devours.

The Minotaur, a monster which, every year, devoured a shipload of victims which Athens was compelled to furnish, is the most horrible monster of legendary antiquity. But the Money Power is worse than the Minotaur. That monster was kept in its den, and could only devour the victims brought to it. The Money Power is an immense Serpent, going at large, and devouring all the victims it can find. More, it is a Crowned Imperialism, which controls governments, and is above all law. It bankrupts the merchant, the manufacturer, the miner, the farmer; and drives them and their families out from their homes into the world, beggared, and perchance to die heart-broken and despairing.

The Money Power is worse than any despot that ever reigned. The despot is restrained from excessive wrong and oppression, lest the prosperity of his people be destroyed.—But it is the aim of the Money Power to destroy the prosperity or all persons engaged in independent business; in order that, amid the ruin it works, it may ravage, and devour industry and wealth.

The Money Power is worse than any monster that ever roamed the earth, or was conceived by human fancy. For the monster needs only to devour a few, to appease its hunger;—but this Serpent is so huge, that it encircles the earth with its folds, and the ruin of nations can not appease its insatiable appetite to devour.

Were a wild beast abroad, destroying as the Money Power destroys, masses of men would gather to hunt it to death.

Were a despot to oppress and ruin his people, as the Money Power is oppressing and ruining our country, he would be blown up with dynamite. or his head would be brought to the block, in less than a year.—The Money Power, like the Serpent, is the Arch enemy of the human race.

Nineteenth Parallelism of Character :—*The color of the dragon is* RED.—This is a *lusus naturae.* Nobody ever saw a red snake. There must have been a special appropriateness in the color here, for it to be applied to the serpent.

This color always, in the book of Revelation, indicates that the power symbolized by a red color is a cruel, bloody despotism. And indeed the red color was indispensable, in order to indicate the bloody character of the Money Power. For the Money Power is a great destroyer—perhaps the greatest destroyer of human life, of all the despotisms that have arisen on the earth.

But it does not destroy its victims on the battle-field. It is described in the third vision of Daniel, where it is said of it: "*In peace, shall he destroy many.*" *Daniel* vii: 25. It does not strike its venomed fangs into the body, but the soul. It reduces its victims to want and beggary; and multitudes of them, in utter despair, turn their faces to the wall and die. Its victims have died—are dying—all over the earth.

Great Britain is the seat of its power; and there, by penury, and want and vain longing and despair, it is, every year, crushing thousands of the poor into untimely graves. I saw in London such poverty, and misery, such utter wretchedness, that the constant spectacle of suffering I could not relieve broke down my health, and I was compelled to leave the country before I had intended, in order to save my life. Among the London poor, you hardly ever see a hoary head. Poverty and want and hopelessness and despair drive them to untimely graves, long before time can furrow the brow or blanch the hair. The whole generation dies in the prime of middle life, destroyed by the conditions with which the Money Power surrounds them. They are as actually murdered as though the dagger were driven to their hearts. It is true, no blood is shed;—but the Serpent never sheds the blood of its victims—they die a bloodless death, crushed in its coils. So the poor people of Britain die, every generation, crushed to death by the constricting coils of the Money Power—crushed into direst poverty and want, till death comes to their relief.

India is completely in the coils of the Money Power.

The Monster killed five million Hindoos with famine, in order to compel them to become its serfs upon its plantations redeemed from the jungle. And now, under the control of industry in India by the Money Power, half a million Hindoos die of starvation, every year.—It is said that, in the wars of Napoleon, waged during twenty years, all over Europe, and in Egypt and Syria, two million men perished. In a time of profound peace, the Money Power, in a single country, *destroys as many lives every four years, as Napoleon destroyed in twenty years!!*

In the United States, during the long oppression of low prices which it has maintained since 1820, with brief intervals, and in the terrible financial crises it has induced, thousands have died of heart-break, and multiplied thousands of penury. During its long continued course of conquest in this country, in which it has been engaged for the last twenty years, it has broken down one branch of industry after another, and devoured them; and it has driven to untimely graves myriads of our countrymen.

There have been, for the last twenty years, about ten thousand failures, every year, of prominent business firms. The men in moderate circumstances who have broke are a great multitude who have not been reported. Only the big fish caught by the Money Power are counted: the multitude of little minnows that it has cast out of its net to die, are left to rot in the sunshine without notice. Not to speak of myriads of small failures, in this country, caused by the Money Power, in the last twenty years, there have been, in the United States, two hundred thousand great failures, for the most part victims of the Money Power.

What became of those victims? Alas, we know not. Some died of heart-break: many drag on hopeless lives in some subordinate position: the sons of ruined families have, many of them, swelled the ranks of the reckless, hopeless multitudes of our cities: many of the cultured daughters are teachers, or seamstresses, or clerks; and many have sunk, through despair, into the great social deep lower than the grave!!

All over the earth, the Money Power has its holocausts of victims. They fall in the midst of peace. They die, and make no sign.—Well is this bloody destructive Money Power represented by the Great RED Dragon.

Twentieth Parallelism of Character:—*Inspiration drops the symbol at last, and calls the Dragon the Devil.*—The Devil was incarnate in the serpent, in Eden, to induce the fall of the human race. In the book of Revelation, Satan is represented as incarnate in the Dragon.

The Money Power is an embodiment of Satanic selfishness, craft, cunning, skill, fraud, deceit, malignity and destructiveness. It constantly breaks down industry in its selfish greed: it destroys the prosperity of the whole earth, in the pursuit of gain: it crushes multiplied millions ol the human race: it overshadows the whole age with darkness.

It would destroy the dawning era of liberty and advancement now rising upon the world, as the serpent destroyed Eden. It would break down our grand Republic, and establish upon its ruins a mighty Despotism, to overshadow the hopes of man: it would, with Jewish hatred of Christianity, break down our churches: it would destroy our rising civilization, and reduce mankind to the condition of serfs, without the possibility of education or enlightenment: it would arrest the progress of the world toward the Millennium, and grind mankind beneath the heel of a despotism worse than that of the Feudal Ages.

The Money Power seeks to destroy our Republican liberties, and to bring the world under a subjection to its own grand Imperialism of wealth and monopoly; in which it, and its agents, will be the privileged Aristocracy, having all culture, and refinement and power;—while the mass of mankind are its serfs, tilling its lands, and doing its work in the various departments of business life, and sunk into abject poverty, with all its concomitants of ignorance, vice and debasement.

Instead of allowing the human race to share in the benefits derived from the power of steam, it seeks to monopolize all those benefits to itself, and use them as a weapon to crush all individual industry, and to subdue the world beneath the imperial sway of its capital. It converts the blessings conferred by Divine Providence upon mankind into a curse. It seeks to introduce a new Feudal Era, in which it, and its agents, will parcel out the world anew, and bring back the wrong and oppression of the Dark Ages.

The iniquity of the Money Power surpasses human depravity. It is Demonic,—in its selfishness and greed—in its cold-blooded heartlessness—in its knavish trickery—in its bold robbery—in its cunning and craft and chicane—in its falsehood—in its lying concealments—in its malignity—in its murders of victims driven by ruin to despair and death,*—in all this—and in all its other unspeakable turpitude, and wrong and baseness, the Money Power is utterly satanic and devilish.*

Who can Doubt That the Dragon is the symbol of the London Money Power? Let us briefly recapitulate the line of evidence:—

There are but three Parallelisms of Character between the Lion with Eagle's Wings and the Babylonian empire; and only two, between the Bear and the Persian empire; and none of them very remarkable.—But here are Twenty Parallelisms of Character between the Dragon and the Money Power;—ten times as many, and far more remarkable.

Review the Entire Career of the Money Power as it has been presented, and its every trait, its every act reveals it as a gigantic Serpent.

1) **It is Like a Serpent** in being essentially a devourer.

2) **It is Like a Serpent in Its Method of Devouring Its Victims**:—it charms its prey, luring them to their doom—it seizes its prey secretly—it paralyzes its victims by its attack—it crushes its prey in its coil—it crushes only to devour, and devours all it crushes—it beslimes its prey before devouring it—it swallows its prey whole, leaving nothing—it swallows it by repeated gulps, and only after repeated efforts engulfs it in its maw.

3) **The Money Power is Like a Serpent in Its Charaeteristics**:—it is full of worldly wisdom and craft—it hides in its agencies, as the serpent hides in the grass—it continually grovels in debasement, lying, fraud and trickery, as the serpent crawls upon its belly—it is cold-blooded, remorseless, cruel.

4) **The Money Power is Like a Serpent in Its Habitudes**:—like the serpent it stretches afar; its head in England, its long body enveloping the whole earth in its coil—it throws many coils of its huge length around many industries, in varous countries all over the earth, every coil a "ring"—it hangs on governments for support, as the Boa Constrictor hangs on a tree—it hides its own bloated gains under the guise of national prosperity, as the Boa hides in the leaves of a tree.

5) **The Money Power is a Veritable Serpent in Its Relations with Mankind**:—it is the necessary enemy of mankind, because its interests are opposed to the well being of humanity, there being as natural an enmity between the Money Power and mankind, as between the serpent and man.—The Money Power, like the Dragon, is RED with the blood of multitudes of victims,

slain by it in its continual wars upon industry—finally, the Money Power is, indeed, the very embodiment of Satanic malignity toward mankind.

In Every Particular, the Symbol has Its Counterpart. Not one point of likeness fails. No other power can possibly be found that embodies all the characteristics of a serpent. In no other power that has ever existed can these characteristics be found. The Money Power is the only Imperialism that has ever risen on the earth, that is like a snake, in any particular. It is like a snake, in every point. And it is like nothing else.—These strange and startling resemblances cannot be fortuitous and accidental. They prove most indubitably that the Money Power is the Imperialism symbolized by the Great Red Dragon.

CHAPTER V.

PROOF THAT THE DRAGON IS THE SYMBOL OF THE LONDON MONEY POWER, CONTINUED.

III. THIRD PROOF:—COINCIDENCES OF FACT.

We have now seen the twenty Parallelisms of Character by which the Great Red Dragon is proved to be the symbol of the London Money Power. But these Parallelisms are only part of the evidence. We have seen that a symbol is also identified with the power symbolized, by Coincidences of Fact, where certain things are stated of the symbol, which represent similar things that are true of the power symbolized. There are twenty-two Coincidences of Fact, which prove that the Money Power is the

Imperialism symbolized by the Great Red Dragon. These will now be presented:—

1st. The Dragon and Beast.

First Coincidence of Fact:—*In the 13th Chapter of Revelation, it is said "the Dragon gave to the beast his power, and his seat and great authority."* And again, *"they worshipped the dragon which gave power to the beast."*

It has already been explained how, according to the 13th and 17th Chapters of Revelation, the Roman empire is to be re-established under the dominion of Prussia, extended over Southern and Western Europe. And it is here stated how the Roman empire is to be re-established under the headship of Prussia,—"the Dragon gave to the Beast [Prussia] his power, and his seat and great authority."

This Establishment of the Prussian Empire over Southern and Western Europe by the aid of the London Money Power is not yet accomplished; but it is so near in the future that we may now see the means of fulfillment. We know that the loans of the London Money Power to the nations of Europe enable them to keep up their standing armies, and to meet the expenses of war. No country in Europe can sustain a war without the loans of the Money Power. In the great war of 1870, between Prussia and France, all the world thought France would be the victor, because she had the greater financial resources. But the Money Power gave to Prussia unlimited loans, and enabled her to put two millions of men into the field, so that she crushed France like an eggshell, in a campaign of only a little more than four months.

If we now observe the state of Europe, we shall perceive that its present condition indicates that the great nations are on the eve of a GREAT WAR; in which Prussia and her allies will triumph through the aid of the Money Power.

EUROPE IS NOW DIVIDED INTO TWO HOSTILE CAMPS:

Russia and France, on the one side; and Prussia and Britain, and Austria and Italy on the other. Of these two coalitions, Russia and France are, in respect of military force, much the more powerful. They are able to bring into the field, in round numbers, six million soldiers; while Prussia and her allies can only bring into the field, in round numbers, four million men.

But the Money Power is a New Force in the Field. It alone has imperial power in our age, sustaining kings, and in war giving the victory by its loans, where it pleases. No nation in Europe can put forth all its strength in war, without the loans of the Money Power. And, in the great war now impending in Europe, the aid of the Money Power will be given to Prussia and her allies. Loans will be refused to France and Russia, and those powers will be unable, for want of money, to bring their vast forces into the field. Prussia and her allies will have unlimited loans, and will be able to equip and keep in the field all their forces: the sure result will be that Prussia and her allies will be the victors in the conflict; and Prussia will become imperial over Southern and Western Europe.

In the New Era of the Imperialism of the Money Power, it needs a grand imperial government that can enforce its demands all over the earth. The British government is now its subservient instrument;—but Great Britain is not sufficiently powerful to enforce its demands against the great nations of the earth. It needs a more powerful nation to be its instrument. And Germany, under the headship of Prussia, is the nation it has chosen.

The Pamphlet given me, in England, shows the

desire of the Money Power to have a great Imperialism capable of ruling the world, to further and support its claims. The writer of the pamphlet said that, in order to support the claims of British capitalists, it was necessary for England to be the most powerful nation on the globe; and that it was the policy of England, in order to this end, that the nations should be divided up into small states, so that England could subdue and control them.

In the Table of Contents of the pamphlet, appear the following headings:—**"England has a Money Interest in Every Nation." "Every War a War upon England." "England Should invariably Chastise." "English Rule a Blessing to Foreign Nations."**—The writer proceeds:—

> "Having her property [the property of the Money Kings] dispersed all over the earth, England should, for her own protection, constitute herself the police of the world; as she is the carrier, the banker, the merchant, the Annuitant, the post-office of the world. When the outrage of war is committed on England's commerce,—that is, whenever any war is undertaken,—it should be the standing order of the people of England to their public servants that, the instant any country marches an army across its own border, the English fleet in the district shall blockade every port of the offending power, and if necessary, bombard the maritime towns; that the British fleet throughout the world shall seize upon and make prize of everything afloat belonging to the offender; and further, that a British army shall, without a moment's delay, be sent to assist the nation invaded, and protect our property."

The writer next proceeds to set forth the power of Great Britain to maintain this imperial position. He sets forth the resources of Britain under three heads,—**"Naval Supremacy:" "The Military Character of**

the People" and "**The Wealth of England.**"—He says:—

"England is the only nation which has at all times maintained its army without a conscription. * * * * * No one doubts our means of supplying the waste of war. The cost [of the Crimean war] that has crippled Russia for twenty years, has never for a moment been felt by us. The large outlay during the Crimean war did not curtail the smallest luxury of the poorest Englishman. The war was thoroughly popular, as all wars are in England. There is no instance of public meetings to protest against a war; for the people of England often urge a war, but never tire of one."

The writer of the pamphlet advocates the breaking up of all the great powers (this was in 1864), into small states, which could not resist the power of Great Britain. He says:—

"A combination of such states as Denmark, Holland, and Belgium would give us little more trouble than a Caffir war, or an attack by the Maories of New Zealand. * * * * * It is England's interest, then, that there shall be no large territories; and, fortunately, nature has limited within comparatively narrow bounds the extent of country which can most beneficially embrace one community. * * * * * England can avail herself of these natural limits without the slightest injury to mankind; and should never fail to assist every people who are struggling for a separate existence."

This writer represents the interests of the Money Power. His statements show that the Money Power feels the need of a great Imperialism able to dominate all nations, in order to further and guard its interests. This writer evidently hoped that Great Britain would become such an Imperialism, by breaking up the great nations of the earth, fomenting discontents, and supporting revolts.—But the tendency throughout Europe and America is toward the growth of great nations. It is now evident that Great Britain is not powerful enough to dominate the earth.

But the Money Power desires such an Imperialism as its agent, as is evident from the foregoing quotations. Such an Imperialism is indispensable to it. And as there is no hope of Great Britain becoming such an overmastering Imperialism, the Money Power has chosen Prussia to become its grand Imperial Agent in the future, and is raising Prussia to imperial power for that purpose. Hence it aided Prussia by its loans to crush France; and it is now preparing, by its policy and its loans, to exalt Prussia to an imperialism over Southern and Western Europe.

Thus will be fulfilled the statement of prophecy:—"*The dragon* [the Money Power] *gave to the beast* [the Prussian empire] *his power, and his seat and great authority,*" *i. e.* imperial dominion.

Second Coincidence of Fact:—*We see from the Dragon giving power to the Beast, that the Dragon does not symbolize a political power.*

For one political power never gives power to another, but exercises it itself. Thus, France will not give political power to Spain, nor Great Britain to Ireland, nor Russia to Poland. Political powers always exercise their own political power, and will not give it to another state. If the Dragon were a political power, it would not give power to the Beast [the Prussian empire], but would exercise it itself.

This fact harmonizes perfectly with the Dragon being the symbol of the Money Power. The Money Power is not a political Imperialism. It needs some political government as its political agent, to legislate in its interest, and fight its battles.

The two foregoing Coincidences of Fact are already in part fulfilled. The Money Power has not yet raised Prussia to imperial rule over Southern and Western Europe. The work is not yet completed. But it is begun, and is far on the way toward accomplishment. The Money Power, by its loans, enabled Prussia to crush Austria and France. Its loans have enabled her to re-establish the German empire, and from being the weakest of the five great powers, to become the mightiest power in Europe. It only needs one more step, which will be taken in the next war in Europe; and then, the Money Power will have completed its work, and given to Prussia imperial power and dominion over Southern and Western Europe.—So much is already done, that we can readily see the way to the single remaining step.

2ND. THE TWO HORNED BEAST.

There is presented in the 13th chapter of Revelation, another beast, a Two Horned Beast, which is seen "coming up out of the earth."

This Beast has been the *vix crucis* of expositors. No expositor has ever applied it to any power that has yet risen, to the satisfaction of himself, or others. This Beast is the Dragon.

John says of it:—"I beheld another beast coming up out of the earth. * * * * * And he spake as a dragon. * * * * * and he causes the earth, and them which dwell therein to worship the first beast whose deadly wound was healed."

1. **I prove that the Two Horned Beast is the Dragon by Three Marks,** mentioned in the above passage:—

1.) **The first mark that proves that this Beast is the Dragon,** is the manner in which John saw it "*coming up out of the earth.*"—This is the action of a serpent, not of a quadruped. When John saw the Beast rise up out of the Sea, the action was instantaneous: "I saw a beast rise up out of the Sea." The beast rose out of the Sea, and that was the end of its rising. But it was different with this Two Horned Beast: John "beheld" it for a long time; and all the time he "beheld" it, it was "*coming up out of the earth,*"—This slow crawl out of the ground is the action of a serpent crawling up out of its den, and of nothing else.

2.) **I identify this Two Horned Beast with the Dragon by its voice**: "*He spake as a dragon.*"—Now, we know a horse by its neigh, and a chicken by its crow, as well as by sight; and we recognize a serpent by its hiss. In all nature, a serpent is the only beast whose voice is a hiss. If this beast spake as a dragon, it hissed; for a hiss is the only sound a serpent utters. *The Two Horned Beast hissed: It was the Dragon.*

But we are not left to inference on this point.

3.) **That this Two Horned Beast is the Dragon, is established beyond the possibility of a doubt** *by Divine inspiration representing it as doing the same thing the Dragon had just before, in the same Chapter, been represented as doing.*—It has just before been stated that the Dragon gave to the Beast whose deadly wound was healed "his power, and his seat and great authority." And here, it is said, this Two Horned Beast "causeth the earth and them that dwell therein to worship the first beast whose deadly wound was healed."—This is just the same thing the Dragon does: The dragon gave to the beast whose deadly wound was healed imperial power: this Two Horned Beast causeth all men to render to the imperial beast worship or homage.—*The act is the same in both instances: this Two Horned Beast is the Dragon.*

I have been careful to prove the identity of this Two Horned Beast with the Dragon, because,

2. **There are eight Coincidences of Fact** between this Two Horned Beast and the Money Power; and all of them so remarkable as to make it absolutely certain that this Two Horned Beast is the symbol of the Money Power.

1.) The following is the text respecting this Two Horned Beast:—

"And I beheld another beast coming up out of the earth:

"And he had two horns like a lamb:

"And he spake as a dragon.

"And he exerciseth all the power of the first beast before him, ['*i. e.*, in his presence']

"and causeth the earth and them which dwell therein to worship the first beast, whose deadly wound was healed.

"And he doeth great wonders, so that he causeth fire to come down from heaven on the earth in the sight of men.

"And [he] deceiveth them that dwell on the earth by those miracles [or wonders] which he had power to do in the sight of the beast;

"saying to them that dwell on the earth that they should make an image to the beast which had the wound by a sword and did live.

"And he had power to give life unto the image of the beast, that the image of the beast should both speak and causeth that as many as would not worship the image of the beast should be killed.

"And he causeth all, both small and great, rich and poor, free and bond, to receive a mark in their right hand, or in their foreheads: and that no man might buy or sell, save he that had the mark, or the name of the beast, or the number of his name.

"Here is wisdom. Let him that hath understanding count the number of the beast: for it is the number of a man; and his number is six hundred and three score and six." *Revelation* xiii: 11–18.

2) Let us note the Coincidences of Fact, presented between this Two Horned Beast and the Money Power:—

Third Coincidence of Fact:—"*He had two horns*

like a lamb."—In prophecy, a horn is a symbol of a kingdom or political power. Thus, the ten horns symbolize the Ten Kingdoms of Modern Europe, within the territories of the Roman empire. The two horns on the head of the Persian Ram, (*Dan.* viii,) symbolize the two kingdoms of Media and Persia, united in the Persian empire. So here, these Two Horns on the head of the Serpent, symbolize two kingdoms whose power the Dragon wields. The horns being *lamb-like* horns, indicates that the two kingdoms under the control of the Serpent are especially Christian kingdoms.

These two horns symbolize the two kingdoms of England and Scotland, which were united, in the reign of Queen Anne, into the United Kingdoms of Great Britain. Great Britain is the name, then established by law, for the two united kingdoms of England and Scotland. And these are the two most pre-eminently Christian kingdoms in the world.

Prophecy only recognizes England and Scotland as the two horns on the head of the Dragon. The Money Power rules Great Britain with absolute sway. The British Parliament always registers its will. No matter what party is in power, Great Britain always legislates for trade, and, when necessary, fights for trade. When the Landed Aristocracy ruled the country, they had Corn Laws, to keep up the price of grain for the benefit of the Land Owners. But when the Money Power wanted free trade in grain and provisions, for the benefit of manufacturers and merchants, Parliament submitted to its will, and threw over the policy of the Tory Landed Aristocracy.

The Tory party, representing the Landed Aristocracy, has had to advance to the ground of the Money Power, and plant itself on the platform of the Whigs, in order to live. The British Parliament is now the creature of the Money Power. The Money Power rules Great Britain. Prophecy, with striking fidelity to fact, represents Great Britain,—England and Scotland,—as the two horns on the head of the Serpent.

Fourth Coincidence of Fact:—*John saw this Two Horned Serpent "coming up out of the earth."*—He looked at it for a long time,—"beheld" it,—and all the time he "beheld" it, it was still "coming up out of the earth." It was always crawling up out of the ground, but never got entirely out. Though constantly crawling up out of the ground, a part of it always remained in the ground.—This is a strange and, seemingly, impossible state of facts,—a snake always crawling up out of its den, and yet never getting entirely out. And yet this strange thing is true of the Money Power.

The Money Power always acts through joint stock corporations. The stockholders and bondholders of the various corporations all over the world, are in London. There is the Serpent's den. The stockholders are hidden from the world in their den. The world only sees the directors and the officers of the corporations, and their hired operatives.—But as the stockholders make more money, they organize more corporations, and elect more directors, and more officers, and employ more operatives. So that the Serpent is constantly growing greater in its den; and as it grows in the den, more of its body crawls up out of the den, and becomes visible to the public eye.

What a strange astonishing similitude is this! and yet it fits the Money Power perfectly. And it will not suit any other power that has ever risen upon the earth. God foresaw the action of the Money Power, and He chose a symbol that resembles it perfectly, and mentioned facts respecting the symbol that exactly suit the Money Power.—It must be a terrible monster which Divine Omniscience took such pains to point out, by making its symbol unmistakable.

Fifth Coincidence of Fact:—*The Two Horned Serpent "exerciseth all the power of the first beast before him,"*—or in his presence.—The first beast, as we have seen, is the Prussian empire; and the statement in the text means that the Money Power will exercise all the power of the Prussian empire in the presence of the empire.

We can Understand how the Money Power will Wield the Power of the Prussian Empire, by observing the manner in which it is now exercising the power of the British empire. In Great Britain, the Money Power is the power behind the Throne, greater than the Throne. It wields the power of the British government by controlling the Parliament, and has been doing so for more than a century. It is avowed that the British government is administered in the interests of the manufacturing and commercial classes. No matter what party is in power, all parties alike do the will of the Money Power.

We had, a few years ago, a remarkable instance of the subserviency of the British government to the Money Kings. When Disraeli was Prime Minister, the Tory Administration entered upon a new career of bold imperialism, in its treatment of other countries. This imperial policy of the Tories was stigmatized by the Liberal party as "Jingoism." Gladstone appealed to the moral sentiment of the Liberals, who are the most religious portion of the British population, against the "Jingoism" of the Tories, and unseated them from power on that issue alone.—But immediately after the Gladstone administration came into power, it outjingoed Jingo.

It happened that the Khedive of Egypt was unable to pay the interest on his debt to the Money Kings. Those capitalists appealed to the British government; and the Gladstone Administration at once proceeded to enforce their claims against Egypt. It did what had never been done before by the British government. It invaded Egypt, conquered the country, discrowned the Khedive, and administered the government in the interest of the Money Power. The British government debased itself to become "RECEIVER" for the Money Kings.

And this high handed outrage upon a weak state was justified before the world by the plea that it was necessary, in order that those imperial capitalists might receive the interests on their loans. And so thoroughly established is this grand Imperialism of Capital, that all the nations of Europe accepted this plea as perfect justification.

A Principle is Established in this Transaction that is full of Menace to the Nations of the Earth. It is now recognized as an established principle that the monetary claims of the Money Power are higher than the right to national existence!! So long as a country which the Money Power has ruined can pay the interest on its debts—well.—But when it is reduced to bankruptcy, and can no longer pay the interest, it thereby forfeits its national existence; and the Money Power has a right to have it conquered, in order to secure its debt!!!

This is the logic of the conquest of Egypt! It is well for the nations to ponder it!!!

The British Government also Conquered Burmah, three years ago, in the interest of the Money Power. The cause of the conquest was kept quiet until, last year, a Mr. Robert Sutherland, in making a trip from India to England, passed through the United States, and in an interview with the reporter of a New York paper stated the facts.

Mr. Sutherland stated to the reporter that he is "Resident Manager of the Burmah and Bombay Trading Corporation, one of the largest Trading Companies [of the Money Power] in the East." Mr. Sutherland further said: "Burmah possesses the only Ruby mines in the world, and they are very valuable. The desire of the French in Tonquin to get control of these, and the Teat forests, led to the recent trouble with King Theebaw, and the overthrow of that monarch's rule. He repudiated a very large claim against him by the Bombay and Burmah Corporation, claiming that the agents had made false returns."

And no doubt they did; for they defraud and cheat everybody. But the corporation appealed to the British government. And, continues Mr. Sutherland:—"To prevent his trading with the French, the British government took up the claim of the Corporation, its members being British subjects, and the war over its enforcement led to Theebaw's capture, and the extension of the British protectorate over the whole of Burmah."

In plain English, this statement means that this corporation of the Money Power claimed exclusive commercial rights in Burmah. They cheated the Burman Emperor, making false returns, and when the Burman government exercised its right to abrogate its trade relations with the corporation, rhe British government, at the instance of the Trading Company, invaded Burmah, dethroned the emperor and sent him prisoner to India, and annexed Burmah as a conquered province.

Some years ago, the British government invaded China, because the Chinese government excluded the opium which the corporations of the Money Power were producing in India, and forced China, at the cannon's mouth, to receive the opium and allow its people to be debauched, in order that the Money Power might continue to reap its profits!

If the British government had conquered China, and made its emperor a captive, and annexed the country to its dominions, the act would have been on a par with the conquest of Egypt and Burmah. The claims of the

Money Power are advancing. Its imperial policy requires the conquest and complete subjugation of any nation that is ruined by it, or which attempts to resist its oppression!

If any have doubted that this London Money Power is a great Imperialism, they can doubt no longer. It may have seemed doubtful to some, while I stated its course in the United States, whether the picture of its imperial power might not be overdrawn. But when we see it reducing Egypt to bankruptcy, and plundering Burmah by fraud, and then having those countries conquered in order to enforce its claims, none can doubt its proud and haughty claims to imperial supremacy.

Great Britain can crush China, and conquer Egypt and Burmah, in the interest of the Money Power.

But Great Britain is not powerful enough to enforce its claims against the United States, or any of the great nations of Europe; and hence the necessity, as already mentioned, of the Money Power raising Prussia to imperial dominion, in order to use its power for the enforcement of its claims. It will have need of the Prussian power to enforce its claims against every country on the globe; for it is bankrupting all nations, as it is the United States; and every country will have to take ground against it, as Burmah did, or be reduced to bankruptcy like Egypt. And the fate of resistance, and of bankruptcy, is the same, — the conquest and the annexation of the victim nation. In this way the Prussian empire would attain to universal dominion, by enforcing the claims of the Money Power.

If the Money Power is not checked in its career, it will carry out its policy to the full extent. It will bankrupt all the nations of the earth, and have them conquered, and their resources administered by a political imperialism in partnership with the Money Power, which will act as "**receiver**" for bankrupt nations, as England has done with Egypt.—The people of that empire would, in the end, become its grand agents, and share with it the plunder of the world.

Sixth Coincidence of Fact.—*This Two Horned Serpent is represented as "saying unto them that dwell on the earth that they should make an image to the beast that had the wound by a sword and did live."*

For a long time, I was perplexed as to the meaning of this "image of the beast." But the meaning is simple and plain.

We have here a remarkable prophecy predicting the representative form of government. In the age when the Revelation was given, the representative form of government had never been thought of. The state always acted for itself, through the Monarch, or a Constituent Assembly in which govermental power was vested. The idea had never occurred to any one to have a representative body in which the governmental power should be vested. Such a Representative Body, whether called Congress, or Parliament, or by any other name, is *the representation or the image of the State.* Each member is the representative or "image" of his constituents, and the whole body is the representative, or "image" of the nation. A Congress "representing" the nation would naturally, and with strict propriety, be called *the image of the nation.*

It is astonishing how perfectly all parts of this prophecy hold together. It is truly wonderful that we should have here, in Revelation, a plain and distinct prediction of the representative form of government, long before it grew up in modern times. This "Image of the Beast" is the Reichstag, or German Parliament, which will be extended over the states of Southern and Western Europe. All the states that become a part of the German empire will represent themselves in the Reichstag. This Reichstag will be the representative body, or "Image" of the empire;

and this "Image" will "speak," and govern the empire.

It is by means of this Parliament or "Image," that "the Dragon shall exercise all the power of the" Prussian empire in the presence of the empire. The Dragon will control the Parliament with its money, and will thus control the Prussian empire, as it has the British empire, during the last century.

Seventh Coincidence of Fact:—*This Two Horned Serpent "had power to give life to the image of the beast [the imperial Parliament,] that the image of the beast should both speak, and cause that as many as would not worship the image of the beast should be killed."*

1. That is, the Prusso-German empire will aspire to universal dominion. Influenced by the Money Power, the Imperial Parliament will enact laws inflicting death upon all who refuse to submit to its sway. It will be the policy of the Money Power to have a grand universal empire, by means of which it will be able to plunder all nations, and get possession of all the property in the world.

2. But there is another fact indicated in this statement:—When the German empire shall first be established over Southern and Western Europe, the several nations which enter the empire will retain their independence in respect of all internal affairs, merely entering into a union for trade purposes, and for the administration of foreign relations.—But with the universal tendency of imperial power to centralize itself, the German Parliament will assume ascendency over the subject states, and will compel all, under penalty of death, to submit to its sway.—And in this encroachment upon the rights of the subject kingdoms, the Dragon will be the active agent, furthering the aims of despotism.

Eighth Coincidence of Fact:—*This Two Horned*

Serpent "doeth great wonders, so that he causeth fire to come down from heaven on the earth, in the sight of men."

This is a startling statement. I used to think that when the power symbolized by this Two Horned Beast should rise, and begin to "cause fire to come down from heaven," I would be sure to recognize it; for, when it should "cause fire to come down from heaven," its identity would be unmistakable.

But the Money Power had been "causing fire to come down from heaven on the earth in the sight of men" for over forty years, before I recognized its identity. "Fire from heaven" is lightning: lightning is electricity. For more than forty years the Money Power has been "causing fire to come down from heaven in the sight of men," to run the telegraph. In all our Cities, it "causeth fire to come down from heaven," to run the electric lights. In all the cities, and many of the towns, "fire from heaven" runs telephones. And in many of the cities, electric motors run street cars by "fire from heaven."

And the Money Power "causeth" all this "fire to come down from heaven." As fast as any new electric invention is made, the Money Power buys the patent, organizes electrical companies all over the world, and sets the invention in operation.—Edison is evidently its paid agent. He has spent over a million dollars in electrical experiments. He has in his laboratory forty assistants, and is expending at least $40,000 a year in his experiments. He can not personally afford any such outlay. He must be the agent of the Money Power; and as fast as he makes a new invention, they buy it, and put it into operation. They only paid him $6,000 a year, for seventeen years, for the telephone—nothing like the value of the invention; but enough, seeing that they paid him while experimenting, and supported his laboratory.

The Money Power owns the telegraph lines, the electric light companies, the electric street car companies, and all the applications of electric force. All over the earth, it constantly "causeth fire to come down from heaven on the earth in the sight of men"!!

Who can doubt that the Two Horned Serpent is the Symbol of the Money Power?!

Ninth Coincidence of Fact:—*The Two Horned Serpent "had power to do great miracles" or wonders.*

We live in an age of wonders. It is a common expression to speak of the "wonders of steam," the "wonders of electricity," the "wonders of mechanical invention."

And all these "wonders" the Money Power has set in operation by its capital. It has built the steam ships—the railroads—the telegraph lines—the telephones—the electric railway lines—the water works—the gas works:—and it has set in operation, by its capital, the thousand mechanical wonders in use in every kind of manufactures.

Tenth Coincidence of Fact:—*The Two Horned Serpent "deceived them that dwell on the earth as to those miracles* [or wonders] *which it had power to do."*

This is perfectly fulfilled in the Money Power, which is now deceiving mankind as to the wonders it is working with its capital. It lauds itself as a great benefactor of mankind. The blessings of Capital are constantly held up before the public. We are constantly told that Capital is necessary to our civilization—that it is beneficent in its operations—that Capital is indeed men's chief benefactor—that the world cannot do without Capital. It is triumphantly asked, where would the world now be without the railroads, the telegraphs and the thousand inventions Capital has set in operation? We are continually reminded that the human race ought to realize the benefits it derives from Capital, and ought to be profoundly grateful for them. And the inference is suggested that, in recognition of these benefits, mankind ought, in all things, to do the bidding and consult the interests of Capital!!

By these self laudations put forth through the press controlled by it, the Money Power is deceiving mankind.

It is admitted that the wonders Capital has wrought have been of the greatest benefit to mankind. No one would be willing to go back to the old days of stage coaches and tallow candles. We can not do without our railroads, and steamships, our telegraph lines, our water works, our gas works, our electric lights, our street railways, and all the appliances of our modern civilization. —But there is a consequence of all this that the Money Power keeps out of view.

By Means of these things, the Money Power is Rapidly Bankrupting Mankind, and getting all wealth into its own hands. There is more work now being done by steam than could be done, with old methods, by five such races as now people the earth. The Money Power has taken possession of steam, and mechanical inventions; and it is making all the profit derived from those sources.—Let a small knot of capitalists make all the profit on the labor of five such races as now people the earth—let them make it, not for one year or one generation, but for ages; and let them constantly reinvest, and enlarge their operations; and let them invest their profits, age by age, in property of all kinds:—and it is only a question of time, when they will do all business, and own all property.

We reach the same conclusion by another course of fact. When the Money Power began its career, 175 years ago, it is a moderate estimate to put its capital at $50,000,000. The commerce of the world has always been needing capital; and business has always afforded the best opportunities of investment. The capital of the

Money Power would certainly double itself once in fifteen years. Then it has doubled 11⅜ times since 1715. If this is the case, the capital of the Money Power now amounts to $163,840,000,000. This is probably below the mark. The wealth of the Money Power can hardly be less than $200,000,000,000.

This is a vast amount; but the facts bear it out. In the First Era of the growth of the Money Power, down to 1775, it had use for all its capital in extending its operations.—In the Second Era,—from 1775 to 1830,—it had sufficient capital to make immense loans to the monarchs of Europe.—In the Third Era,—from 1830 to 1864,—it had money enough to make loans for building railroads, water works, gas works, &c.; but it waited for the people to come for the money.—But since 1864, in the Fourth Era of its growth, it has been going into all kinds of enterprises; and now it is seeking new investments, and begging people to sell it their property, all over the earth. The Money Power has so much money, now, that it can not find investment for it. *In one more double it will about have all the property of the earth.* In the beginning of its career, a double of its capital meant $100,000,000. Now a double of its capital means $400,000,000,000. And all the property of the world is less that $600,000,000,000.

The labor wrought by steam and invention is too vast, for a few capitalists to be suffered to monopolize these grand agencies of industry for their own exclusive benefit. The monopoly of those appliances in the hands of a few capitalists is ruining the world.

The monopoly of steam industry must be stopped, and some way must be discovered by which the masses of mankind may be allowed a chance to share the profits derived from steam and invention.

How well Divine Inspiration foreknew the craft of the Money Power, and how thoroughly it has exposed it. In exposing the pretense of the Money Power as to the beneficent influence of capital, it has completely unmasked the deception of the claim that the operations of Capital, as now carried on, are beneficent to mankind. The exposure of its deception is the first step toward a new and better order of things, in which the operations of steam and invention, instead of inuring to the exclusive benefit of the Money Power, shall be used by the people of every country for their own national and individual prosperity.

Mankind is slow to accept a new thought, and some persons may be unwilling to believe that the Money Power is thus taking possession of all the property of the world. But divine Inspiration declares that such is its purpose:—

Eleventh Coincidence of Fact.—*This Two Horned Serpent "causeth all, both small and great, rich and poor, free and bond, to receive a mark in their right hand or in their forehead; and that no man might buy or sell, save he that had the mark, or the name of the beast, or the number of his name."*

This "mark" is the brand in the hand or on the body, by which slaves were marked, in ancient times. It is the aim of the Money Power to get all industry and all business into its hands, and reduce all mankind to the condition of its paid servants, branded in the hand, or on the forehead, with the badge of servitude.

A very intelligent man, after hearing my lecture, suggested to me that the "mark in the hand" designates the multitude of operatives who render manual service to the Money Power; while the "mark in the forehead" designates those who render to the Money Power brain service. This would include all great agents, having control of departments of industry or trade; all editors who wield their pens in the service of the Money Power; all lobbyists and legislators who sell themselves to promote the aims of the Money Power; and all in any department of business,—lawyers and other professional men,—who render brain service to the Money Power.

The mind shrinks from the idea that a grand Imperialism of Capital should get every department of industry and enterprise into its possession, so that none except its paid agents can do any business. But we have seen how entirely the Money Power has obtained control of all business, in India. We have seen how it is monopolizing almost all business in the United States, except farming and retail traffic—and how it is rapidly getting possession of these. We have seen how one more double, which will only take fifteen years, will give it more than all the property of Christendom, and two more doubles will give it all the property in the world.

A. T. Stewart broke down one thousand retail merchants in New York City, so that they could not buy nor sell, until they failed in business; then they took the "mark in the hand," and went behind his counters; and they could sell all the goods the New York people wanted to buy.

Some time ago, Armour began a campaign against the butchers of Davenport, Iowa. He wanted them to sell his meats. They refused: they wanted to buy and kill their own cattle; for there is a grand profit in buying and killing cattle and selling beef, at present prices. But Armour determined to coerce them: he began to sell dressed beef in Davenport so low that the butchers could sell no beef. They surrendered, and agreed to sell Armour's beef; they took the "mark in the hand"; and then they could sell all the beef the people of Davenport wanted to buy.

Business men are now being driven out, not of the beef trade only, but of many lines of business. The Money Kings have already obtained possession largely of the wholesale trade, and of all the great lines of business in the country. They have the import and the export trade: they buy all our products of every kind. They have almost everything except merchandizing and the farms; and, as we have seen, they are rapidly getting possession of the retail trade, by the retail stores which they are establishing throughout the country; and will soon have possession of our farms, by their foreclosure of mortgages.

The New York *Times* expects the Money Power to get possession of the farms by foreclosure of mortgages, and in a leading editorial, published Aug. 12th, 1877, it anticipates this result, and prepares the public mind for it. It says:

"There seems to be but one remedy, and it must come,—a change of ownership of the soil, and a creation of a class of land owners, on the one hand, and of tenant farmers on the other—something similar in both cases to that which has long existed and now exists in the old countries of Europe. * * * * * *Everything seems ripe for the change.*

"Then will begin a new era in agriculture, and one that seems very desirable. * * * * * Those farmers who are land poor must sell, and become tenants, instead of owners of the soil."

The *Times* regards the farmers losing their farms as inevitable, and it looks forward with complacency to the time when all our farms will be devoured by the Money Power. When that event occurs, the farmers will be serfs upon the soil redeemed by their fathers from the wilderness.

In a few years more, if things go on in their present grooves, this prophecy will be fulfilled; and no man in America can buy or sell, unless he is the paid agent of the Money Power. And if it is not checked, it will, ere long, extend its ownership over the whole world, and make all mankind its employees and servants, with its brand in their hand, or on their forehead.

Twelfth Coincidence of Fact:—*The number of the name of the Beast:—"Here is wisdom. Let him that hath understanding count the number of the Beast: for it is the number of a man; for his number is six hundred and three score and six."*

The manner in which this number of the name of the Beast is mentioned makes it evident that the number of the name is a very important means of identifying this two horned beast with the power it symbolizes.

From a very early period, the Christian fathers turned their minds to the exposition of this symbolic number. Irenæus, Bishop of Lyons, in Gaul, who lived in the Second Century, gives three names that have this number 666.—The first name was *Euanthes*, which he merely mentions, and passes by, with the remark, "but we affirm nothing respecting this."—The second name he gives is *Lateinos*. This name has been very generally adopted by expositors, who supposed this Serpent to be the Papacy.

The third Name which Ireneus Gives as Containing the Number 666, is Teitan; and this name he himself adopts.

It may be that this is not the name intended by divine Inspiration; and that, when this Dragon Imperialism shall be fully developed and known to the world, and its history be complete, it shall have a ruler or king, in whose name the fated number will appear. But in the present state of our knowledge of the subject, I accept *Teitan* as the fated number; and it is my belief that this is the number that was intended in the text; and for the following reasons:—

1. Titan was the Great Legendary Giant

of the Olden Time. We still use the name to designate any colossal power. I believe that one reason why divine Inspiration called this Serpent Titan, was to indicate its immense power, its huge proportions, its Titanic strength.

1) The Money Power is the most colossal empire that has ever risen upon the earth. It is a *Titanic* empire; the greatest that has ever existed. And the Serpent, its symbol, is a "GREAT" Serpent, stretching its mighty folds all over the earth. It is a TITANIC Serpent.

2) In its relations with the Beast, the Dragon has all the power; for "The Dragon gave power to the beast;" and this Serpent "exerciseth all the power of the first beast in his presence."

3) So, in the third vision of Daniel, the Little Horn which was the symbol of the Roman empire, grows so great, at last, that its top stands up among the stars. It becomes a "TITAN" Horn. And the vision of it was so terrible that it entirely unnerved the prophet, so that he was sick for three weeks.

This horn became a Titan Horn only after the re-establishment of the Roman empire, under the joint rule of the Money Power and Prussia. The power of this Joint empire shall be so collossal that nothing can represent it but a Titan Horn rising up above the earth, till its top is among the stars.—The fact that this "Little Horn" became a "TITAN" Horn has never been observed by expositors.

2. BUT THE SPECIAL REASON WHY THE DRAGON IS DESIGNATED BY THE NAME "TITAN," IS ITS ANTAGONISM TO GOD.

1) The Titans, according to the Heathen legend, warred against Jupiter, and hurled their missiles against Olympus; and they were only beaten, at last, by Jupiter smiting them with his thunderbolts. Titan, according to the legend, was the king of the Titans, and was thus the Arch-rebel against the gods.

2) It is believed that the legendary war of the Titans

against the gods, was the heathen mythological form of the rebellion of Satan and his angels against God. So that, the Satan of the Bible is the mythological Titan.

3) In the biblical idea, Satan is embodied in the serpent. And the Dragon, in the book of Revelation, is called the Devil and Satan. This indicates that the Dragon symbolizes that power which, in the political world, is the great antagonist of God, as Satan is in the spiritual world.

4) **The Dragon is the Great Antichristian Power of the Latter Days.** In its full development, the head of the Dragon power is the Antichrist.

1] We have seen how the Jews are even now hoping and expecting to overthrow Christianity. A very intelligent Jew once, in the heat of discussion, gave me the idea of the Christ which the modern "reformed" Jew holds. He said the *prosperity* of the Jews in the earth—he did not choose to say their *dominion*—is what is set forth in the writings of the Prophets under the figure of the Christ.

In the Jewish idea, the Dominion of the Jew Money Power is the Christ. And, at the last, I think that the head or king of the Money Power will claim to be the Christ.

Christ means "The Anointed One," in allusion to his being the promised royal descendant of David, the promised King of Israel. The Money Power, it seems, will at last choose a king, who is to be the acknowledged king of Israel,—the long expected, the long promised One,—the Christ. They will not claim that he is Divine, or the Son of God. For they deny that, in the Deity, there is the relation of Father and Son. They deny the Divine Trinity. They "deny the Father and the Son." They recognize only the unity of God.

The Jews have always expected a temporal sovereign as the Christ. They rejected the Lord Jesus, because He said "My Kingdom is not of this world." They expect a Christ whose kingdom is of this world—who is merely a temporal monarch. The time will probably come when, in the plenitude of its power, the Jew Money Power will set up a king, and declare him the promised Messiah. They will declare him the founder of a new Dynasty that is to rule the earth forever.

They will proclaim him the first of a line of kings,—Anointed Ones,—who, in their expectation, will all bear the title of "the Christs;" as the kings of Egypt were called "the Pharaohs," and the emperors of Rome, "the Cæsars."—The present attitude of the Jew Money Power is a stern menace to Christianity.

2] **The Jew London Money Kings would break down our churches.** In monopolizing the trade of our towns, and getting possession of our farms, the Money Power hopes to succeed in accomplishing the aims against Christianity which the Jews are known to entertain. If the Money Power should succeed in its aims, our churches will inevitably be broken down. Strike down our farming yeomanry and the tradesmen of our towns, and who would sustain our churches? our schools? Our churches in town and country would be pastorless for want of support. Our school systems would fall into wreck in the universal poverty that would prevail. Our Christian civilization would lie in ruins.

It is well known that the Jews, in our day, entertain strong hopes of overthrowing Christianity.—Prof. Godet, of Lausanne, utters the following warning of the danger threatening Christendom from the hostility of the Jews. He says:—

"On hearing this word 'Jewish,' many of you perhaps smile. That which bears that title does not seem to them very dangerous for the Church. They do not say, 'Can there any good thing come out of Nazareth?' but 'Can anything dangerous to us come out from thence?' To this contemptuous smile, I will oppose another, that of the Israelites themselves,—I mean the intelligent Israelites,—when they see us Christians bestirring ourselves for the propagation of the gospel, * * * * * and carrying the religion of the Bible to the ends of the earth. 'This religion,' they say quietly, 'is our religion. All these pains you are taking for us. * * * * * For the God of the Christian is the God of Abraham, Isaac and Jacob,—the God of the Jews. The doctrine of Jesus is none other than that of our prophets. One thing only separates us from these Christians,—the worship of the Christ. Let this absurd dogma of the divinity of a man,—one that is contrary to the most elementary principles of Monotheism,—let this last remnant of the ancient paganism living on in Christianity fall to the ground, and the gospel, thus purified, is Judaism. Christians, we are waiting for you! It is not we who are coming over to you; it is you who are coming over to us.' * * * * * So think, and so speak clear sighted Jews."*

Inspector Lictor Platt, in a recent course of lectures before the University of Berlin, said:—

"Everywhere one thought rules the Jews—the thought that the Christian idea shall at last be vanquished by the Jewish; and their common effort is directed to this end,—to supplant Christianity in the collective life of the nations." †

The Christian Editor of one of the leading evangelical papers of North Germany writes in the same strain:

"Among the Jews themselves, the conclusion is reached, not that the Jews will have to return to Christianity, but that the Christians will have to be turned to the Jewish faith."—*Neue Evang. Kirchen-Zeitung*, Feb. 4, 1882.

A Jewish writer, quoted in the same paper, asserts with all assurance: "Reformed Judaism is the confession to which the dominating church must return, if she will com-

---

* *Lectures in Defense of the Christian Faith*, pp. 316, 317.

† *Neue Evang. Kirchen-Zeitung. Berlin*, Aug. 27, 1881.

plete her reformation." — *Neue Evang. Kirchen-Zeitung*, Nov. 19, 1881.

I have taken the above quotations from Dr. Kellogg's book, *The Jews*. The author of that work says:

"This attitude of aggressive antagonism to Christianity, which the Jews are assuming, however little noticed by the unthinking many who never look behind acts and events for agents and causes, is a sign of the times as grave as it is remarkable. The confident expectation and determination of these enfranchised Jews, that not Christianity, but Judaism,—divested indeed of what was ceremonial and temporary,—shall yet win the world against Christianity, when we remember their control of the Capital of the world, their profits, and their confessedly marvelous success in modern life, acquires a serious significance."—*The Jews*, page 210.

The Jews are fully conscious of their Imperialism of Capital, and are looking forward to the time when, in full possession of all the industry, and wealth and property of the world, they can give entire direction to secular affairs, and form to religious belief. Let them get possession of our farms, and the business of our towns, and they will not hesitate to attempt to crush out our churches, by reducing their members to such poverty that they will be unable to sustain the expense of public worship.

If the Dragon empire, in its ultimate development, is the Antichrist, there is a peculiar fitness in Divine Inspiration calling it "*Titan*," the Satan of heathen mythology.

The Greeks had a well known method of expressing names by numbers. Each letter of the alphabet had as its equivalent a definite number. According to this system, the name Titan has the number 666. The Greek spelling of the name was *Teitan*. The numeral equivalent of these letters are as follows:

$$T\ 300 + \varepsilon\ 5 + \iota\ 10 + \tau\ 300 + \alpha\ 1 + \nu\ 50 = 666.$$

3RD. THE DRAGON AND THE MAN-CHILD.

We now turn to the symbol of the Dragon in the 12th Chapter of Revelation, where are presented ten other Coincidences of Fact. Until now, we were not prepared to take up the exposition of the Coincidences of Fact set forth in this symbol of the Dragon, inasmuch as it was necessary, first, to understand the relations of the Dragon to Great Britain and the Prussian empire.

The following is the text in the 12th chapter of Revelation:

"And there appeared a great wonder in heaven; a woman clothed with the sun, and the moon under her feet, and on her head a crown of twelve stars.

"And she, being with child, cried travailing in birth, and pained to be delivered.

"And there appeared another wonder in heaven; and behold a great red dragon having seven heads and ten horns, and ten crowns on his heads.

"And his tail drew the third part of the stars of heaven, and did cast them to the earth.

"And the dragon stood before the woman which was ready to be delivered, for to devour her child as soon as it was born.

"And she brought forth a man-child who was to rule all nations with a rod of iron.

"And her child was caught up unto God and to His throne.

"And the woman fled into the wilderness, where she hath a place prepared of God, that they should feed her there a thousand two hundred and three score days.

"And there was war in heaven: Michael and his angels fought against the dragon: and the dragon fought and his angels; and prevailed not: neither was their place found any more in heaven.

"And the great dragon was cast out, that old serpent, called the Devil, and Satan, which deceiveth the whole world: he was cast out, and his angels were cast out with him.

"And I heard a loud voice saying in heaven, now is

come salvation and strength, and the kingdom of our God, and the power of his Christ: for the accuser of our brethren is cast down, which accused them before our God day and night.

"And they overcame him by the blood of the Lamb, and by the word of their testimony; and they loved not their lives unto the death." *Rev.* xii: 1—11.

In the remaining portion of the chapter there are other Coincidences of Fact, which prove that the Dragon is a symbol of the Money Power; but, as they require, in order to bring them to bear on the question, a comparison with other prophecies not yet explained, they are omitted. But, without them, there are, in the part of the chapter already quoted, ten Coincidences of Fact, which prove beyond the possibility of doubt that the Dragon is the symbol of the Money Power.

Before presenting these Coincidences, it is first necessary to give an

1. Exposition of the Other Symbols.

In the 12th Chapter of Revelation, the scene is laid in

1) *The Lower Aerial Heaven.*

The Lower Aerial Heaven, in the Book of Revelation, is Always the Symbol of America, considered geographically as a country. The principle on which this symbolism is based is very simple and clear.

John received his Revelation on the Isle of Patmos, in the Ægean Sea. The Revelation, like all the other prophecies, was given by vision. The Isle of Patmos is in the Southeastern part of Europe.—As the Seer looked out toward the West, he beheld Europe spread out before his eye; and, beyond it, was another country, up in the air above Europe; and above this country was the highest Heaven, where the Throne of God was placed. Above the earth of Roman Europe was a sky, in which sun and moon and stars were beheld.

This was the Apocalyptic Landscape which John beheld in his vision. He was, no doubt, familiar with the geography of his time, and recognized the outlines of Roman Europe, which he called "the Earth." He naturally, in accordance with the ideas of his age, supposed the Eastern Continent to be the whole of the world, and that there was nothing on this earth beyond. He therefore called the country which he saw in the air, above Europe, "Heaven." But that country was America; and was placed in the Apocalyptic landscape above Europe, in the air, in perfect accordance with the laws of perspective.

In Accordance with the Laws of Perspective, the Foreground of a Landscape is always at the bottom of a picture, and the background, at the top. As John looked toward the West, therefore, he saw Roman Europe at the bottom of the landscape, as though on the ground, while America would appear above, at the top of the landscape.—But, with three thousand miles of perspective, America would be diminished to a point, and be invisible. In this respect, the law of perspective would have to be set aside; and America would be brought into the foreground sufficiently to be clearly visible, and placed above Europe, as though in air. In accordance with the law of perspective, America, in the book of Revelation, is always presented in the landscape in the lower aerial heaven.

2) *A Glorious Woman*

appears in the Lower Aerial Heaven,—America,—"clothed with the sun, and the moon under her feet, and on her head a crown of twelve stars." Expositors generally agree that this Woman is the symbol of the Christian

Church. The Two Witnesses, in the 11th Chapter of Revelation, are also the symbol of the Church. As the Two Witnesses prophesy clothed with sackcloth "one thousand two hundred and three score days," so the Woman is in the wilderness "one thousand two hundred and three score days."

The mistake into which expositors have fallen, in supposing that the woman is presented here before she fled into the wilderness, has been the cause of much error in the interpretation of this vision. Owing to this error, expositors have looked for the fulfillment of the vision in events that occurred in the Early History of the Church.

But, in the sixth verse, where it is said, "The woman fled into the wilderness, where she hath a place prepared of God that they should feed her there a thousand two hundred and three score days," *it does not mean that the woman then fled into the wilderness for the first time.* Several considerations make this evident:—

1] The Greek verb rendered "fled" is not in the imperfect tense, so as to indicate action beginning and continuing; but it is in the aorist, indicating completed action. The woman was not then making her first flight into the wilderness: she had been there for a long time, and only emerged from obscurity for a brief space, at this time, and now returned to it again.

2] The woman fled into the wilderness, "where," says the Seer, "she hath a place." She had been in her "place" a long time; she now returned to her "place."

3] This return to her "place" is like her subsequent return, in the 14th verse, where the woman again flies to her "place" in the wilderness. In both instances, the woman flies to her refuge; but it does not mean, in either case, that she flies thither for the first time.

Hence, the woman flying to her "place" does not give

us any clue to the era of the vision: that must be learned from other facts.

3) A Man-Child

was born of this woman,—the Christian Church,—in the Lower Aerial Heaven, "who was to rule all nations with a rod of iron."

This Man-child is the symbol of the United States; as is evident from the concurrent teachings of prophecy:—

1] The Man-child is born in the Lower Aerial Heaven, which is America as a country.

2] The Man-child is represented as born, the child of the Church. And the United States is, in a remarkable manner, the child of the Christian Church, as I have shown in my lecture on *The United States in Prophecy*. All the American Colonies were founded and settled by Christians seeking a refuge in the New World, where they might worship God according to the dictates of their conscience. There were the Puritans in New England, the Baptists in Rhode Island, the Dutch Calvinists in New York, the Swedish Lutherans in New Jersey, the Scotch Covenanters from New York to North Carolina, the English Quakers in Pennsylvania, the Episcopalians in Virginia, the French Huguenots in South Carolina, and the German Moravians in Georgia. The United States is emphatically the Child of the Church.

3] In the first vision of Daniel, the United States is represented under the symbol of the "Stone" which was "cut out of a mountain without hands"; which is interpreted by the Prophet as a kingdom set up by the God of heaven. This is very similar to the representation of the origin of the United States,—the Man-child,—in the book of Revelation. In Daniel, God is represented as the founder of the country, without anything being said of any human instrumentality: Here in Revelation, the human instrumentality, the Church, is especially mentioned. But the divine or Providential origin of the country is set forth in both instances.

4] The Man-child was "to rule all nations with a rod of iron." And it is the accordant voice of prophecy that the United States is to be a world-wide Republic, ruling all the nations of the earth.

5] "The Man-child was caught up unto God and to His Throne." This indicates the providential deliverance of our country in the War of Independence, and the providential protection that has kept us throughout our entire career as a nation.

Having identified all the other symbols of this vision of the 12th chapter of Revelation, we are now ready to identify the Dragon, beyond the possibility of doubt or question.—We have identified the Woman, the Man-child, and the place of his birth. This being done, we cannot mistake the interpretation of the Dragon.

2. Coincidences of Fact.

Thirteenth Coincidence of Fact:—*In the birth hour of the Man-child, "the Dragon stood before the woman, which was ready to be delivered, for to devour her child as soon as it was born."*

The United States was born as a nation in the War of Independence. At that time, the Great Red Dragon attempted to devour the infant nation. Great Britain was the power which then attempted to destroy our national existence. We must, therefore, either identify the Dragon with the British government, or with some power in Britain, behind the throne, greater than the throne.

As we have seen, the Dragon is not the symbol of Great Britain. The Dragon is the seventh grand form of Imperialism in the world: Great Britain is no such Imperialism. England and Scotland are Two of the Ten Kingdoms of Europe. They are represented in prophecy as the two horns on the head of the Dragon. Moreover, Prophecy represents Great Britain and the United States as united in the great future war against the Dragon and the Beast.—The Dragon is not the symbol of Great Britain as a nation.

Hence, the Dragon must represent some power having its seat in Britain, and having the British government under its control; and which influenced Great Britain to war against the United States, in our War of Independence. — This is just the historical status of the Money Power. It controls the British government with autocratic sway. It has controlled it for over a hundred years.

The Money Power was the prime mover in the oppression of the American Colonies, which drove them to revolt. The Landed Aristocracy, the Moneyed Capitalists, and the Mercantile Class of Great Britain were all united in holding stock in the British East India Company, which was then the Money Power; and their combined influence had complete control of the British Parliament.

During the trial of Warren Hastings, there were, in the administration party, a large number of the stockholders of the East India Company who had seats in Parliament. But the Administration party was in a minority in the Company, which sustained Hastings against the government. Many of the Opposition in Parliament were, no doubt, also stockholders. The connection of the Company with the government was very close; so that it would carry in Parliament any policy on which the Company was united.

In England, the Money Power is a Third Estate, greater than King and Parliament. In 1775, as now, the British Parliament was the pliant tool of the Money Power, and registered its will. It was not yet the age of steam, and the Money Power looked to Colonial dependencies as the chief source of gain. With its experience in India, it naturally desired to make another India of the American Colonies; and it derived great profits from their commerce, and great revenues from their taxation.

No sooner was the Seven Years War over, than the Money Power, impelled the British Parliament into a system of oppressive taxation and commercial restrictions, which drove the Colonies into Revolution. The whole question in dispute between the Colonies and the Mother country was taxation, industry and trade; matters in which the Money Power was specially interested, and in which it wished to enforce the policy that would promote its interest. The tax on tea, which drove the Colonies to revolt, was enacted for the special benefit of a corporation connected with the East India Company, which had a great quantity of tea on hand. While the nominal tax was retained, the tea was made lower than before in the interest of the Company, so as to enable it to sell. The law of the British Parliament for the benefit of the East India Company was the special occasion of the Revolution.

The Money Power through its control of Parliament drove the Colonies to revolution; and then, instead of attempting to allay discontent by concession, it attempted to destroy our national existence, by war.

There can be no doubt that the Dragon, which wished to devour our infant nation in the War of Independence, *was the Money Power*, which then ruled the British Parliament.

This Coincidence of Fact, alone, is sufficient to prove that the Dragon is the symbol of the London Money Power.

Fourteenth Coincidence of Fact:—"*On his heads*,"

were "seven crowns." The Seventh or Dragon Head was, at that time, a crowned Imperialism.

In 1775, the East India Company which was the head of the Money Power was a crowned Imperialism.. According to history it became an imperial power in 1757, at the victory of Plassy. In 1764, it was ruling an empire in Bengal of forty million subjects, having greater revenues than the most powerful kingdom of Europe.—In 1775, the Dragon head had just become a crowned Imperialism.

Fifteenth Coincidence of Fact:—*The tail of the Dragon "drew the third part of the stars* of heaven and did cast them to the earth."

In the Revolutionary War, the British forces overran about one-third of the United States. In the latter years of the Revolution, the British forces held their headquarters in New York City, and broke down all organized resistance in North Carolina, South Carolina and Georgia, and overran part of Virginia. About one-third of the country was thus "cast down" by the invading forces. The tail of the Dragon "cast down one-third of the stars" that glittered on our flag.

Sixteenth Coincidence of Fact:—*But the Dragon did not succeed: "the Man-child was caught up unto God and to His Throne."*

This catching up of the Man-child to the Highest Heaven, as beheld by John, symbolized the providential deliverance of the United States in the Revolutionary War, and the Divine protection of our country ever since. Our Revolutionary fathers all recognized the hand of Divine Providence in the success of our country. Washington, speaking of the events of the Revolution, said:—

"The hand of Providence has been so conspicuous in all this, that he who lacked faith must have been worse than an infidel; and he more than wicked who had not gratitude to acknowledge his obligations."

Seventeenth Coincidence of Fact:—"*And there was war in heaven: Michal and his angels fought against the Dragon: and the Dragon fought and his angels.*"—Here is a future war represented as occurring in America,—the Lower Aerial Heaven,—between the Dragon and Michael.

The place where this war occurs is clearly set forth: It is the same Lower Aerial Heaven where the Man-child was born. The Man-child is now grown up to man's estate, and is called Michael. In the fourth vision of Daniel, also, Michael is presented as the symbol of the United States.

I could not for a long time see the basis of this symbolism. I could not see the point of similarity between Michael and the United States, which always lies at the foundation of all symbolism.

But it is very plain. Michael is the Archangel—the Chief of the Hosts of God in heaven. Divine Inspiration always regards the United States from the standpoint of its future grandeur and glory, when it shall rule the whole earth in righteousness, for God. There is a striking fitness in the Leader of the Hosts of God in heaven being made the symbol of the United States, the great future leader of the Hosts of God on earth, during the grand millennial age.

Only the fact that there is to be a future war between the Dragon and Michael, between the Money Power and the United States, can be learned from this passage.

In the fourth vision of Daniel, there is a synchronous prophecy, which represents the Prussian empire as invading the United States. Speaking of the King who "shall do according to his will"—which is the Prussian empire—the angel tells Daniel that he shall overthrow many countries, and says:—"He shall enter also into the glorious land." *Daniel* xi: 49.

In Daniel VIII: 9, it is said of the Roman empire, there presented under the symbol of "a little horn," that it "waxed exceeding great toward the South, and toward the East, and toward the glorious land." As the Roman empire actually grew great toward the South, and East and West, it is manifest that its Westward growth is here set forth as a growth "toward the glorious land," the growth toward the East and South being previously mentioned. This shows that "the glorious land" lies toward the West of Europe. That designation can only point out the United States.

The Angel Called our Country "the Glorious Land," in view of its future destiny, as an Universal Republic, giving religion, liberty and civilization to the world throughout all coming ages. The warlike entrance of the Wilful King,—the Prussian empire,—into the Glorious Land, foretells a Prussian invasion of the United States.

Putting the two Prophecies Together, they Foretell an invasion of the United States, by the Prussian empire as the agent of the Money Power. In the future, the Money Power will exercise the power of the Prussian empire, as it now exercises the power of Great Britain. As it influenced the British government to invade China, and to conquer Egypt and Burmah, so it will influence the German empire, when extended over Southern and Western Europe, to invade the United States.

Prophecy does not say what cause of quarrel the Money Power will have against our country. It does not say whether we shall be utterly bankrupted as Egypt was, and unable to pay the interest on our vast debt to the Money Power; or whether we shall attempt to resist its encroachments before we are finally ruined, as Burmah did.

Whatever its ground of umbrage, the Money Power will set the Prussian empire upon us.

And Prussia will not be reluctant to undertake the conquest. Our Republic is a standing menace to monarchy. We are the most powerful nation on the globe; and our influence in the world is even mightier from our moral power, than from our national greatness. If things could go on prosperously with us for thirty years more, Europe would become Republican by the progress of liberal ideas. The despotic Prussian empire over Southern and Western Europe will never be safe while the Great Republic of the West stands. The stability of monarchical institutions requires that the American Republic shall be overthrown and subjugated.

The Invasion would not be Attempted with a small Army. Prussia, at the head of Southern and Western Europe, and backed by the unlimited loans of the Money Power, might easily put two million men in the field. It is probable that the army of invasion will reach that number. The British government, under the rule of the Tories, will give its support to the Prussian empire, and lend its fleets for the transportation of the invading army and its supplies. According to military probabilities, the line of invasion will be the St. Lawrence River and Lake Ontario, and thence down east of Lake Erie, in an attempt to take possession of the line of the Alleghanies, and cut off the Eastern and Middle States from the West and South.

And together with this, having command of the ocean, the invaders will probably attempt to seize and capture New York City from Long Island, and renew the attempt of Burgoyne to cut off New England from the West, by taking possession of the line of the Hudson.

The statements of Prophecy indicate a conflict of unexampled magnitude. Prussia invaded France with one million men; the rest of her forces being kept at home to guard the frontiers. And the invading army crushed France almost without a struggle. But when Prussia shall invade America, it will be Greek meeting Greek, and the mightiest conflict will ensue on which the sun has ever shone.

Eighteenth Coincidence of Fact:—"*The Dragon prevailed not; neither was their place found any more in heaven. And the great Dragon was cast out, he was cast out into the earth, and his angels were cast out with him.*"

When this great future conflict comes, we shall understand the design of Providence in permitting the outbreak of the late War. It will then be seen that our Civil War saved our country and the world. If, when this future invasion comes, we were distracted by a sectional issue, and unarmed, as we were in 1860, our position in the face of a grand invasion would be hopeless. Before we could prepare for war, the heel of the despot would be upon our neck. But when the invasion comes, we shall be thoroughly armed with the weapons of our Civil War; and, all distracting issues past, North and South will present a solid front to the foe. We shall be fighting for religion and liberty, for home and property rights. The country will be fired with unexampled enthusiasm. The fiery valor of the South will be united with the cool stubborn courage of the North; and together they will be irresistible. We learned in the late War the value of flanking movements, and developed a new arm of war in mounted infantry. When the invader shall march into the country, we will meet him in front, and envelope him with flanking movements. He must either fight or retreat. There will be quick, hard rapid fighting. Prophecy indicates that we press the fighting, and put the invaders on the defensive.

We attack; we defeat them; We drive them out of the country.

Thenceforth, the Money Power has no place in the United States.

Nineteenth Coincidence of Fact:—*It is said that the Dragon "deceiveth the whole world."*

The Money Power has deceived the whole world down to the present time. It has deceived the whole world as to its existence. It has hidden itself in its London den, and made the world believe that the agents it appointed to manage the companies it organized in the various countries, were the owners of the companies they manage. It has deceived the whole world as to the right laws of industry, making the world believe that the system of industry which is reducing the world to bankruptcy is beneficial to mankind. It has deceived and betrayed everybody who has trusted it, systematically "freezing out" those who have put money into enterprises controlled by it. It has deceived the whole world by booms in city property, and by booms in business enterprises, which it has started for the purpose of robbing the public of its money invested in them. It has deceived the whole world, and made it believe that prices should be left to regulate themselves by the law of supply and demand;—when it constantly regulates prices, by the might of capital, through the instrumentality of Boards of Trade, which are absolutely controlled by it. It deceives the whole world in making people believe that Capital is beneficent;—when it is using its capital to bankrupt the world, and reduce mankind to the condition of serfdom.—The Money Power is the Arch-deceiver.

Twentieth Coincidence of Fact:—*The Dragon is called "the accuser of our brethren."*

This will probably be fulfilled in the future. When the Money Power shall be exposed, the people of God will denounce it from pulpit and platform. Then the Money Power, through the papers which it controls, will denounce all who take ground against it with all manner of false accusation.

So fearful will be its accusations, that only they will dare assail it, who take their life in their hand, and "love not their lives unto the death." In many papers, the Jews own a majority of the stock, and have them completely under their control. Others they will suborn with bribes. The Shimeis of the press will be manifest as the mouthpieces of the Dragon, by their accusations of those who expose the Money Power.

Twenty-first Coincidence of Fact:—*But the accused overcame the Dragon, "by the blood of the Lamb, and by the word of their testimony."*

God reigns. The Money Power shall fall, though all wealth and influence and power be on its side. They who expose it, though they be "the weak of this world shall confound the mighty."

But they will "overcome him," not by human might, but "by the blood of the Lamb, and by the word of their testimony." The "blood of the Lamb" has redeemed the human race from the thralldom of evil; and He, unto whom "all power in heaven and earth is given," will not suffer the Money Power to deprive mankind of its promised Millennium of blessedness, and grind it down beneath oppression and wrong. He will guard His servants,—will give "the word of their testimony" power to rouse the people.—Let them present "the word of their testimony,"—the testimony of prophecy against the Dragon, which will be the power of God to overthrow this titanic evil.

Twenty-second Coincidence of Fact:—*Divine inspiration here calls the Dragon "that old serpent called the devil and Satan."*

The Jew Money Power is the embodiment of evil in the Latter Days. It is the enemy of God and man. The Jew Money Kings are infidel to a man. They embody the very spirit of Antichrist: holding only to the unity of God, they "deny both the Father and the Son." They wish to break down all industry, as it has heretofore existed in the world: They wish to break down all business men, and reduce them to poverty, and dependence on themselves: They wish to break down society as it now exists, and reorganize it on the basis of their own ascendency, and the subordination of mankind to them: They loathe Christianity, and wish to break it down and substitute for it an infidel Judaism. Hoping to establish a universal monarchy under the rule of a Jewish king, they are in principle opposed to Republicanism. Desiring, in this country, to take from the people all their property and reduce them to the condition of peasants, they know that they can not accomplish their aims while Republicanism exists. They know that a free people will not submit to such wrong, and that they can only establish their power by the overthrow of Republicanism.

Already from some of their agents we have ominous utterances of a purpose to subvert Republicanism. If the Money Power should get possession of our farms, and succeed in breaking down the business men of our towns, the days of the Republic will be numbered. Then we may fear that the state of things suggested in the following article in the Nevada *Chronicle*, will be inaugurated:—

"We need a stronger government; the wealth of the country [the Money Power and its agents] demands it. * * * * * The Capital of the country demands protection. The wealth of the country has to bear the burden of the government, and it shall control it. The people are becoming educated up to this theory rapidly, and the sooner this theory is recognized in the constitution and the laws, the better it will be for the people. * * * * * To avert fearful bloodshed,—a *strong central government should be established, as soon as possible.*"

The Money Kings will establish an empire in this country, if they get possession of all industry and property.

It will not be difficult for them to bring it about. With their absolute control of industry, they can make times so hard as to cause intolerable suffering. Stopping the construction of railroads, and city improvements, and manufactures and iron mills, they can fill the country with hundreds of thousands of starving tramps. They can then get their paid emissaries to pretend great sympathy for the people, *as their emissaries lead the Nihilists of Russia, and the Liberals of Central Europe and Italy.* And when they become popular leaders, they can easily excite the starving people to outbreaks and insurrections. Such outbreaks are always easily suppressed by military force; and in the victory over the outbreaks, an Imperial government might be established. Such outbreaks are always suppressed; and their suppression is the method by which Republics are converted into imperial despotisms.

Let the Money Power succeed in carrying out its aims, and our country is ruined. The grand yeomanry of our country is our pride and safety. It is the backbone of the Republic—the strong column that upholds the temple of our liberties and our Christian civilization. Let our farmers lose their farms, and our yeomanry become peasants, and all is lost.

This is the greatest crisis the world has ever known. Upon its issue depends the destiny of mankind forever. It will determine whether the world shall go on to a millennium of liberty, peace and blessedness, or be crushed by the triumph of the forces that are striving to arrest the progress of our age, and bring upon the world a new Feudal Era, in which the mass of mankind will be reduced to the condition of serfdom beneath the yoke of an Aristocracy of Jew Money Kings, who will grind man down beneath the heel of oppression forever.

For, that yoke, once fixed upon the world, can never be shaken off. The Money Kings, with a mighty government under their control, would keep the masses of mankind reduced to the condition of peasants in hopeless bondage. In this age of warfare with cannon and gunpowder, an unarmed peasantry could never cast off the yoke of the Money Power, in control of the government, and having possession of all wealth.—There are two Millenniums before the world: one, a millennium of peace and blessedness, under the reign of Liberty and Religion; the other, the reign of Oppression and Wrong, under the rule of the Money Power. The present crisis will determine which shall dominate the earth, from now to the end of time. The destinies of the Future are now hanging in the balance. Either the Money Power must go down, or the hopes of humanity must set in darkness.

Well is the Money Power called Satan, for it is the very incarnation of Satanic malignity and evil.

Who can doubt that the Great Red Dragon is the symbol of the Jew London Money Power? Its identity with it is proved by six Historical Marks—by twenty wonderful Parallelisms of Character—and by twenty-two strange and startling Coincidences of Fact. There are thus forty-eight separate and distinct points of resemblance; in respect of historical facts, of resemblances of character, and of coincidences between facts mentioned of the symbol and facts true of the Money Power. The proofs that the Dragon is the symbol of the Money Power are just eight times as numerous as those which prove that the Lion with Eagle's

Wings is the symbol of the Babylonian empire, or the Bear, the symbol of the Persian empire; and, in their strange and wonderful similarities, these proofs are a hundredfold stronger than those which identify any of the other symbols of the prophetic scriptures with the powers they set forth. Divine Inspiration has heaped proof upon proof, evidence upon evidence, until the mind almost wearies of it; and until no dispassionate mind can resist the mass of evidence that forces conviction.

The proof presented in this work is not one-sixth of the evidence presented in the prophetic scriptures, that the London Money Power is the grand Imperialism so bitterly denounced in the Bible as the great Archenemy of God and man; and which is foretold in prophecy, as destined to rise and be overthrown, in the Latter Days. When all the evidence is before the public, it will convince the most incredulous mind that God, in the inspired prophecies of scripture, has depicted the Dragon in this perfectly unmistakable manner, in order to save mankind from its power.

PART III.

THE REMEDY.

As I have lectured on the Money Power, I have frequently been asked what is the remedy for our present evils? And I have been compelled to promise that, when I published my work on the Money Power, I would present my views as to the proper remedy for the evils that now afflict our country. This must be my excuse for discussing questions pertaining to political economy in a work having for its special aim to present the Money Power as set forth in prophecy.

If further excuse be needed, it may be found in the fact, that when, thirty-four years ago, I discovered that the prophecies of the Latter Days set forth especially the events of our age, I perceived that, industry being the grandest factor in the march of advancement in our time, no one could understand the prophecies of the Latter Days without understanding the laws which govern industry. I was therefore led to study the principles of Political Economy, not from the standpoint of Adam Smith, who wrote in the days of household hand manufactures and wagon transportation, but from the standpoint of the Age of Steam.

As I discovered the evils of the Money Power from its violations of the Laws of Political Economy, it seems proper, after tracing its rise and its ravages upon industry, to present the principles of Political Economy violated by it, and the proper means of remedying the evils it has caused.

CHAPTER I.

PREREQUISITES TO ANY REMEDY.

A great and fundamental error exists, as to the proper means of remedying the industrial evils of our time. People think they are to be *remedied by governmental legislation.* But the industrial evils of our time arise out of *a false industrial* System. To remedy the evils, the False Industrial System must be overthrown.

There are measures of governmental legislation that are essential, in order to the remedying of these evils. But the evils that now exist in the business world can not be remedied by legislation alone. Before we can even think of discussing the legislative remedies, there are two preliminary points necessary to be attained.

I. FIRST PREREQUISITE TO A BETTER STATE OF THINGS: MORE LIGHT.

The first essential to a better state of things is for our people to understand what is the cause of our present industrial evils. The physician must diagnose a case before he can suggest a remedy. Everybody knows that the times are out of joint, but nobody seems to know what is the cause. The American people must know what the Money Power is doing. The whole country must know that the cause of all our troubles is a knot of Jew Capitalists in London—that they have been breaking down our business men, for over twenty years—breaking ten thousand great business houses, every year, besides many thousands of small business men whose failure in not recorded — that they are now breaking down the business men of our towns, and are putting prices of farming produce so low as to ruin our farmers:—our people must know all this—and I do not believe they will suffer the Money Power to continue its work of ruin.

Light must be diffused by the dissemination of the views presented in this work.

THE CHRISTIAN MINISTRY,

especially, needs to be awake on the subject.— The Christian ministry should set before the people the teachings of the Word of God with regard to the Money Power. They can do it without leaving their sphere of bible teachings. The moral sentiment of the age is shocked by the course of the Money Power; and the exponents of the principles of truth and righteousness, as set forth in the precepts of the Christian religion, cannot afford to be silent.

No great cause has ever triumphed in Modern Times, without the advocacy of the pulpit. Many wrongs have been stricken down in the past; but this, the mightiest of all wrongs, remains. It too must fall; and it would shame the church, were the Christian ministry to have no share in the honor of freeing the world from this Titanic evil.

The Ministry has had, perforce, to remain silent in the past, because the people have been divided in sentiment: Labor has made the mistake of confounding all employers with the Money Power; and the Ministry could not take part in a class feud, but had, of necessity, to remain neutral. In this work, the proper distinction is made; and it is shown that the Money Power is oppressing our merchants and farmers even more than Labor.

We now have the right issue presented. There should, in future, be no division of sentiment among our people. In taking ground against the Money Power, the pulpit will be championing the rights of the people in the pews,— business men, farmers and wage earners.

The Christian Ministry have weightier obligations resting upon them, in our age, for the promotion of the well-being of the human race, than in any past era. By taking the lead in enlightening the people, and aiding in the suppression of the fearful wrongs that are now prevailing, they have an opportunity that rarely occurs in the history of the world, to gain the highest place for Christianity in the confidence and gratitude of mankind. By taking ground against the Money Power, and presenting it as it is foretold in the prophetic scriptures, they may render the highest service to the cause of God, and take their stand at the head of the united movement of our people for the preservation of the rights we hold most dear from the encroachments of the Money Power.

As, in the midst of primeval Chaos, God spoke the word of power, "LET THERE BE LIGHT,"—and order began its reign, until Chaos disappeared; so now, from the inspired fountain of revealed truth let light beam forth upon the world from every pulpit, and the Chaos that pervades our business will disappear, and the harmonious laws which govern industry will resume their sway, giving to mankind in the greater industrial advantages of our time, a grand era of prosperity and advancement such as the world has never known.

II. SECOND PREREQUISITE TO A BETTER STATE OF THINGS:—UNITY AMONG OUR PEOPLE.

Our People Must Stand Together. Our greatest misfortune has been the divisions among our people. Every class of industry has, unfortunately, been forming *class organizations*, and the different classes are full of the spirit of rivalry.—The farmers have a separate organization, and seek their own interests, without any thought of the interests of the other industrial classes; and often, in the pursuit of their own interests, they work an injury to the mercantile class.—The Labor of the country organizes separately, and consults its separate interests, without consideration for the other classes of industry.

This is the first great evil that needs to be remedied. Until this is effected nothing can be done; all measures of legislation will be hopeless, and even if enacted, will be fruitless of beneficial result.

The Money Power finds Strength in our Divisions; and it can be Proved that it Foments them.—Every Imperialism that has ever risen on the earth has risen through the disunion of those whom it conquered.—Thus, Macedon rose through the disunion of Greece. The states of Greece were, if united, much more powerful than Macedon. But their disunion prevented all concerted action. At last, Athens and Thebes opposed Macedon at Cheronea, with almost equal forces, and their defeat prostrated Greece before the Macedonian power.—Rome also rose through the disunion of the states which she conquered.—And so, the Money Power is establishing its Imperialism over our industries, and breaking our business men, *through the disunion of our people!!*

The Working People have seen the evils of the times, and have known that something is wrong; but they did not know the cause of the evils which prevail. They rightly attributed the evils of the times to Capital. But, not knowing that the evils are all owing to a knot of foreign capitalists, they have drawn the line at the wrong place between Labor and Capital,—just above Labor. They have confounded our business men with the Money Power.

We need to draw the line at the right place,—just below the Money Power and its agencies. All below that line,—the business men and Labor class,—are in the same boat: their interests are identical. Men engaged in individual business never injure Labor: Labor has nothing to fear from independent business men: independent business men have nothing to fear from Labor. They are allies. Both have everything to fear from the Money Power.

The Money Power has not, as yet, greatly injured Labor in this country: wages are generally as good now, as they were twenty years ago. The Money Power has been busy warring upon the business class. It has been breaking the business men, rank after rank, year by year, for twenty years.—When it gets the business men all broke—when the merchants and grocers of our towns are all ruined, and our farmers are all reduced to serfdom—then the time of the laboring men will come. Then, when none can resist, the Money Power will oppress Labor in this country, as it oppresses the Labor of India, as it oppresses the Labor of Great Britain, as it now oppresses the coal miners of Illinois and Pennsylvania. Then, it will grind down our whole population into a writhing mass of poverty and wretchedness, earning barely wages sufficient for subsistence—barely sufficient to sustain a weary, wretched loathed life.

The Money Power is the source of danger to all classes of our people; and, if we are to be saved from it, our people of all classes must unite together against it for self-preservation.

I repeat it, we must draw the line high up, just below the Money Kings, and their agencies. All those below that line—if they wish to escape the ruin the Money Power is purposing to inflict upon us all—must all unite, to check its encroachments, and to promote the common interests of all. All must unite,—all classes of business men engaged in independent business, and all classes of wage earners. Manufacturers, merchants, grocers, bankers, builders, miners, farmers—professional men of all kinds—all employees, of railroads, farms, mines, mills, shops, stores,—men of all classes—and men of all political parties, republican, democratic, labor, Temperance—all must unite, and stand shoulder to shoulder in this common cause, to protect our property and our homes from the clutches of the Money Power.

No effort of any one class, or any one party, will be of any avail. The experience of the past proves that. The farmers tried it in the Grange movement, and it accomplished only partial results: the Labor party has tried it, and without success.

The Money Power knows that these class movements must of necessity fail, *and it encourages them, on purpose to have them fail.*

The American Grange movement originated in England. The very name proves it. "Grange" is not an American word: it is in use in England, to designate an old farm manor. The Money Kings, when they favored the Grange, thinking to divide the American people, did not know that the name assumed would betray the English origin of the movement. They wanted the American farmers to go into a separate movement, in which, like Ishmaelites, their hand would be against every man, and every man's hand against them, in order to deprive them of the sympathy of all the other business classes; so that when the time came for the Money Power to devour them, there would be none to sympathize with them, or interfere in their behalf. It was a shrewd move on the part of the Money Power, and it had, in some measure, its effect.—The Money Power is an Imperialism, and, as is the case with all rising empires, its policy is to divide and conquer. If it can keep the American people divided, it will surely devour us all, and complete the ruin of the country.

The farmers can do nothing alone: the Labor people

can do nothing alone: the business men of the towns and cities can do nothing alone. But united all together in a grand defensive "UNION," they will be irresistible by the Money Power. Let such a "UNION" be formed, and the country will be safe. The Money Power can do what it pleases against a divided people: against a united people it can do nothing.

The Money Power is afraid of such a "Union" of the American people against it; and with its consummate shrewdness, it has taken measures to prevent, by law, any such Union. In the beef Convention which met in St. Louis last spring, the emissaries of the Money Power who were in large attendance on the Convention, and opposed the adoption of some measures that were proposed, made no opposition to the law that was proposed against Trusts, but were pleased with it. For, that proposed law, not only prohibited combinations of Capitalists in Trusts to raise prices, but it prohibited all union of individuals for the purpose of raising prices. If that law should be passed, and the necessary combination of the people be prevented, the country will be ruined.

Trusts,—combinations of Capital,—ought to be prohibited. But it is absolutely necessary that the right of the people to unite for self-protection should be distinctly recognized. It is not necessary, in order to prevent capitalists from combining to ruin the country, to prohibit the people from uniting in their own defense. It would be a foolish law, which, in order to suppress burglary, should prohibit honest men from having weapons in their houses.

The effect of such a law against Trusts, unless carefully guarded, would be evil. It would only prevent the union of our people for self-defense. Capitalists would evade it.

The proposed law shows the wish of the Money Power. It is like its cunning to avail itself of the inadvertence of the people to get a law passed in all the Western States, which prohibited the united effort of the people to resist its domination. Once placed upon the statute book, the Money Power would see that it was enforced, and would thus suppress all efforts of the people to unite against it. Let the proposed law against Trusts be passed everywhere;—but let it simply prohibit Trusts, or combinations of Capital for the purpose of raising prices; and let it distinctly state that the law does not prohibit a combination on the part of the people of the country to regulate prices in the interest of the people.

For a "Union" of the American people is imperatively necessary, to enable us to protect ourselves. An organized "UNION" of the whole American people, of all classes, and all parties, is an indispensable condition of any successful effort at self-protection. Without it, no public legislation, by the state or the Federal government, will do any good. Without it, no separate combination of farmers, or of labor, or of the merchants of our towns, will be of any avail. We want a "UNION" of the farmers, of the business men of our towns, of Labor in all its departments,—a general

UPRISING OF THE WHOLE AMERICAN PEOPLE.

Such an organization alone, without any legislation, will be far more effective than all legislation without such organization. Such an organization is indispensable. We can not do without it. It is mere driveling folly to talk about a remedy for the evils of our time without it. I wish to emphasize this point. For, to seek a remedy in an organization of any one class, farmers, or Labor, or merchants, is merely a waste of time. Nothing will save us but an organization of the whole American people against the Money Power.

The work we have to do is the work of such an Organization. The remedy for the evils of our time will be found in certain remedial measures to be carried out by such an Organization, and which only such an Organization can carry out and make effective. All legislation is merely to help this Organization in its work.

But before entering upon the subject, I wish to explain my position, that I may not be misunderstood.

III. THE AUTHOR'S POSITION.

I am very conservative. I am not in favor of any measures more radical than are absolutely necessary to save the country. I do not desire to suggest any measures which are not necessary to this end. I am not in favor of Communism or Socialism. I want no new state of things; but I want to preserve the old state of things, and to maintain the rights that are still left us.

I want our farmers to be able to pay off their debts, and keep their farms. I want the merchants of our towns to keep their business, and not be driven out by Jew stores. I want good prices to be restored for farm products, and good times to be re-established in our towns. I want to stop the loss of their farms by farmers through low prices; and the breaking down of our merchants, by the stores started by the Money Power all over the country.

If the Money Power would consent to a compromise, stop its encroachments, and re-establish good prices, I, for one, would be willing to accept the compromise. I would be willing to let the Money Kings keep what they have already plundered from our people. But I do want to defend the rights, and the property, that still remain to us. I do want to oppose a firm barrier of a united people against the deluge of destruction that is overspreading our land, and to say to the Money Power, "Thus far hast thou come, here let thy rage be stayed." I do wish to say to these Money Kings, "Keep what you have, but you cannot have anything more: you cannot ruin the merchants of our towns, and take their business away;

nor oust our farmers from their farms, by forcing down the price of farming produce so low that the farmers cannot support their families and pay their debts."

We need no radical measures to restore prosperity, if the Money Power will now do right. We only need fair prices for farming produce. Let the farmers have fair prices, and they will be able to pay wages and interest and taxes—and support their families so well that they can spend enough in town to give prosperity to the merchants and townsfolk, and still have something toward the payment of the principal of their debt, every year. Four or five years of fair prices will enable the farmers to pay off their mortgages.—And we have a right to demand fair prices for our produce. The Money Power should not be suffered to crush our farmers and merchants in the folds of its capital, as it has crushed the New York merchants, the oil well owners of Pennsylvania, the pork packers of Louisville, Cincinnati and St. Louis, and other classes of our business men.

But the Money Power will not consent to any compromise. It will never agree to do right. It is bent upon crushing down prices and getting possession of all the farms, and crushing out all the merchants of our towns. Therefore, we must, despite the Money Power, raise the prices of farming produce; or we are ruined. This is the issue between the American people and the Jew London Money Power. And upon this issue, there will arise a stern conflict; and, in that conflict, the whole American people must be united. Our whole people must enter into an organized "UNION," in a grand general purpose to control the Money Power.

We must "Bind the Dragon." The Binding of the Dragon will be done effectually, by and by, just before the Millennium begins. We must do it now, at least so far as is necessary to save our country and the world from its domination, and prevent the destruction of all our property and all our rights.

We now come to the consideration of the practical **Remedy** for present industrial evils.

Chapter II.

RIGHT PRINCIPLES OF POLITICAL ECONOMY, IN ACCORDANCE WITH WHICH ALL BUSINESS SHOULD BE CONDUCTED.

All the troubles of our age have arisen out of violations of fundamental principles of Political Economy, without which there can be no general or enduring prosperity. Before we can properly understand the remedy for our present evils, we must comprehend the principles of Political Economy, whose violation has caused them.

It is time for us to re-establish the broken down principles of Political Economy, whose violation has brought our country to the verge of ruin.

FIRST PRINCIPLE of Political Economy:— Every Country, and Every Section of Country Should Have Currency Enough to Raise and Ship its Own Products, and Do its Own Business.

The justice of this principle, in its application to nations, is apparent as soon as it is stated. We can see that it would be ruinous for France to be dependent upon England for currency to raise and market its products.

But this is our own present condition. We are one of the countries of which the Englishman in his pamphlet said " English capital ships the products of all countries, and does almost all the interior production." He says that the wheat of Russia and the cotton of Egypt and the lumber of Norway and Sweden and Poland are carried by English capital to the port of shipment. And it may now be added that the cotton, the wheat, the hogs, the beef and all the other products of the United States are shipped to market by English capital.

It is necessary, not only that each country should have money enough to raise and ship its own products, but that every section of country should have enough money to raise and ship its own products. Our country is more extensive than half of Europe; and it would be as reasonable for all Central and Western Europe to be dependent upon Italy for currency, as for one section of the United States to have all the currency, and the other sections to be dependent upon it for money to carry on their business.

And here is to be found one great trouble in our condition, at present: our currency is not equally distributed throughout the country. The greenbacks and the gold and silver are not localized, and have almost all drifted into the East, and are owned there. And our National banks, are, most of them, owned in the East. Massachusetts has more national banking currency than all the states North of the latitude of the Ohio river, extending from the Alleganies to the Pacific; and more than all the states south of the Ohio river, extending from the Atlantic to the Pacific. And Massachusetts has not nearly so much national banking capital as the Middle States.—Indeed, almost all our capital is in the East. The West and South have not nearly enough currency to raise and move their products.

This state of things is utterly incompatible with any degree of prosperity to those moneyless sections. We need imperatively the equalization of our currency, in its distribution in the different sections of the country.

SECOND PRINCIPLE: — Every Section of Country Should Have an Equable Currency, Not Liable to Sudden Contractions Causing Wide-spread Panic and Disaster.

This was the trouble with our old State Bank System. The currency was then upon a specie basis; and the Money Kings could, at any time, withdraw enough Specie from the country to cause a panic and compel a suspension of specie payments, followed by a great contraction and wide-spread ruin.

And the Money Power, now, has our currency in a condition in which the Money Kings can bring on a Money panic, whenever they wish, as bad as those of 1837 and 1857 and 1873. Our currency is now in a wretched condition, placing our prosperity completely at the mercy of the Money Kings, enabling them to crush it at any time they choose.—This question will be treated at large further on.

THIRD PRINCIPLE: — The People of Every Section of Country Should Always Do the Business of the Section; Shipping its Produce, and Buying and Selling All Articles Imported for Consumption.

Any section of country that fails to do this, will necessarily fall into poverty, while the people who buy its products and sell to it its imports will be enriched at its expense.

This is what is the matter with our country now: the London Money Power is buying and shipping all our products, and selling us all our imports. Until this condition of things is stopped, and our own people in every section do all the trading for the section, buying and shipping its products, and buying and selling its imports, we cannot have any general and enlarged prosperity.

FOURTH PRINCIPLE:—Every Country and Every Section of Country Should First Supply its Own Wants Out of Its Produce, Only Shipping Abroad the Surplus. And it is an Advantage to the Country for this Surplus to be Exported, as Far as Practicable, in a Manufactured Form.

The whole system of British commerce is based upon a violation of this great cardinal principle of Political Economy. The Money Kings buy produce from all over the world and transport it to England, and import food for their operatives, and then send their British manufactures all over the earth for a market. And the Money Kings have introduced the same system into the domestic consumption of this country. The wheat of the West is carried to the East to be manufactured into flour, and the flour is brought back to the West for consumption. The hogs and beef cattle of the West are taken to Chicago to be killed, and the bacon and lard and dressed beef are brought back to the West for market. The cotton of the South is carried to England for manufacture, and the manufactured goods are brought back to the South for sale.

This system is good for the railroads and shipping of the Money Kings, who make the profit on the transportation. But it is ruinous to our country; and such a system ought to be broken up.

FIFTH PRINCIPLE:—On the other hand, if any community does not produce enough of any article for its consumption, it is the interest of the community to import the article in a raw state, in order to diminish its cost, and secure the profit of its manufacture at home.

It is obedience to this principle that has made England so rich, and its violation has impoverished the rest of the world. England imports raw products, and sells manufactured articles. The United States sells raw products, and buys manufactured articles. England buys cheap raw products, and sells high manufactured goods. We sell cheap and buy high. England gets rich; we grow poor.

What is true of nations is true of sections Each section should, as far as possible, sell its produce in a manufactured form; and each section should, as far as possible, buy its imports in a raw state, and manufacture them for the supply of its own wants.

This single principle is so important that it would revolutionize the industrial life of our country and our age.

SIXTH PRINCIPLE:—The Prices of Every Country For Agricultural Products, For Manufactured products, And For Labor, Should All be Fixed at An Equable Standard, and Properly Adjusted To Each Other.

The evils of our country are largely owing to a violation of this principle. We have no equable standard of prices. Some industries are flourishing, while others are languishing. Our manufactures flourish; our farmers are on the verge of bankruptcy. Some of our wage earners, protected by Trade Unions, are getting fair wages; while others, without any protection, as the coal miners of Illinois and Pennsylvania, are receiving starvation wages.—With us, prices are the result of conflict and war, rather than the subject of proper and equable adjustment. Laborers who can combine in Trade Unions, secure fair prices for labor as the result of the war of strikes; while laborers in industries where such combination is not practicable are crushed down at the will of the employer. Lines of business which can regulate prices by combination secure fair profits; while other lines of business in which such combination is impracticable, are being reduced to bankruptcy.

This state of things should not be suffered to endure any longer. The industries owned by the Money Power can combine and secure protection for themselves; but, except certain classes of wage earners who can protect themselves by Trade Unions, all classes of American independent industry are now helpless, and at the mercy of the Money Power. We want a grand "UNION" of all classes of independent American industry, which will secure to all equally fair prices, mutually and equably adjusted in relation to each other. This will be a great advance upon anything that the world has ever hitherto known, and will be a grand stride toward the great coming Age of blessedness to the world.

Mankind never makes any advance, except under stress of imperative necessity. It is thus that a benign Providence overrules evil for good. In the end, the outrageous wrongs of the Money Power will work a great advantage to humanity, by compelling the world to organize for self-protection against it, in a grand "UNION," where each will care for the interests of all, and bring into the relations of business life the principles of strict justice, and the brotherly love embodied in the Golden Rule.

SEVENTH PRINCIPLE:— The Price of the Entire Products of a Country Ought Not to be Fixed By the Price of a Small Surplus Exported to a Foreign Country;— But, In Every Country, The Standard of Prices Should Be Fixed At Home, And Adjusted to the General Status of Prices Maintained By Tariff and The Amount of Currency, Without Regard to the Price of The Small Amount of Products Exported to the Foreign Market.

The Money Power violates this principle constantly, in its dealings with this country. We have no standard of prices. The Money Kings are constantly crushing prices down. They are at continual war with the farmers, crushing down the price of agricultural produce; at constant war with our merchants, putting down the profits of business by rival stores established by them; and at constant war with Labor, crushing down the rate of wages.

And they put down the price of our entire production, to accord with the price of a small export to England. For instance, we export one-fourth of our crop of wheat; and they put down the price of the other three-fourths, which is consumed at home, to the price of the Liverpool market.—They ship a few cargoes of wheat from India, raised on their own jungle plantations, and store it in Liverpool at a nominal price, in order by that means to put down the price of the whole crop of American wheat.

This is an outrage; for India cannot supply the English market with wheat. Its small export should have no effect upon the market at all.—Suppose two butchers should combine, and buy an ox in the spring of the year, and put it in a farmer's pasture and hold it at two cents a pound; and then should want to put down all the beef of the county to the same price, by means of the single ox. Suppose the butchers should say to the farmers, "There is an ox out in Blank's pasture which is held at two cents a pound; and you must sell me your beef cattle at the same price!" The farmers would laugh at them, and tell them to go and buy the cheap ox and kill it, and then come and pay them their price for their beef cattle. —And yet these Money Kings, with their few cargoes of India wheat, owned by themselves, and held in store for the purpose of "*bearing*" the market down, are putting down the price of the entire wheat production of the United States! We should tell them, as the farmers would tell the butchers about the ox, "Buy the India wheat, and grind and sell it, and then pay us a fair price for our wheat." But instead, we allow them to put down the price of our entire crop by this shallow trick!

By this outrage, and by fixing prices arbitrarily in Boards of Trade, under their absolute control, they annually cheat our farmers out of hundreds of millions of dollars, and thus keep our country in poverty.

This way of allowing the Money Kings to fix our prices at their own will, must be broken up. The prices of our country are fixed upon the basis of a high tariff: those of England, upon a free trade basis. Our prices are fixed upon the basis of a liberal paper currency, and a basis of bimetalism, using both silver and gold: those of England are based upon a scarce paper currency, and a basis of monometalism, using gold only. Our high tariff, and our larger currency place the United States upon a basis of liberal prices: the free trade and sparse currency of England place her upon a basis of low prices.—How oppressive, then, to fix our prices at the English standard. We must have our prices equalized, in accordance with our basis of tariff and larger currency, and not have them regulated by the standard of English prices. We should take a firm stand here, and resolve that we will no longer submit to this trickery of the Money Kings, but that we will regulate the prices of our own country upon an equable standard for everything, fairly adjusted in relation to each other.

EIGHTH PRINCIPLE:—The Railroads Of Every Country Should Be Owned By the People of The Country.

The Railroad Question has been a very perplexing problem. Many persons, in order to solve the difficulty, have proposed that the Government should own all the railroads. Governmental ownership of railroads may do for a centralized monarchy; but it will not answer for a free Republic. It centralizes too much power in the hands of the Government, and such large ownership of property by the Government is inconsistent with the safety of Republican institutions.—And besides, it is too much wealth to be taken out of the sphere of investment. When, after a while, the world shall be fully developed, the corporate property of the earth will amount to many thousand billions of dollars. This vast corporate property will greatly add to the wealth of mankind. To lock it up in the hands of Government will always keep mankind poor, and make the Government corrupt.

The railroads of every section of country ought to be in the ownership of the people of that section. This is the only proper disposition to make of the Railroad Question.

If the People of one country own all the transportation of another country, they are sure to reduce the people of that country to utter poverty, and get possession of all their property. It is absolutely essential to the prosperity of a country that its people shall own its railroads.

This principle is violated in the ownership of our railroads by the Money Kings. It will be a most important part of the work of the proposed "UNION" to rectify this matter.

NINTH PRINCIPLE:—Every Country Should Have Half Enough Shipping to Do Its Import And Export Trade.

The necessity for this is apparent, without argument. If a nation had shipping enough to carry *all* its imports and exports, it would thereby have such an advantage over the people of other countries, as would, in the end, result in its engrossing their wealth to itself. But, by every country having half enough shipping to carry its imports and exports, all is equalized, and the wealth of the world remains in equilibrium.

We feel deeply, as a nation, the loss of our commercial marine. It will be a most important work of the proposed "UNION" to adopt measures that will bring about the rebuilding of our commercial navy, until we shall have at least half enough shipping to carry on our export and import commerce.

TENTH PRINCIPLE:—A Foreign Imperialism of Capital Can not be Allowed to Own Vast Bodies of Land and City Property, In A Country, Without Thereby Reducing the People of That Country, In The End, To Poverty.

This principle has been violated in the wide ownership of real estate in this country by the Money Kings. They have planted parasite investments on every side, which *are eating into the heart of our national life.* The investments which they have made are theirs. If ever obtained from them, they should be honestly paid for at a fair price. But it is necessary to the well-being of our country that those investments should be in the ownership of our own people. In the end, the proposed "UNION" would crown itself with honor in bringing about this desirable end.

The above principles are undoubtedly correct. Their truth might easily be demonstrated; but the deplorable condition of things in our country which has been caused by their violation, is sufficient evidence of their correctness. The violation of them will surely lead to the centralization of all industry and wealth in the hands of some one nation, and the ruin of all other nations. On the other hand, the maintenance of them will secure the prosperity of all nations, and prevent the centralization of all wealth and industry in one country, or one section of a country.

From the above principles it is evident that all our evils arise out of a Grand Industrial System established by the Money Kings. The evils do not rise out of measures of legislation; and consequently measures of legislation will not cure them. They rise out of a False Industrial System; and the only remedy is the overthrow of the False Industrial System.

The False Industrial System cannot be overthrown by

legislation. It can only be overthrown by an organized "UNION" of the whole American people.

Certain legislation is necessary, in order to enable the proposed "UNION" to properly perform its work. But it is only such an "UNION" that can make the legislation effective.

I shall treat the subject in the following chapters under the following divisions:—

1st. Measures of legislation Necessary to be adopted in order to enable the proposed "UNION" to remedy the Industrial evils of our times;

2nd. Proper Method of organizing the "UNION;"

3rd. Work of the organized "UNION."

The Remedy for the evils of our time is to be found in no one of the above, but in them all,—in the "UNION" and its work; and in the measures necessary to enable the "UNION" to do its work.

We must put these principles into operation. Some of them may be furthered by legislation; but most of them must be carried into effect by the organized "UNION" of the people. And the only use of legislation is to enable the "UNION" to act with effect.

CHAPTER III.

MEASURES OF LEGISLATION NECESSARY, TO ENABLE THE PROPOSED "UNION" TO REMEDY THE INDUSTRIAL EVILS OF OUR TIME.

As has been said, the special evils to be remedied are the low price of farming products, and the breaking down of the Tradesmen of our towns by the establishments of stores run by agents of the Money Power. It will be readily seen that these objects can not be accomplished by any public legislation alone, but can only be effected by an organized "UNION" of all industrial classes.

But, in order that the "UNION" may do its work properly, certain acts of legislation are necessary to enable it to act efficiently; and other legislation, also, is needed, that will so control the Money Power, as to prevent it from crushing the people with its capital, while they are putting things to rights.

I. FIRST MEASURE:—**Trusts Must Be Suppressed.**

But the legislature, as has already been stated, should be very careful, in framing the act, to avoid putting any hindrance in the way of the organization of the people for self-protection.—This measure can be best effected by State legislation.

II. SECOND MEASURE:—**Dealing in Futures in Agricultural Products Should be Prohibited.**

Where agricultural products are purchased, there should be in all cases actual delivery. This, to prevent the artificial fixing of prices by the Money Kings, by fictitious transactions in Boards of Trade.—This measure, also, can be accomplished by State Legislation.

III. THIRD MEASURE:—**All Joint Stock Corporations Should be Required to Enter The List of Their Stockholders Upon Public Record.**

The public ought to know who are the stockholders of these grand corporations which are owning so much property in this country. The Money Kings should not be suffered to hide their personality, any longer, behind joint stock corporations.

And there should be the strictest precautions against fraudulent entries. Any fraudulent entry of false stockholders should be penal, and should forfeit the stock. And, to prevent agents from holding the stock in Trust, and entering it in their own name as their own property, it should be the actual property of the person so entering it, as against any other claimant; and, if the entry were afterward found to be fraudulent, the stock should be forfeited by the original owner.—This legislation, also, can be established by State Legislation.

IV. FOURTH MEASURE:—**In All Cases of Strikes of Employees of Large Corporations, There Should be a Board of Arbitration to Arrange the Difficulty on a Just Scale of Wages.**

The justice of this is apparent without discussion. Strikes are only a species of Industrial warfare. In the Dark Ages, when courts of judicature did not settle business disputes between individuals, such disputes were brought to the arbitrament of "Private War." With the advance of civilization, "Private War" has been banished from society, except that a remnant of it continues, in the industrial world, to distract business by great strikes. Public adjudication should adjust these disputes in respect of wages, without leaving them to the arbitrament of "Private War." For there is no greater justice in the arbitrament of "Private War" in strikes, than when differences were settled by jousts in the lists. It is only a question whether the poor can endure frightful suffering long enough to exhaust the purse of the Money Kings. *It is a question of money against life.* The Money Kings should not be suffered, by the might of capital, to crush down labor into starving wages; but the ægis of public protection should be extended over the working people, to protect them from the oppression of the Money Kings.

If the proposed "UNION" is to succeed, it can only do so by the hearty co-operation of all industrial classes in the "UNION." If the working people, who are the great mass of consumers, come into the "UNION" to help raise prices, and save the farmers and the merchants of our towns, then those classes, in turn, must be willing to accord their hearty protection to the Working People against the wrongs and the oppression of the Money Power.—This, also, can be accomplished by State Legislation.

V. FIFTH MEASURE: — **The Half Bushel Should be Made the Legal Measure for all Grain.**

This will prevent the cheating of the farmers, by making No. 1 wheat rate as No. 2, and No. 2 rate as No. 3. And it will also secure to the farmers fair weights and measures for their grain.—This measure also may be accomplished by State Legislation.

But there are measures of very great importance, for which Congressional legislation will be necessary:

VI. SIXTH MEASURE:—**All Railroads owned by foreign Stockholders, or Bonded to Foreign Bondholders, Should be Operated by a Commission Appointed for the Purpose.**

This is essential, in connection with the operations of the proposed "UNION," in order to prevent the Money Kings from thwarting all efforts of the people for self help, by their manner of operating the roads. The railroads are their property, and they should have all the income derived from them. But they should not be suffered to operate them, while the proposed "UNION" is carrying out its work, because they would use their power to thwart all efforts to control them. This is an essential measure of self-protection; and if it cannot be carried out by a concerted State legislation, it should be enacted by Congress.

VII. SEVENTH MEASURE:—**We Need a New Currency System; Which Will Equalize Our Currency, and Secure it From Being Contracted In**

Periods of Financial Crisis Brought about By the Money Kings.

This is the most important measure of all.

1st. Present Dangerous Condition of Our Currency.

1. **The present state of our currency illustrates the evils** of our present currency system. It is almost wholly in the hands of the Money Kings; so that, though we have $1,700,000,000 of money in the country, there are only about $400,000,000 in circulation.

This may be denied; but it is assuredly true. In 1860, we had only $207,000,000 of currency. That amount was sufficient to do the business of the country at the scale of prices then prevailing. *Our prices are lower now, than they were in* 1860; so that we only need an amount of currency to do the business of the country now, at present prices, greater than that of 1860 by the amount of increase of population and business. And if $207,000,000 was sufficient to carry on the trade of the country in 1860, $400,000,000 is sufficient to carry on the business of the country now, at our present scale of prices. It is certain that we have now not more than $400,000,000 in circulation in the channels of business.

This fact shows the nature of our need. We need a proper amount of money; *and we need it all in active circulation, in the channels of business.*

2. **Furthermore, our currency is, at present, in a most precarious condition.** We have now in the country, it is stated, about $1,700,000,000 of money. Of this, about $239,000,000 are national bank notes; and a little over $346,000,000 are greenbacks. The remainder of the money consists of gold and silver; much of it held in reserve, and as a basis for the National Bank circula-

tion; but a part of it in circulation as coin, and a part, represented by gold and silver certificates.

The gold and silver that are in circulation are perfectly good, while they remain in circulation. But they are liable to be withdrawn from the country at any time by the Money Power. They have an intrinsic value, and can be used by the Money Power in its traffic, in any other quarter of the globe.

3. **Let us notice the effect upon us** of the Money Power withdrawing the $1,100,000,000 of gold and silver from the country, and keeping the greenbacks retired from circulation.

1.) By presenting the gold and silver certificates at the Treasury, and drawing the gold and silver they call for, the gold and silver certificates would be withdrawn from circulation.

2.) Then, by withdrawing the rest of the gold and silver, we would be left with nothing but the greenbacks and the National Bank circulation.

3.) But the $346,000,000 of greenbacks have already been, in great measure, retired from circulation. They are all owned in the great money centers, chiefly by the Money Kings, or their agents. When the Money Kings shall be desirous of bringing on a crisis, they will, of course, keep the greenbacks retired.

4.) This would leave us only the National Banking circulation of $239,000,000. By presenting the National Bank circulation at the counters of the banks, and drawing out the gold in their vaults, the Money Kings could compel the National Banks to suspend specie payments, and contract their circulation at least one-half. Then we would be left with only about $120,000,000 of National Bank notes in circulation.

But the greater part of the national banks are owned by the Money Kings, who could withdraw their circulation, if they chose to do so.—It is evident that the Money Kings can, in three months, if they wish, reduce our currency in circulation to less than $100,000,000.

They have got the greenbacks locked up now: and a banker has recently proposed to retire all the greenbacks, and substitute for them silver coin. If this were done, the Money Kings could ship our silver and gold to India, and Africa, and China, and Japan, and South America, to stimulate the industry of those regions, and would leave us almost entirely without currency.

They can easily do this. They only need the excuse of a panic to justify them in doing it. And they could start the panic at any moment by breaking a few National Banks; which can easily be done by drawing out their specie and forcing them to suspend specie payments. In 1837, the Money Kings brought on the panic, by continuing to draw gold from the banks of New York City until they were compelled to suspend specie payments. They brought on the crisis of 1857, by drawing several million dollars of gold from the vaults of the Trust Company Bank in Ohio. That bank was evidently on a sound basis. It was able to bear extraordinary drafts upon it. But they started the run, and they continued to draw until the bank failed. So now, they can break any or all of our National Banks in a week, and force them to suspend specie payments, or go into bankruptcy.

Our currency is now a *trap*, with the triggers all set, ready to fall whenever the Money Kings choose to touch it off. The condition of the currency needs to be remedied, or we shall have, some day, the most terrible crisis that ever ruined a country. It will not do to have our currency so completely at the mercy of the Money Kings.

This is the state of things we need to remedy.

2ND. THE CURRENCY SYSTEM TO BE ADOPTED MUST BE ACCOMMODATED TO EXISTING CONDITIONS.

We can not establish a perfect currency system. Any currency system we may adopt must be adjusted to existing circumstances.

1. **All the Specie that is in circulation** must be held at par.

But we can not consider specie as fixed currency; since the Money Kings can withdraw it from the country whenever they choose. We must expect the Money Kings to withdraw it, and base our currency system on that expectation. We must, therefore, recognize it at par value, when in circulation; but we must have currency enough to do without it, when it is withdrawn from the country, as it assuredly will be when we put the proposed measures into operation.

We should, therefore, coin silver to the maximum amount authorized by law, and recognize its par value when in circulation, but provide an amount of currency sufficient for our needs, if the Money Kings ship all the specie out of the country.

2. **The National and Individual Banks will need to remain** as they are; except that they should be relieved from the obligation to maintain specie payments, and should be placed and kept under such supervision as would secure their safe and proper management, and the safety of their circulation.—The reason for relieving the banks from the obligation to maintain specie payments will be given further on.

3. **The greenbacks**, which are all in the hands of the Money Kings and are retired, in great measure, from circulation, should be withdrawn by the government, for reasons soon to be given, and should be replaced by the currency system herein presented.

4. We will only count $260,000,000 of specie, because it is liable to be taken out of the country at any time by the Money Kings. This, with the $239,000,000 of national banking currency, will give us $500,000,000 of currency. And we should make up the deficit of currency by the issues of the proposed currency system.

The next question to be considered is

3RD. THE AMOUNT OF CURRENCY NECESSARY.

I am not an advocate of unlimited inflation. But we need enough money to do the business of the country with a fair scale of prices. We had good prices in 1869 and 1870, and all our currency was then in circulation. So that it required all the money we had in 1870 to do the business of the country at the scale of prices then prevailing. I think wheat should be about $1.25 per bushel; beef cattle should be about 4 to 8 cents, according to quality; and hogs should average about 5 cents. Cotton also should bear a fair price,—10 to 12 cents.

If we needed $900,000,000, in 1870, to sustain fair prices, we should now need, in the same ratio of currency to population, about $1,450,000,000.*

Of this amount, the National Bank notes constitute $239,000,000. And we might estimate the specie circulation at $260,000,000. This would leave about $950,000,000 of the new issue of currency under the proposed currency system.

The next question to be determined is

4TH. THE BASIS OF THE DISTRIBUTION.

I think the Currency Should be Distributed in proportion to the *population*. It may be thought by some

* This cannot be called inflation. For we have now in the country $1,700,000,000. But it is almost all locked up. We do not need an excessive amount of money. But we want enough to sustain fair prices; and to have it all in active circulation.

that the amount of *trade* should also be considered. But the object to be kept in view is, to equalize industry and prosperity as far as possible. If the poorer parts of the country are deprived of currency on account of their poverty, the poverty will be perpetuated. The only way to promote the prosperity of the poorer sections of the country is, to give them the currency needed, and then their business will grow up to it.

If we issue more money to the present trade centers, in proportion to their population, than to the less developed portions of the country, it will increase the preponderance of wealth in the trade centers, and keep the new sections of the country depleted of currency, and poor. Let the currency be issued to each portion of country in proportion to its population, and the money will be invested in productive industry, and thus the poorer sections will grow up in wealth, and prosperity will be equalized.

There is a natural tendency for currency to leave the remote portions of the country, and drift to the great trade centers. This tendency, together with their natural proportion on the basis of population, will give to the trade centers currency enough for all business purposes. If it were afterward found necessary to give to the trade centers an additional amount of currency, it could be done.

In the construction of the currency system, one of the main points to be provided for is, to prevent the currency from drifting to the great trade centers and settling there, until the rest of the country would not have money enough to carry on its business. The currency ought not only to be distributed, but the system should be so constructed as to keep it distributed, and equalized in proportion to population.

The next question to be considered is,

5TH. THE BASIS OF THE CURRENCY.

This is a most important question. There are several points to be held in view, in order to avoid evils of which we are warned by past experience.

1. THE CURRENCY SHOULD NOT BE ON A GREENBACK BASIS.

1) A grave objection to a greenback currency is, that it is not based upon anything in the way of value received. If the Government should introduce the greenback currency by paying out the greenbacks for work or property, the greenbacks, in such case, would not be equally distributed. On the other hand, if the Government did not pay out the greenbacks for work or property, then, in order to get the greenback currency into circulation, the Government would have to make the different parts of the country a present of so much money.—It is a grave objection to the greenback currency that there is no proper method of getting it into circulation.

2) It is a decisive objection to a greenback currency that is not located anywhere, and would, at once, be drawn to the great centers of trade, and would be owned there. It would pass into the hands of the Money Kings as soon as it went into circulation. We want a currency that will be equally distributed throughout the country, and that will stay distributed, in proportion to population.

2. HENCE, THE CURRENCY MUST BE BASED UPON A BANKING SYSTEM.

A Banking System is necessary in order to properly distribute the currency, in the first instance; and it is also necessary in order to keep it distributed and equalized. A bank only lends money on a secured note, binding the borrower to pay it back over the counter at a certain time.

Money placed in a bank is localized, and remains in the community where the bank is placed. It may go abroad into the channels of business, but the channels of business will bring it back again to the bank from which it started.

3. THE CURRENCY MUST NOT BE A BANKING SYSTEM BASED UPON NATIONAL BONDS, AS AT PRESENT.

1) One objection to such a system is that it will require a national debt to be maintained, in order to be a basis for the currency.

2) But the greatest objection to a currency based upon national bonds is, that such a system places all the currency of the country in the hands of capitalists, who are able to own national bonds. This makes a *favored class;* and it gives them so great an advantage as to make them a *wealthy caste*, perpetuating the wealth of the country in their hands.

The very thing we wish to get rid of is having our currency in the hands of an Imperialism of Capital, which uses it to take possession of all the business of the country. We can never break up this domination over all business by the Money Power, while we have a system of currency which makes all our money the property of those capitalists and their agents. There is no use of issuing more money, if we base it on government bonds, and thereby place it in the hands of the Money Kings who own the bonds. We want our currency to be owned by our people. And we must adopt a currency system that puts and keeps our currency in the hands of the great mass of our people.

3) Moreover, this system of currency, based upon national bonds, is incompatible with the equal distribution of the currency. The capitalists who own the bonds, will start a bank where they please, or they will not start it at all. This will continue to keep the newer states of the West and South in want of currency, perpetually, and will

keep them too poor to raise and market their own products, and will keep those sections dependent upon the Money Kings for capital, which is the very thing we wish to avoid,—the evil that needs to be cured.

4. THE CURRENCY SHOULD NOT BE ON A SPECIE BASIS.

A specie basis for currency is liable to several objections :—

1) In the great expansion of industry in modern times, there is not nearly enough gold and silver in the world, to afford a basis for an amount of currency adequate to the needs of business. And as business shall continue to grow with the development of industry, the difficulty will increase until, before many years shall have passed, there will not be gold and silver enough in the world to constitute one dollar in twenty of the currency that will be necessary to transact the business of the world. Then no one will think of making currency rest upon a specie basis.

The requirement of a specie basis would now limit *our* currency to an amount far short of the needs of our business. Just now, the Money Kings are buying up our property; and they have allowed us to keep our silver, and have flooded the country with gold. This is done, probably, in order to lull us into security, and afford an argument against any change; and also, no doubt, to have us in a condition in which they can utterly prostrate us, at any time, by withdrawing all the gold and silver from the country. They are now draining the rest of the world, to flood the United States with specie. They are only doing it temporarily, while they are buying up our property. When the property is bought up, they will certainly withdraw the specie; and then, if we are on a specie basis, we shall not have nearly currency enough to do the business of the country.

2) In the early ages of the world, when there was no

public credit, it was necessary to use a metallic currency as the standard of value. But the time has passed away when a metallic currency is possible; or a specie basis in any country with which the Money Kings are trading. A paper currency on a specie basis was a mere expedient, when there was not specie enough to afford an exclusively specie currency; and the continual crises which it has caused, show what a poor makeshift it was. And now that the Money Power has risen, which has a special interest in bringing about financial crises, by breaking down banks which are on a specie basis of three for one, it is perfectly suicidal for any country to have its currency upon a specie basis.

3) Even if we could obtain specie enough to be the basis of an adequate amount of currency at the ratio of three for one, yet it is an insuperable objection to a specie basis, in our time, that the Money Kings could break any bank that had a circulation three times the amount of the specie in its vaults. A bank might be perfectly sound, and yet the Money Kings could continue to draw upon its specie, until it would be compelled to stop specie payments. They did so with the Trust Bank of Ohio, in 1857, which was a perfectly sound institution. It is easy to start a "run" on a bank. And they could do this to one bank after another, until a general panic was started. And they would do it. When they were determined to start a panic, they would continue to break banks until their object was accomplished.—A specie basis is no longer suited to the condition of our age. It puts the currency of every country completely at the mercy of the Money Power.

We have now seen, 1) That our currency should not be a greenback currency; because greenbacks can not be equally distributed, nor can they be caused to remain equalized; 2) That the currency should be located in banks, as the only method of equally distributing it, and of keeping it distributed; we have seen, 3) That the currency must not be based, like our present national banking system, upon national bonds; becanse it puts all the currency into the hands of capitalists who are able to own the bonds; and because it prevents the equal distribution of the currency; and we have seen 4) That the currency should not be upon a specie basis; because the Money Kings would withdraw the specie from the country, and cause such a panic as swept the country in 1837 and 1857.

Our present currency system is a conglomerate, composed of portions of all these objectionable systems. It is part specie, part gold and silver certificates, part greenbacks, and part national bank notes, based both on government bonds and on a specie basis.

5. The Currency System must be a System of County National Banks.

1) For the only way to distribute and equalize the currency in such a manner as to keep it distributed and equalized, is to put it in banks. Money paid into a bank is located. The bank never lends it to any one except upon a secured note, binding the borrower to pay it back over the counter at a certain time.

2) But it will not do for the Government to issue the currency to *individuals*; for it would make of them a favored class, which would soon become the Money Kings of the country.

3) There is but one way in which the banks can be organized. The currency must not be based on specie, like the old state banks: it must not be based on Government credit, like the greenbacks: it must not be based on national bonds, like the present national bank notes. *The currency we need must be based on the credit of the American*

people, not the Government, and be based on the bonds of the Anerican people, not the bonds of the Government.

The United States Government should issue the national bank notes to the Counties of every state and territory, upon the county bonds, issued dollar for dollar, and deposited with the Government. These county bonds should bear one per cent. interest, which would be sufficient to meet the expense of issuing the currency, and reissuing it as occasion required, and maintaining a proper supervision of it.

4) The currency should be issued to each county in proportion to its population. And it should be provided by law that the currency should be loaned at a specified rate of interest. There is no objection to interest, provided it is equal everywhere. And it would seem that money, which is the representative of the value of property, must itself have a value, represented by the rate of interest which it bears.

Besides, it is necessary for the currency to bear interest when loaned, in order not to interfere with the existing national banks and individual banks. But by means of these new national banks the rate of interest would be equalized throughout the country.

There is an advantage in issuing the currency to the counties, inasmuch as the county authorities would have no interest in evading the law respecting the rate of interest to be charged upon loans. And, as the prosperity of the county would be deeply involved in the successful management of the banks, their management would be carefully guarded. It would also be an advantage for the counties to realize the profits upon the loans of the banks, as it would save the people of the counties taxation to that extent, and would enable the counties to establish many educational and other advantages which they could not otherwise support.

5) In issuing this new currency, the present national banks and all individual banks would stand just as they are. The circulation of the national banks would count as a part of the $1,450,000,000 of needed currency, and would be credited to the place where they are established. Those places, consequently, would get none of the new issue until the rest of the country was brought up to an equality with them. Hence, the East would get less of the new issue than the other portions of the country.

6) THE NEW BANK ISSUES SHOULD BE LEGAL TENDER

for all taxes, and customs, and debts. It may be objected that, in this case, the Government would not be able to pay the gold interest on its bonds. I admit that this is a point of financial difficulty; but it is not a difficulty of very great importance. The country is now ruined, as things stand at present. If things go on as they are, the American people will lose at least $20,000,000,000 worth of property within the next ten years. The System I propose will save all that to them, and a great deal more. And if it costs the Government $100,000,000 a year, for five years, to buy gold with which to pay interest on the bonds, it will be a cheap price to pay for the immense advantages obtained through the system here proposed.

6TH. THE FINANCIAL SYSTEM MUST BE MADE FLEXIBLE.

1. **The Money Power Would Lock up the Currency,** if we have a fixed amount, and thus maintain a scarcity of money. To lock up $1,000,000,000 will be a small matter to them. It would only cost them $40,000,000 a year, at four per cent. interest on the amount. When, by keeping our currency scarce and prices low, they can make an annual profit of $1,000,000,000 in the purchase of our products, they can well afford to lock up

our currency, in order to cause a scarce currency and low prices. It would be a paying speculation.

All the currency in the country passes through their hands once in every three or four months. They receive our currency from every man who buys coal from them, or lumber, or dry goods, or groceries; and from every man who pays them for railroad tickets, or telegraph messages, or freights, or electric lights, or any of the numerous necessary things which they own and furnish to us. If they choose to keep the money they receive, and not pay it out again, they would, in a few months, have all the currency of the country in their possession, and business would be at a standstill for want of money to carry it on.—To prevent such a state of things,

2. It will be Necessary to have a Central Bureau of Currency,

to which all the banks in the country should make weekly, or semi-weekly returns of the amount of currency on hand. Whenever the returns showed that there was less than $1,450,000,000 in circulation, the banks in counties showing a deficit should have more currency issued to them in exchange for county bonds. And these bonds should be redeemed, as soon as the returns showed an excess of currency in circulation, by the return of the currency so issued to them to the Government, and the redemption of the bonds.

Such a currency system as the above would secure to us an abundant supply of currency, uniform in quantity, and equally distributed throughout the country.

VIII. EIGHTH MEASURE:—The Tariff.

This is a delicate question in the present attitude of parties. But, fortunately, my views do not either fully agree, or absolutely conflict with the views of either of the two great political parties which now divide the country. My views are a middle ground, on which both Republicans and Democrats can unite. For the Republicans and Democrats are both right, and both wrong, on the Tariff Question. Each has partial truth on its side.

1st. The Proper Scale of Tariff Duties

depends upon the general scale of prices prevailing in the country.

1. **If we are to have a low scale of prices,** as at present, then manufactures must, in common justice, be low also, and we want a low scale of tariff duties. But if we are to have a general scale of fair prices, then we want a general scale of tariff duties to correspond.

When the farmers are being destroyed by ruinously low prices, and when the merchants are only able to continue business by the most pinching economy, it is unjust to keep up a high scale of prices on manufactures by a high scale of tariff duties. On the other hand, if we are to have fair prices for farming produce, and if all prices and earnings are to be at a fair rate, then it is fair and right to protect our manufactures from the competition of foreign goods, manufactured abroad under a scale of low prices.

Our factories, manufacturing under a low scale of prices, can compete with foreign manufactures manufactured at a low scale of prices; but if we have a liberal scale of prices, then our factories, manufacturing under a high scale of prices, can not compete, without protection, with foreign manufactures manutactured under a low scale of prices. In such circumstances, they will need protection; not otherwise.

2. The Question is, Is it Better for Us to Scale Up, or to Scale Down?

Had we better reduce the tariff, and bring all prices down to the ruinous rate of farming produce? or, on the other hand, is it better to raise farming produce, and all our prices, up to the generous scale of the tariff? This is the question for the American people to consider, at the present juncture.

One thing is certain: everything ought to go up, or go down together. If the tariff is to stay up at a high rate of duties, then all prices must go up to the same level. If all prices are to stay down, then the tariff must, in common justice, come down also. The question is, Shall prices go up? or go down? Shall the tariff come down to the level of the prices of farming produce? or shall the prices of farming produce, and other prices, go up to the level of the tariff?

If we have a low tariff, and bring all prices down to the level of farming produce, in that case, a farmer may save about $30 a year in store bills. But will that enable him to pay for his farm machinery, and pay off his mortgage and save his farm? It will not. A reduction of the tariff is no remedy for the present evils that afflict the country. The tariff may be reduced, and the farmer may save his $30 a year in store bills; and still, at the present low scale of prices, he will fail to pay his mortgage, and will lose his farm.

3. Nothing Will Save the Farmers But a Rise of Prices.

If the farmers have fair prices, they can afford to pay present prices for the goods they buy, and can still pay off their mortgages and save their farms. Any one can see that our true policy, at present, is, instead of reducing the tariff to the low scale of the prices of farming produce, to let the tariff stand, and raise the prices of farming produce to the level of tariff prices.

4. The Key to the Present Situation

is the condition of the farming population. If the farmers can not pay off their mortgages and save their farms, the country is lost; and the Money Power will get everything, and have everything its own way. We *must* save the farms to the farmers from the clutch of the Money Power. If we can do this with a low tariff, and a scale of low prices, I am in favor of a low tariff and a scale of low prices. But if the farmers can not pay off their mortgages and save their farms under a scale of low prices, then let us have fair prices for farming produce, and let the tariff stand.

We cannot separate the two things: A low tariff and low prices for farming produce go together; and, on the other hand, a high tariff and fair prices for farming produce go together. If we have a high tariff, we must have an equal rate of prices for farming produce: if we have low prices for farming produce, we must have a low tariff also.

5. The Proposed Measures, Compromise Measures.

It is well, perhaps, that the principal measures to be adopted in our proposed system are compromise measures, in which each party will have to yield some of its own views, and accept some of the views of the others. If the Democrat has to give up his ideas of low tariff, he obtains the concession of his idea that prices must be equalized. If the Republican has his idea of a high tariff conceded, he must, on the other hand, concede the equalization of all the prices in the country, and accept the measures necessary to give fair prices for farming produce and establish a fair scale of prices in all departments of business. If the Greenbacker has to give up the greenbacks and excessive inflation, he ought to be content with an equalized currency, adequate to give us fair prices, and secure the prosperity of the country.

1) If we are all to unite on a common platform, we must have a compromise basis on which to unite. No party can expect all others to come to it. There must be a compromise ground on which all can unite.

And, fortunately, truth lies in the middle. All extremes have only part of the truth. The real truth blends into itself the partial truths held by both extremes, and forms out of them a blended harmonious whole.

2) **The proposed "Union" will need to start and foster many new industries**, which will need the tariff to protect them against the importations of the Money Kings. It is not a question of protecting the manufactures already started, so much as of protecting new enterprises, to be started by the American people all over the country. The establishment of such new enterprises will be essential to start the country upon a career of grand prosperity.

6. The protection of the tariff should be made more perfect than at present, by making the duties payable when the goods enter the warehouse. This will prevent the Money Kings from storing goods in New York City, not for sale, but for the purpose of "bearing" down our markets.

7. And it will be necessary to cover with tariff protection all agricultural products; in order to prevent the Money Kings from interfering with the system of prices we shall establish, by throwing the products of India and Australia upon our markets. We propose to establish fair prices for the benefit of our own producers, not for the benefit of Australians, or the India plantations of the Money Kings. And, in order to keep the benefit of our scale of prices to ourselves, it will be necessary to shut out the products of foreign industry by tariff protection.

2ND. TO BRING ABOUT COMMERCIAL TREATIES should be one great aim of a tariff policy. By this means our foreign commerce might be greatly extended.

But the subject is too extensive to be further discussed here.

The above are the measures which are necessary to remedy the evils that are afflicting our country. They are so reasonable, and their necessity is so apparent, that it is hoped they will be readily accepted by the great body of the American people.

IMPERATIVE NECESSITY OF AN ORGANIZED UNION.

But if it be asked, Will this legislation stop the encroachments of the Money Power? the answer must be in the negative.

The Money Power can not be controlled by legislation alone. But this legislation will enable the American people to control the Money Power, by having *a proper Organization.* The Money Power can be controlled, only by a grand organized "UNION" of the great body of the American people. Such a "UNION" is mightier than the Money Power: nothing else is.

With the legislation above mentioned, our people, by a proper Organization, can carry on the industry of the country in accordance with correct principles of Political Economy, and can soon restore the country to such a condition of prosperity as will enable the farmers to pay their debts, and our entire people to grow rich.

No legislation will be needed other than that already mentioned. Most of the legislation needed is state legislation; and it can be enacted as soon as the will of the people is made known. The Congressional legislation may be slower.

But a good currency system is the only point of national legislation that is of essential importance, and it is not necessary to wait for that. The people can organize the "UNION," and with the necessary state legislation, the "UNION" can put things in good condition with our present currency system, unless the Money Kings cut us short by keeping the money of the country locked up. We have money enough in the country—$1,700,000,000—to give us good times. If the Money Kings prevent us from making good times, the eyes of the American people will be upon them, and Congress will obey the wish of a United People, and pass such proper legislation as will soon enable us to put things to rights.

The organization of the American people for self-protection is more important than any Congressional legislation. With such an "UNION," we can do without national legislation until the public sentiment of the people shall induce Congress to pass needed laws.

CHAPTER IV.

PROPER METHOD OF ORGANIZING THE PROPOSED "UNION."

I. STYLE OF ORGANIZATION.

The proposed movement should be A PATRIOTIC UPRISING of the whole American people, to save our country, our property, and our homes from the Money Power. As has been said, the organized "UNION" should include people of all political parties, and all industrial classes. It should include all except the Money Kings, and their agents engaged in managing their business. The Labor employees of the Money Kings need protection against them as much as any other class of our people, and should be included in the "UNION."

1ST. THE NAME OF THE "UNION."

The proposed "UNION" will be a patriotic movement, having for its motto, AMERICA FOR AMERICANS.

It will be a patriotic uprising of the people, to protect every thing that is most dear to us from foreign domination. Its aims will be wholly patriotic. It will be an uprising against the establishment of a grand Imperialism over us—an uprising, to throw off the yoke of the Money Power, and to protect our country from the power of this foreign Despotism.

This Uprising Against the Oppression of the Money Power, now, will be as patriotic a movement as the uprising of our Revolutionary Fathers against the oppression of the Money Power, in 1776. The name of the "UNION" should indicate its patriotic character. The best name for the organization, therefore, will be

"THE PATRIOT UNION."

The PATRIOT UNION should be above all sectional feeling, and all party prejudices; and it should include in its membership persons of all sections, and all political parties; the only requirement for membership being a resolution to enter into a union of energies and resources, for the purpose of protecting and delivering American industry from the domination of the Imperialism of Capital centered in Great Britain.

And its name should indicate the fact that, as the PATRIOT UNION includes people of all sections, and all political parties, and all business classes; so, under its auspices, all past differences are blotted out and forgotten in the grand united movement to save our country from the domination of the Money Power. The name should indicate that it is a Patriot Union of the North and South, of the East and West, in which all sectional feeling and prejudices are buried. It should indicate that, as the PATRIOT UNION includes men of all classes of industry and all political parties, so, in it, all class interests are blended in the promotion of the common interests of all.

2ND. ORGANIZED BY LODGES:

The organization of the PATRIOT UNION should be by Lodges; in order to the proper consideration of all measures, and efficient action in promotion of the interests of the Union.

3RD. THREE ORDERS OF LODGES.

In order that every industrial class may be properly represented, and in order to avoid conflict of interest or opinion, it will be better to have three Orders in the Patriot Union,—the Farmers' Patriot Union, the Townsmen's Patriot Union, and the Labor Patriot Union. By this means, each great branch of American industry will be kept distinct, and its interests will be distinctly represented, and effectually fostered and protected.

1. **The Farmers' Patriot Union** should include all branches of production from the soil: viz:

1.) All American farmers owning their own farms, or renting farms owned by Americans in actual legal right. But no renter or manager of a farm owned by corporations whose stockholders are not known to be Americans exclusively, should be eligible to membership. 2.) Stock-raisers, including all graziers and owners of cattle ranches owned and managed by individuals, or by companies whose stockholders are exclusively Americans. 3.) Cotton growers, and owners of sugar plantations. 4.) Market gardeners and horticulturists; and all who are engaged in any department of agricultural production.

2. **The Townsmen's Patriot Union** should include all the business men of our towns and cities, and men in the various professions: viz:

1.) All American merchants, and grocers, and owners of shops and stores, who are engaged in independent business; including all companies, as well as individuals, whose stockholders are Americans not connected with the London Money Power. 2.) Boss carpenters, and masons, and architects, and builders, who are not connected with the Money Power. 3.) All American manufacturers of every class whose owners or stockholders are Americans, and not connected with the Money Power. 4.) All professional men having no business connection with the Money Power or its agents. 5.) All capitalists and banks whose stockholders are all Americans having no connection with the Money Power. 6.) Mine owners, of coal, and iron, and gold, and silver and other metals, whose mines are owned by American stockholders. 7.) And all other classes of business men, whose business is run on the individual basis, or by companies whose stockholders are exclusively Americans, and which are not bonded to the Money Power.

3. **The Labor Patriot Union** should include all classes of Labor: viz:

1) Farm operatives; 2) Clerks; 3) Employees of all the trades; 4) Employees of railroads and other corporations; 5) Factory, mill and shop operatives; 6) Working miners; and, generally, all Wage Earners engaged in any department of industry.

4. **A grand branch of industry in any of the three foregoing Orders** might organize a special order of the PATRIOT UNION, so that its interests might be specially represented and considered.

1) Thus, **in the Farmers' Patriot Union**, there might be special branches; as The Stock Growers' Patriot Union, and the Cotton-Growers' Patriot Union.

2) **In the Townsmen's Patriot Union**, there might be, in large cities, a need for Lodges composed of men in various branches of industry; as, the Merchants' Patriot Union, the Builders' Patriot Union, the Manufacturers' Patriot Union, the Miners' Patriot Union.

3) **In the Labor Patriot Union**, there might be also various Branch Lodges: In the country, there might be the Farm-Labor Patriot Union, and the Mine-Labor Patriot Union. In the towns and cities, there might be the Railroaders' Labor Patriot Union, and Labor Patriot Union Lodges of craftsmen in the various branches of industry, who might prefer to be associated together.

All the foregoing classes of American industry have identical interests, and should unite in the PATRIOT UNION, in order to conserve the general interests of all. The three great Orders of Lodges of the PATRIOT UNION should include all branches of American industry, and all persons who are not associated with the management of joint stock corporations owned by the Money Kings, or mortgaged to foreign capitalists.

II. BASIS OF ORGANIZATION.

The basis of organization should be: 1) By counties; 2) By states; and 3) National.

1st. County Patriot Organization.

The Various Patriot Union Lodges in each county should annually elect a County Conference Board; which should meet at the county seat once a month, or at such time as should be appointed, to consider and carry out measures for conserving and promoting the industrial interests of the people of the county.

In counties where the towns are not large, the Townsmen's Patriot Union, the Farmers' Patriot Union, and the Labor Patriot Union, might have equal representation in the County Conference Board.

In the counties where the towns are important, the County Conference Board might consist of an equal representation of Townsmen's Patriot Union Lodges, Farmers' Patriot Union Lodges, Town Labor Patriot Union Lodges, and Country Labor Patriot Union Lodges.

2D. STATE PATRIOT ORGANIZATION.

In each state, there should be a State Conference Board, consisting of eight men, which should meet once a month, or at such times as might be appointed, to consider the best means of promoting the industrial prosperity of the state, and of protecting the industrial interests of its people from the aggressive oppression of the Money Power.

The State Conference Board might be elected in the following manner. The County Conference Boards might each nominate eight men, two representing the Townsmen's Patriot Union, two, the Farmers' Patriot Union, two, the Town-Labor Patriot Union, and two, the Country-Labor Patriot Union. Then, in an election in which all the Patriot Union Lodges of the State should vote, the State Board, consisting of two Townsmen Patriots, two Farmer Patriots, two Town-Labor Patriots, and two County-Labor Patriots, might be elected out of the whole number of nominees.

3RD. NATIONAL PATRIOT ORGANIZATION.

An Annual Convention of the PATRIOT UNION should be held, which should consider questions pertaining to the general policy of the PATRIOT UNION, and elect the President, and the National Conference Board of the PATRIOT UNION.

The National Conference Board might consist of a President, and of four Vice-Presidents, and sixteen Members. One Vice-President and four Members might be appointed from each of the four great sections of the country, divided as might be deemed best.—The Farmers' Patriot Union, the Townsmen's Patriot Union, the Town-Labor Patriot Union, and the Country-Labor Patriot Union might be equally represented in the National Conference Board.

The National Conference Board should meet annually, or semi-annually, at such suitable place as might be appointed, to consider measures pertaining to the industrial prosperity of the whole country. But it might be called together at any time, by the President.

The above mode of organization is merely suggested as a basis from which the organization might start. On some such basis as the foregoing, the PATRIOT UNION would be able to pursue its work effectively; and it would soon remedy existing evils, and bring our country into a state of such general and exalted prosperity as would introduce by our example a New Era in the history of the world.

For, this new Organization, once inaugurated, would be maintained perpetually. It would put an end to the jarring conflicts of warring class interests: it would harmonize the interests of all industrial classes: it would adjust the price of labor, and of all industrial products, upon a basis equally fair and just to all; and it would promote, in a manner unexampled in the past history of the world, new enterprises in every direction of industrial development.

Its advantages will prove so great as to make it indispensable. The time will come when every country on the globe will have a PATRIOT UNION, to develop its industry, and to harmonize and promote the interests of all industrial classes. In its full development, it wtll diffuse among every class in each nation the principles of justice; and, in the end, it will unite all nations in industrial harmony, under the principlè of fraternity embodied in the Golden Rule.

Chapter V.

WORK OF THE PATRIOT UNION.

The power and efficiency of the Patriot Union will arise, especially, out of its

I. MODE OF ACTIVITY.

The Patriot Union will not be a political party. It will be a sort of General Trade Union. Its fundamental principle, from which it will derive all its power, is the

1st. Agreement of the Members to Trade with Each Other.

The members of the Patriot Union should agree that they will buy from each other, in preference to purchasing from the Money Power, in all cases of competition. They should agree that they will buy from a Patriot merchant or grocer, rather than from a Jew Store, or any branch store established by the Money Power: that they will buy all manufactured articles,—building materials, articles of food and clothing, and all other manufactures,—from a Patriot manufacturer, rather than from factories of the Money Kings, when such articles can be so obtained: that they will buy their flour from a Patriot mill owner, rather than from mills owned by the Money Power: that they will buy meat from a Patriot butcher, rather than from a store selling Armour's beef; and that they will buy bacon from a Patriot packing house, rather than from a packing house of the Money Power.

Such an agreement is very simple, and yet it is

The Key to the Situation.

All parties would abide by this trade regulation; their own prosperity being so deeply involved in the movement.—The grocer would buy flour and bacon and lard and dried beef from Patriot packing houses, rather than those of the Money Power—and the merchant would buy articles of household consumption, and goods sold in his business, from Patriot houses; for both merchant and grocer would find in the Patriot movement their only salvation from the competition of Stores established by the Money Kings.—The farmer would quit dealing with Jew Stores, and buy his goods altogether from Patriot merchants and grocers; for the success of the movement would be his only hope of paying off his mortgage, and saving his farm.—The workingman would buy his articles of household consumption from Patriot grocers and merchants; for by means of the Patriot Union, the Working People will be backed in their conflict with Money King employers by the sympathy and the might of the whole American people.—There can be no doubt that this agreement would be universally and faithfully observed.

This agreement of the members of the Patriot Union to buy from each other, in preference to the agents of the Money Kings, is the one grand central point of power which would make the Patriot Union master of the situation. For this agreement will afford a secure basis for established trade. It will prove an adequate and secure basis for the investment of money to supply the immense demand that will be everywhere afforded to new enterprises by the Patriot Union.

In every County, flour mills should be built, to supply the people of the county with flour. Such mills would afford an adequate market for the wheat grown in the county; for, in the greater part of the country, each county does not raise more wheat than enough to supply the home demand.—Where a county does not raise wheat enough to supply the home demand, a flour mill should be erected, notwithstanding; and wheat should be purchased from the wheat-growing sections and manufactured into flour for the supply of the County demand.

For, as already stated, it is a most important law of Political Economy that, where a community needs to import any article for its consumption, it should buy, not the manufactured article, but the raw material: it should buy the article in its cheapest form, and let the community make the profit of manufacturing it. This is a principle of prime importance, and its observance in all cases will greatly promote the prosperity of the community.

Packing houses should be built in every county, to kill at least enough pork and beef to supply the people of the town and county with beef and bacon and lard. And, if the county did not raise hogs and cattle enough for its home consumption, packing houses should be built, notwithstanding, and beef cattle and hogs should be imported for slaughter, to an extent sufficient to supply the county demand. In this way, the people of the county would save hundreds of thousands of dollars of profit realized by its own people, which now go to swell the hoard of the Money Kings.

Tanneries and shoe and harness manufactories should be established in every county, to tan leather and make shoes and harness enough for the county consumption. Even if the county had not tan bark, it would be better to import it than to buy leather, or leather manufactures.

It would probably not pay to establish manufactures for boots and shoes of fine quality; but heavy articles of ordinary domestic wear, and all harness, should be made at home.

A foundery should be established in every district of country, to supply the common grades of ironware to the people of the district.

In every county, there should be a Factory for manufacturing the coarser grades of cotton and woolen goods for ordinary domestic wear. Finer goods it would not pay to manufacture; but much the greater quantity of goods consumed in every county are the substantial grades for every day wear. And it would greatly promote the prosperity of the county to establish such a Factory, import raw wool and cotton, and manufacture a sufficient quantity to supply the county demand.

In hemp and flax growing districts, manufactures should be established that would supply the demand for those articles, of which we now import $33,000,000 worth annually.

We now import $83,000,000 worth of sugar and molasses annually. The culture of sorghum and the sugar beet, would supply this demand, and give great prosperity to the fertile farming regions of the West.

The above system of industry, in which each community supplies, as far as possible, its own wants, is the only system that accords with sound principles of Political Economy. Such a system will tend to equalize wealth, and give to every county the advantages which wealth confers.

It will also greatly add to the national prosperity. At present we annually import, in a raw or manufactured condition, sugar, flax, hemp, cotton, leather, wool, to the value of $216,000,000, which it requires almost all our exports of breadstuffs and provisions to pay for. Supplying our own demand in those articles will greatly enrich our people, and promote our national prosperity.

And it would be entirely practicable to put this system in operation, at once, by means of the PATRIOT UNION. For that organization would give a sure and steady market everywhere, at fair prices, to the extent of the county demand for consumption; and enterprising people in every county would be glad to avail themselves of the opportunity to engage in the new enterprises which the PATRIOT UNION would call into existence.

And what a rush of industry would at once be started, all over the country. In every county seat would be erected flour mills, cotton and woolen and shoe factories, harness shops, iron founderies, packing houses and tanneries. In all the county towns stagnation would cease at once, and the towns would ring with the hum of industry.

2ND. THE PATRIOT UNION MUST REGULATE PRICES.

1. In the nature of things the right to regulate prices would belong to the PATRIOT UNION. This would be the only way to prevent a great evil.

The dealers who belong to the PATRIOT UNION might want to take advantage of the people being bound to trade with them to charge excessive prices for their goods. This could only be avoided by the PATRIOT UNION having the right to regulate prices.

The Right to Regulate the Standard of Prices would belong to the PATRIOT UNION in the very nature of the relation of its members to each other. If the members agree to patronize Patriot business houses, the Patriot business houses, on the other hand, must agree that they will not make excessive charges, nor demand excessive profits. The PATRIOT UNION must have the right to say that the farmer shall not charge excessive prices for his produce: that the butcher shall not charge excessive prices for his meat: that the merchant and grocer shall not charge excessive prices for their goods.—In the very nature of things, the PATRIOT UNION would have the right to regulate the standard of all prices, so far as the home demand goes.

This Regulation of all Prices by a Regular System in which all prices are fairly and equally adjusted in relation to the general scale of prices will be a grand advance in the industrial condition of the world.

2. **No Method of Regulating the Standard of Prices** has ever yet been discovered.

1) The price of imports has been regulated by the tariff. The price of those products of a country in which the home demand is not fully supplied have also been regulated by a tariff.

2) But the price of the great mass of production, in which the country fully supplies its own wants and has a surplus for exportation, is left unregulated as to its price. This has always been the greatest evil in the industrial condition of past times.

3) It has, indeed, been held that the price of such products is sufficiently regulated by the amount of money in a country, and by the law of supply and demand. But it is found, in our time, that the price of such products is not regulated by the amount of currency, nor by the law of supply and demand.

1] In the hard times from 1873 to 1878, we had in the country $900,000,000 of currency; while prices were so low that it only required $300,000,000 in circulation to do the business of the country, $600,000,000 being locked up. At the present time, we have $1,700,000,-000 of money in the country, paper and specie; while prices are lower than they were in 1860, when we had only $207,000,000 of currency in the country—lower than in 1850, before prices were affected by the gold of California.*

It only requires, at present, about $400,000,000 to carry on the business of the country with the present low scale of prices. The rest of the money,—$1,300,000,000,—is locked up.—It is evident that, in our time, a sufficient amount of currency has no influence whatever in raising the prices of a country.

2] On the other hand, the law of supply and demand no longer regulates prices. Our experience two years ago proves this. When our wheat crop was fifty million bushels short, and there was an active demand for wheat in Europe, and wheat ought to have gone up to over $1 a bushel, we have seen how the Chicago buyers put wheat down to 60 cents a bushel, in defiance of the law of supply and demand.

The events of our time prove that the old methods of regulating prices do not answer the purpose any longer, but that the Money Kings regulate prices to suit themselves, by the power of Capital.

This State of Fact must be Recognized. And it brings a most important question before us for determination.

3. **The old Method of Regulating Prices has been Overthrown** by the Money Power. We must either let the Money Power continue to regulate all prices, and thereby ruin us all, or we must find some method of regulating prices at a fair standard, that will be effectual.

This is the great question now before us. *What new method of regulating prices?*

4. **Prices cannot be regulated by Law.** A legis-

---

* This is ascertained by an actual comparison of the prices.

lative body is not usually the best agent to properly regulate prices. Such bodies have not the necessary experience; and, they are too liable to be influenced by other than industrial considerations, and would be too apt to frame Laws with a view to the furtherance of local interests. And besides, it would too greatly increase the power of the Government.

5. **The only proper method of fixing prices** is by a special Organization of the people, formed for that purpose, and for the promotion of the general prosperity of the country. The world has reached a point at which prices must be fixed by the proposed PATRIOT UNION, or else they will be fixed by a combination of Capital.

The old way of leaving prices to be regulated by the amount of currency and the law of supply and demand will not do any longer.

We cannot regulate prices by law; and if the *People* will not do it by means of the PATRIOT UNION, Capitalists will continue to do it, and will thereby ruin the world. The organization of the people in the PATRIOT UNION, to regulate prices, and to otherwise promote the general prosperity, is, in our age, an imperative necessity. Nothing else will save our country and the world from absolute ruin.

3RD. OUR PRESENT FALSE INDUSTRIAL SYSTEM.

It is necessary to remind the reader that the evils that are afflicting our country have their immediate cause in the low prices which the Money Power is putting upon all farming produce. In order to save the country from the grasp of the Money Power, the price of farming produce must be raised, and all prices properly adjusted by the PATRIOT UNION.

1. Present False Industrial System Crushes Farmers and Retail Merchants.

At present, the Money Kings are making all the profits of handling farming produce; and, to increase those profits, they have cut down the prices of the farmer, and the profits of the retail merchant.

The wholesale merchant used to be content with fifteen per cent. profit, the amount of his sales making up his income; while the retail merchant, had to have from 25 to 50 per cent. profit, in order to be fairly prosperous. But now, after leaving the farm, produce pays from 35 to 50 per cent. profits before it reaches the retail dealer; and the retailer is cut down in his price accordingly, until his profit hardly reaches 15 per cent.

The farmer and the retail dealer are cut down in their profits, and the consumer pays a high price for his food, in order that the Money Kings may realize all the profits of the Industrial System.

The manner in which this System works may be readily illustrated:—The farmer's wheat, raised ten miles out in the country from a Western town, instead of being ground into flour at the county town, and eaten at home, must be sent to New Jersey to be ground into flour, and then hauled back, and sold in the town where the wheat was raised.

Before reaching the retail dealer who sells to the consumer, the flour has paid profits to the buyer of the wheat, to the railroad that hauled it East, to the wholesale dealer, to the miller who ground it, to the wholesale dealer who sent it West, and to the railroad for hauling it back. In order to pay all these charges, the farmer must take a low price for his wheat, and the retail dealer must make a low profit on his sales, while the consumer pays a high price for his flour.

This is good for the Money Kings, whose agents buy

the wheat, whose railroads haul it East, whose wholesale dealer delivers it to the miller, whose mills grind it—who, in a word, make all the profits between the farmer and the retail merchant who sells the flour to the consumer. It is a good thing for the Money Kings who make all the profit; —but it is very bad for the farmer and the retail merchant, who are both cut down in their prices, in order to enlarge the profits of the Money Kings on the much-handled produce.

2. This System Being Made Universal.

The Money Kings now want to make this system of business universal. They are enforcing it to a great extent; greatly to their own profit, and to the injury of the general public.—The beef of Iowa, grown ten miles from Davenport, cannot be sold in Davenport; but it must be shipped to Chicago, and there killed by Armour, and then shipped back to Davenport for the people to eat.—The beef of Colorado must be shipped to Kansas City, to be killed by Armour, and be shipped back, to be eaten by the people of Colorado.

The butchers do not want to do this business; they prefer to kill their own meat; — but Armour is forcing them into it, by selling beef at a loss, till they are compelled to submit.—The beef of the West is all to be carried to the East for slaughter, and the meat brought back to the West for consumption; and the hides must be tanned in the East, and made into shoes for Western wear. Western hogs are hauled on railroads to Chicago, to be killed, and the bacon and lard brought back to the West for consumption.

3. This System an Absurd Violation of all Principles of Political Economy.

In this system, the Money Kings make all the money. They make the profit on the double transportation, on the killing, and on the handling.

This system of sending all our produce away in a raw state, to be put into shape for use, and then bringing it back for consumption, is a gross absurdity. To illustrate:—A farmer has a barn in which he stores his provender and keeps his stock. Will he not be a fool to have another barn at the other end of his farm, a mile away, where he keeps his cutting box and his steaming apparatus, so that he has to haul all his provender away from barn No. 1 to barn No. 2, to be prepared for use, and then haul it back to be fed to his stock? It is equally ruinous to the people of this country to send all agricultural produce to a distant market to be prepared for use, and then buy it back in a manufactured form for home consumption.

If the farmer who sends his provender to the distant barn, to be prepared for use, should sell it to a speculator out of barn No. 1, and allow him to haul it away and prepare it for use, and then haul it back again and charge him an additional price for it, sufficient to pay a fair price for hauling and handling, it would not be long before the speculator would own the farmer's farm and stock.—The Money Power is the speculator who is doing this by us. It is buying our raw produce, and doing the hauling both ways, and preparing our raw products for use by manufacturing them; and it is making all the money, and is now in a fair way to get possession of all the property of our people.

The only way for the farmer to save himself, in such a case, will be to put up a cutting box and steaming apparatus in the barn where his provender and his stock are kept, and prepare his provender for use himself, and thus save all the hauling, and the cost of all the handling. Then he will make money. The speculator will lose his profits, because the farmer has no longer any use for him. But the farmer, saving all that the speculator made, will soon grow rich.— So we must quit our absurd System of sending our raw products away from home for manufacture, and buying them back again in a manufactured form.

4TH. THE TRUE INDUSTRIAL SYSTEM.

1 **Each County Should Manufacture at Home, at least so much of its own Products as are Needed for Home Consumption,** and only send away the surplus. The consistency of this with sound reason is apparent at a glance.

1.) **If Every County Ground its own Wheat,** and killed its own hogs and cattle, and tanned and manufactured its own leather, the farmers could get a fair price for the hogs and beef and wheat; while the consumer in the county would get his food supplies as cheap as now. And moreover, the business men in the County, who are now making nothing, would get rich on the profits of grinding the wheat, and killing the hogs and cattle. Every County in the West might, in this way, make hundreds of thousands of dollars that are now made by the Money Kings.

We Want a System of Industry in which all the Counties shall prepare the produce of the Counties for home consumption, without sending it abroad and bringing it back again for consumption; and in which the produce of the County should, as far as practicable, be placed in the manufactured condition before being sent to other markets for consumption. By this system the farmers would pay their debts, and get rich: the towns would flourish with new business they are now not doing at all; and the consumer would pay no more for food than he is paying now.

2. COUNTY BUYERS SHOULD SHIP ALL PRODUCE.

The better price obtained by the farmer for his produce sold to supply home demand would be a great benefit to him. It would enable him the better to stand the lower price he would have to take for the portion of his produce that was sent away to market. And, in the end, the home demand would regulate the price of the produce shipped, as well as that sold to supply the home demand.

For, if the Money Kings would not give fair prices for the produce that was shipped, the home buyers would soon be able to buy all the produce and ship it to the great markets of the country. For the home shippers could do the work much cheaper than it can be done under the present system.

For example: Flour mills owned in Kansas could sell flour cheaper in Chicago than New Jersey mills, which bought their wheat in Kansas, and had to ship their flour back to Chicago. For the Kansas miller, buying his wheat at home, can get it cheaper than its cost to the New Jersey miller; and the shipment to Chicago from Kansas is cheaper than the shipment to Chicago from New Jersey.—And so of the other products of the country.

Besides, the county manufacturer of home products, --flour, bacon, lard, prepared beef, etc.—having a good price at home, could afford to ship abroad on a close margin of profit. In the end, the county buyers would be able to ship all the products of the county that were sent abroad, so that the profits made on the shipments would be kept at home and add to the county wealth.

5TH. THE PATRIOT UNION MUST BREAK DOWN THE FALSE BUSINESS SYSTEM

which has been established by the Money Kings in this country for their own profit, to the ruin of our people, and establish the proper system of industry, and thus promote the public prosperity and the betterment of every class of industry.

1. **Only a Grand Industrial Organization** can effect this result. Only such an organization can break down the false system of industry that now prevails, and establish a right system of industry. No man could now enter into business in competition with the Money Kings. But the PATRIOT UNION, existing all over the country, would give sure and profitable markets to the home buyer, both for the products which he sold to the home markets, and for those shipped away to other points.

The System Would Soon be in Universal Operation, and the whole country in the full tide of prosperity. The farmers would be getting good prices, and would soon be out of debt; the merchants and grocers of the towns, freed from the danger of Jew Stores, and doing business at a fair scale of profits, would grow rich; and Labor, sharing the general prosperity, out of good wages would begin to accumulate savings. The West and the South would have a prosperity such as they have never known.

The East also would hum with industry,—building ships, and establishing Patriot mercantile houses, to carry on the grand import and export trade of the country.—For, the prosperity of the East, at present, is not so much the prosperity of our own people, as the prosperity of the Money Kings and their agents.

The PATRIOT UNION would not only take the whole business of our counties out of the hands of the Money Kings, and give it to our home people, but in its full extension, it would take the wholesale trade of the country and the import and export trade away from the Money Kings, and place them in the hands of members of the PATRIOT UNION.—When Western and Southern merchants would furnish a market all over the country for imports sold by Patriot houses, it would not be long before an abundance of Eastern Capital would go into the business and supply the demand.

In the last twenty years, the Money Kings have broken down in this country two hundred thousand great business establishments, whose failure has been reported; besides many thousands more of small establishments that have gone down unnoticed. The change of the business of the country from the hands of our own people into the hands of the Money Kings has wrought wide-spread ruin. So, on the other hand, the taking of the business of the country out of the hands of the Money Kings and putting it into the hands of our people again, will be like life from the dead.

It will call into operation again two hundred thousand great business establishments in the place of those destroyed by the Money Kings; and it will summon into life ten times as many moderate establishments all over the country as have gone down in the last twenty years. The industry of the country will have a Grand Resurrection, and will move forward with the freshness of a new life into the era of unprecedented industrial prosperity to which the PATRIOT UNION will give birth.

II. OBJECTIONS ANSWERED.

1. **It may be objected** that the establishment of a higher scale of prices by the PATRIOT UNION might lose us the foreign market for our wheat. To this I answer

1) This is a mistake. England only buys from us what she has to buy; and she would buy the same amount, if she had to pay a fair price for it.

2) As it is, the English market for our wheat is a great disadvantage for our farmers. We now sell one-fourth of our wheat crop to England; and the Money Kings make our farmers take the Liverpool price, not only for the wheat that is sent abroad, but for the three-fourths which

is sold and consumed at home. The farmers would be better off if the wheat sold to England were burned up, if they might so get a fair price for the three-fourths sold in the home market.

3) Furthermore, the Money Kings raise wheat enough on their bonanza wheat farms to supply the English markets. When the PATRIOT UNION is established, we will have no need of their bonanza wheat to supply the home market, and they can send it abroad to England; while the American Patriot farmers having the home market will get a fair price for their wheat consumed at home.

4) At present, we are raising too much wheat. We had better raise less wheat, and more sugar, and flax and hemp and wool, in the West. The Western people can not now go into the raising of sorghum and the sugar beet, and the production of sugar on a grand scale; because the Money Kings hold our market for their Sugar Trusts, and they would destroy any American who went into the sugar production. But with the assured demand at a fair price which the PATRIOT UNION would afford, the West would go into sugar production on a large scale, at once, and we would very soon fully supply our own market with sugar. We would also soon cease to import hemp and flax and wool and leather.—By doing this, we would save more than we now get as the price of all our exported wheat and beef and bacon put together.

2. **It may be objected** that, while the rise of prices effected by the PATRIOT UNION would be good for the Western farmers, it would be an injury to the Southern planter, raising cotton for the foreign market. It may be said that, if we raise the standard of prices in the country, the cotton grower would have to raise his cotton at a greater cost, while he got for it the same price he now receives in the foreign market.—I reply that this is founded on error.

1) The Southern planter would get a better price, in the new scale of prices, for his cotton sold in the home market. In fact, the *American Patriot* cotton grower, under the new system, would be better off than now. There are an immense number of our cotton plantations now in possession of the London Money Kings. These would be shut out of the home market, and they would have to send their cotton abroad; and this would leave the good price of the home market to the American Patriot cotton grower.

2) Furthermore, during the Late War, the Money Kings tried the experiment of raising cotton in India, and Egypt, and elsewhere. It was found that they could not raise it for less than 12 cents a pound. And if American cotton were now held at 12 cents a pound, the English manufacturers would have to pay that price for it. And we ought to fix our prices at such a point as to get the highest price for our products in the foreign market that they will bring. The Money Kings ought to be compelled to pay a fair price for all the cotton they buy from us.

3. **It may be objected** that it would disorder the business of the country, if we supplied our home consumption in our counties in the West and South by home manufactures; as this would shut out the products of Eastern factories, owned by the Money Kings, from the Western and Southern markets, to that extent.—This objection also is founded on error.

1) The Money Kings have the markets of the world; and if they were shut out from the home market of the West and South by their being supplied with the County manufactures of the PATRIOT UNION, it would only cause them to seek a foreign market for their manufactures in the East, greatly to the prosperity of the country.

2) We ought to supply our home market with woolen and cotton goods, with leather products, with iron, and all

other things consumed in our market; and, more than this, we ought to export a large surplus to the markets of the world. The Trusts of the Money Kings are now attempting to prevent this; limiting our production to a point short of the full supply of our home market; thus leaving a part of our demand to be supplied by English manufactures. The Money Kings never will supply our home market, if it is left to them. The only way to have our home market fully supplied and have a surplus to ship abroad, is to take the home market out of the hands of the Money Kings, and supply it in great measure by county manufactures; thus leaving the manufactures already established by the Money Kings in the country to seek, in part, a foreign market.

The PATRIOT UNION would effect this, and thereby greatly promote the national prosperity. It would diminish our imports of sugar, cotton and woolen goods, iron, leather, wool, and hemp and flax, to the amount of over $200,000,000 annually; and it would add perhaps an equal amount to the value of our exports. At present, our people are doing a losing trade with the rest of the world, our imports exceeding what our people get for our exports by many millions. Under the new industrial system furthered by the PATRIOT UNION, this state of things would be reversed, and the price obtained by our people for our exports would exceed our imports annually, by several hundred million dollars. Not only would individuals in our country grow rich under the system, but the country itself would rapidly grow in wealth, until our prosperity would surpass anything even dreamed of hitherto, in the history of the world.

CHAPTER VI.

INVESTMENTS FOR THE PEOPLE, SECURED BY THE PATRIOT UNION.

The grand industrial system inaugurated by the PATRIOT UNION would not injure any American interest, or any American industry. It would greatly benefit them all.—The Money Kings might suffer in the transition, it is true. But the English Cuckoo hatched in our national nest has thrown most of our business people out of the nest, to make room for itself. When we put our expelled fledgelings back into the nest, if they crowd the Cuckoo in its quarters, any inconvenience it may endure will be only the fate due to such intruders.

Better that the Money Kings should lose some of their bloated gains, than that the rest of our people should be deprived of all their property, for the enrichment of these foreign intruders upon our industry.

I. THE PATRIOT UNION WILL SECURE INVESTMENTS.

A liberal scale of prices is better for the people of any country. And, in establishing a scale of fair prices, the PATRIOT UNION will merely break down the present abominable industrial system in which the Money Kings are making all the money; and will substitute for it the most perfect system of industry the world has ever known. One great advantage of the proposed system is that

1ST. THE PROFITS NOW MADE BY THE MONEY KINGS WILL BE MADE BY THE AMERICAN PEOPLE,

to the enrichment of them all.—The farmers will be enriched by fair prices. The laboring men will get better wages, and have but little more expense. The merchants and grocers will get rich by the more liberal expenditure of the farmers, and working people, and people of all classes of industry. The towns will flourish with industries established by the PATRIOT UNION. Everybody will be making money; and everybody will soon be seeking investments. A very little time would elapse after the PATRIOT UNION was in full operation before, in the general prosperity, all classes of industry would have money for investment.

Then the Patriot Union would enter upon a new era in its existence. It would find investments for the people,—solid investments, that would yield regular, safe dividends.

Heretofore, in every era of prosperity, our people have gone wild with excitement, and embarked in wild-cat speculations in real estate. The investments which they made added nothing to the wealth of the country; and the excitement was always followed by financial collapse. But this evil would be guarded against by the PATRIOT UNION.

Our country is full of property owned by the London Money Kings, which ought to be the property of our own people. It will be remembered that it is a fixed principle of Political Economy that the people of every country ought to own its own railroads. It would be the office of the PATRIOT UNION to secure the purchase of this, and other property hereafter to be mentioned, for our people, and thus divert them from unprofitable speculations in undeveloped real estate.

But it will be asked

2ND. HOW CAN WE GET THE RAILROADS?

We should not deal unjustly with the Money Kings. We should not retaliate upon them the wrongs they have inflicted upon our people. We should treat them with perfect justice. I would take no property they are not willing to sell; and we should pay a fair value for all we buy from them.—Many persons would shrink from compelling the Money Kings to sell their property by public law. But it is perfectly right for the American people to compel the Money Kings to sell their property, if it can be done by fair business competition.

The Money Kings have acted on this principle, availing themselves of their superior might of Capital to compel weaker parties engaged in business to give place to them. The Money Kings are stronger than any individual business man, or any single business company. But the American people, banded together in the PATRIOT UNION, are mightier than the Money Power. When the American people unite their resources and energies in the PATRIOT UNION, to engage in any line of business, they will take that line of business away from the Money Kings.

For instance; if, acting through the PATRIOT UNION, the American people should combine their means, and parallel the Great Trunk Line railroads of the Money Kings with other roads owned by companies organized under the auspices of the PATRIOT UNION—these new Patriot roads would do all the business, and make the railroads of the Money Kings worthless. The PATRIOT UNION would have a perfect right to avail itself of its superior might, and compel the Money Kings to sell us property we ought to own—the profits of which, indeed, if long continued in their possession, would enable them to bankrupt and ruin us.

Hence, when money for investment was offered to the PATRIOT UNION on every side, — when farmers, and merchants, and all business men, and all employees in every kind of business had money they were anxious to invest, the PATRIOT UNION could easily find investment for it. A great Trunk Line Railroad from the Mississippi to

New York would be a grand investment. Such a road would only cost some thirty millions of dollars. In less than a year after the PATRIOT UNION was in full operation, offers of money for investment coming from all over the country would far exceed that amount. The railroad would be built. It, with its branch lines, would do all the business between the East and the West; for, of course, all Patriots would travel upon the Patriot road, and all Patriot business men would ship their freights over it.

But if the Money Kings were wise, before matters reached this pass, they would offer all their railroad property to the PATRIOT UNION, to be purchased at a fair price.

The PATRIOT UNION can make its own terms with the railroad owners. And it might make some such arrangement as this:—The Money Kings to restock the railroads at the price which it would cost to build them and furnish the rolling stock; and to hold them at that specified price, subject to purchase by the American people, in shares of one hundred dollars ($100). But until the entire stock should be purchased from them, the Money Kings to receive the dividends on so much of the stock as remained in their possession.

3RD. THE AMERICAN PEOPLE COULD EASILY PURCHASE THE RAILROADS.

Under such conditions, how long would it be before the American people would own the railroads? Before five years had elapsed we would own them all.

Even now, hard as times are, our people spend in spirituous liquors $900,000,000 per annum, and $600,000,000 for tobacco; and in other things they would be better off without, at least $2,000,000,000 more. It is safe to estimate that the American people spend every year $3,500,000,000 for things that do not benefit them at all, but are really harmful.

The greater part of this astonishing amount of waste is spent by the working people. For though the waste of each individual among wage earners may be less, their vastly greater number brings up the aggregate of expenditures to a much larger amount then that spent for those things by wealthier people.

In the fact of this vast expenditure, and in the opportunity for economy and profitable investment made possible by the possession of so large an amount of money, above the actual cost of living, lies the best hope for the uplifting of the great mass of the American people. If the American people are to be uplifted, the work must be done by themselves. They must exercise the self-denial which lies at the foundation of all improvement in the financial circumstances, the mental development, or the spiritual ennoblement of man.

This waste of money in drink, tobacco and sensual self indulgence is largely caused by want of inducement to economize. The man working for wages who saves fifty dollars cannot find investment for it. He cannot invest in land; for he cannot attend to it. He cannot find safe stocks that will yield a good dividend; for such stocks are not put upon the market except at such a premium as he would not care to pay, the stocks in the market being only baits for the unwary.—Having no opportunity for investment, the wage earner spends his money in self indulgence, or wastes it in vice.

Start the American people in a race of accumulation, by affording them safe investments that will yield fair dividends, and they will all begin to economize.

This will do more for the promotion of temperance and habits of morality, than any fact in human history. It will, indeed, inaugurate a New Era in the social and moral, as well as in the business world. A boom for investment would soon arise: everybody would be eager to economize, and invest savings in stocks that would yield good and sure returns. Every man would have a longing to belong to the property class. No one would any longer be content to be moneyless and poor. The distinction of men of property and the non-property class would soon no longer exist. All men would be men of property; the only distinction being that some would own more property than others.—Such a state of fact would do more to lift up the great mass of mankind into the region of self-respect and aspiration, than any event that has ever occured in the business world.

The condition of the country would soon be transformed. In five years, the American people might own all the railroads: in ten years, they might own all the manufactures in the country now owned by the Money Kings; and, in twenty years, the American people might own all the possessions of the Money Kings in the United States.

II. THE MONEY POWER RENDERED A BLESSING.

One of the greatest advantages of the proposed industrial system remains to be stated. In the new state of things, the Money Kings would become a blessing to the country, instead of a curse.

1st. Pioneers of Industry.

The Money Kings would be paid for their possessions in currency, which would be of value in this country, and nowhere else. They could use it in the United States, for all business purposes,—to hire labor, to buy products of industry, and to start new enterprises.

We would stipulate with them that they might start any new enterprises in the country, and have them in full possession and be admitted to all business advantages, for twenty years; but, at the end of that time, they should be open to purchase by the American people at a fair price, not exceeding the cost of the original investment.

This would keep the Money Kings constantly on the lookout for new investments. They would build irrigating canals, to redeem the Rocky Mountain dėserts and restore them to fertility: they would drain and redeem the swamp lands of the Mississippi Valley and Florida: they would build new canals and new railroads: they would build ships with which to transport our commerce on the ocean: they would push forward new inventions: they would build up new cities. For we would stipulate that they might build new houses and hold them for twenty years, before setting them at purchase; but that they should not buy houses, or factories, or other property, already built or improved. They would thus become the pioneers of industry in every department of industrial progress. They would be getting richer all the time; but their wealth would be a blessing to the world, and not a curse.

An incidental advantage will arise out of this that has already been briefly touched upon,—the suppression of all speculation in real estate. The Money Kings could not profit, as now, by the labor of other people enhancing the value of their investments; for it would be held that their possession and use of the property for twenty years would be a sufficient advantage, so that when the property was purchased from them, they would receive for it only the cost of their original investment.

And the property of the Jew Money Kings, being offered at cost twenty years after the investment, would be a constant stream of new property coming on the market. It would be the cheapest property that could be bought; and all persons would seek those investments. And such investments constantly coming into market at the same rate of value, would prevent any undue inflation of property, and all speculative excitement. Such a state of facts would tend to keep all property at an equable value, and put a stop to all wild speculation.

2ND. THE NEW RULE, PERPETUAL.

The rule of making the property of the Money Kings purchasable by the people of the country in which their investments lie, is destined to revolutionize the world. This principle, started in America, will be perpetuated, and will be extended all over the earth.

Palestine is the natural trade center of the world; and the Jews, when restored to their own country, will be, throughout all ages, the Merchant Princes of the earth. It will then be necessary to establish the principle that they shall not hold property in any country, outside of Palestine, longer than twenty years; as the only method of preventing them from bankrupting mankind, and getting possession of all the property of the earth.

It should be a principle of universal application, in all countries, and throughout all time, that the Jew Money Kings, either now while they are in London as their center, or after a while when they will center their operations in Palestine, shall, after holding property for twenty years in any country, place it on purchase by the people of the country, at the price of the original cost of the investment.

This will make the Jews a blessing to all nations. It will fulfill the prophecy that their influence upon all nations shall be like the bounteous dew, which relieves drought and makes vegetation flourish in luxuriant growth.

The Jews, holding property perpetually, are a curse to mankind. Holding property for twenty years, they become the pioneers of industrial advancement. They will be constantly adding to the property of the earth, which the rest of mankind will purchase from them as soon as it is fully developed. They will be constantly conquering acquisitions from the realm of undeveloped nature; and mankind will, after twenty years, take their conquests at a fair price, as the heritage of the race. This system of purchasing the property of the Jews will cause the *People*, who make the purchase, to become in the course of ages immensely rich. The earth will be full of wealth; for the Jews will be always getting new property; and, as fast as they develop it, they will be paid for it, and it will become the wealth of the people of the country in which it lies.

Here is the destined

III. SOLUTION OF THE QUESTIONS BETWEEN LABOR AND CAPITAL.

In the present Age, Capital is concentrated in the hands of the Jews. It will be so in all future time. In all future time, the Jews are the destined great Capitalists of the earth. The great question between productive industry and Capital will always be a question between the Jews and the Gentile world. It will not be a question of how to keep the Jews on an equality with the Gentiles. For that is impossible: the supremacy of the Jews in wealth is a foregone conclusion—from their being practically a great National Syndicate, and from the superior advantages of the location of Palestine for making and keeping it, in the future, the commercial center of the Earth.

The question between Productive Industry and Capital will be,—How to make the supremacy of the Jews a blessing to the world and not a curse—How to keep them in a recognized position of beneficial leadership of industry, and prevent them from getting possession of all business and all wealth.—This question can find no other solution than the one given in this work.

How much better thus to utilize Capital and make it the ally of Productive Industry, than to antagonize it and treat it as an enemy. In a proper adjustment of industrial questions, there is no antagonism between Capital and Labor. They are allies.

While Capital holds all it gets, and bands itself into an Imperialism for greater accumulation, it is a crushing despotism. But when Capital is bridled by law, and compelled, after twenty years possession of the property it acquires in foreign countries, to sell the property to the people of those countries at a fair price, then Capital becomes the helper of Labor. It does the hard pioneer work of development, which it ought to do, on account of its superior might, and as the price it pays to the world for its superior advantages. But Industry becomes its heir; and the accumulations of Capital become the heritage of mankind.

How much better such an adjustment of the questions between the Money Kings and the people of the country where they operate, than putting all property into the hands of the Government, as Socialists have proposed. Socialism would impoverish mankind, in order to increase the wealth of the Government, and the patronage of office holders: this adjustment will increase the wealth of mankind in a degree inconceivable in the present age. Socialism depresses the whole human race into the common level of a hopeless poverty: this adjustment lifts the whole race into the self-respect of constantly increasing wealth. Socialism destroys energy by the hopelessness of all aspiration: this adjustment starts mankind onward in a career of boundless enterprise and activity, inspired by the emulation of example and the consciousness of increasing attainment.—This adjustment will open to mankind the door of hope that leads into the Higher Era for which the World is almost hopelessly longing.

In this adjustment the antagonism between Capital and Labor will be finally allayed. Capital is "the Lion" that has been devouring "the Lamb,"—the People engaged in industrial occupations. Capital is "the Bear" that has been destroying "the Cow" of industry. By this adjustment, "the Lion and the Lamb shall lie down together; and the Cow and the Bear shall feed" together in the pastures of industry.

In the end, it will probably be held that the property thus bought from the Money Kings should be held by the purchaser for only twenty years, and that then it shall be purchasable by some one else, and the owner of the stock made to seek some other investment. In this way, young people just starting in life would always have a place to put their savings, and an encouragement to economize.—But this feature is a refinement for which we are not yet prepared, though future times may adopt it.

Chapter VII.

CONCLUSION.

I wish to disclaim all prejudice against the Jews. They are the destined Merchant Princes of the earth, in the great Coming Age.

I am glad that Palestine is the natural center of the world's commerce; and that the Jews, at a future time, when they shall be restored to their own land, will be the great commercial agents of the earth. According to Prophecy, they are the destined leaders of the world in its onward career of industry.

I am willing, now, to recognize the rights of the Jew Money Kings, and to treat them justly. But they have no right to ruin the world, as they are now doing. Their present course of fraud and injustice should be stopped.

They have no right to break down industry by commercial crises, in which they seek their own advantage in the ruin of multitudes of people.—They have no right to force down the price of all produce, to the ruin of farmers and merchants, for their own profit.—They have no right to start booms in towns, by forcing a temporary rapid growth; thereby making people believe the boomed towns destined to become large cities, and inducing removals and investments which ruin the lives of thousands.—They have no right to get, and hold permanently, property in all countries, when such holding of property will surely reduce to utter poverty the countries in which such possessions lie, and make their people peasants.

I protest against these evils, and propose a remedy for them. The proposed System of Industry is an effectual remedy. It is the only remedy. There is no other. If it shall be adopted now, it will save our country and the world from the most gigantic evil that has ever threatened the well-being of man. If not adopted now, it will be adopted in the future, when the Dragon shall be bound.

There is no remedy for the evils now afflicting our country, except the Union of our people under the principle of the Golden Rule.

Our only hope is for us all to unite in a PATRIOT UNION, whose members all agree to act toward each other in the spirit of mutual fairness and brotherly kindness—all agree to promote, each the interests of the others, equally with his own: the employer agreeing to give fair wages to his employees: all agreeing to eat the produce of the Patriot Farmer, and buy the goods of the Patriot manufacturer, and merchant, and grocer; and all agreeing that they will charge only fair prices, and that they will leave it for disinterested parties to say what prices are fair and right.

This certainly is a noble principle of action. It stops all trickery and chicanery in trade. It makes business a bond of union and mutual benefit, as it ought to be. It enables each person to prosper through the common prosperity of all. It makes all mankind a band of brethren, united for their common protection and common benefit.

It will have to conquer the selfish Jew Money Power, it is true, and stop its ravages upon industry, by the might of a great united people. But, this accomplished, it will give fair and equal terms of adjustment to the vanquished; and will establish a system of mutual fairness, that will continue down to the end of time and bless the world forever.

The PATRIOT UNION will be needed to endure all through the Millennium. Its establishment will inaugurate the principle of the Golden Rule in business, and will introduce a New Era in the progress of the human race.

The Money Power ought to accept an arrangement that is so fair and just. If it will not, upon its head be the consequences!—

But even though the Money Kings should antagonize all our measures of relief—still, the PATRIOT UNION will do them no wrong: it will go steadfastly forward, marshaling our Patriot movement; and, with God's help, it will save our country despite all opposition.

MAY THE LORD SAVE OUR COUNTRY AND THE WORLD FROM THE RUIN THAT IS NOW IMPENDING—AND MAKE THE EVILS THAT ARE HANGING OVER OUR AGE THE OCCASION AND THE CAUSE OF A GRAND MOVEMENT THAT SHALL INTRODUCE A HIGHER ERA IN THE HISTORY OF OUR RACE, AND MARSHAL MANKIND ONWARD INTO THE GLORY OF THAT BETTER AGE OF UNIVERSAL LIBERTY, EQUALITY AND FRATERNAL LOVE.

Published by

Facsimile Publisher
Ashok Vihar, Delhi-110052 (India)
Website: www.facsimilepublishers.com

Distributed by

Gyan Books Pvt. Ltd.
5, Ansari Road, Daryaganj, New Delhi-110002 (India)
E-mail: books@gyanbooks.com, Website: www.gyanbooks.com

9 789332 897984